LITERATURE AND ART.

BY S. MARGARET FULLER,

AUTHOR OF A SUMMER ON THE LAKES, WOMAN IN THE NINETEENTH CENTURY, ETC., ETC.

Two Parts, in One Volume.

CONTAINING:

With an Introduction,

BY HORACE GREELEY.

NEW YORK:

PUBLISHED BY FOWLERS AND WELLS,

CLINTON HALL, 131 NASSAU STREET.

1852.

Boston, 142 Washington-St.] [London, No. 142 Strand.

INTRODUCTION.

THE MEMOIRS OF MARGARET FULLER OSSOLI, lately published, have inspired many readers with a profound regret that they had not, during her life, made or improved the acquaintance of one whom impartial judgment must pronounce the most capable and noteworthy American woman the world has yet known. Criticism has not spared the writers of that Memoir; yet no critic, so far as I am aware, has hinted a doubt that it portrays, truly and vividly, its heroine, though she had previously been more widely misapprehended—perhaps I should say uncomprehended—than any of her cotemporaries. Especially is that portion of the Memoirs contributed by Ralph Waldo Emerson entitled to the praise of being the frankest, fairest, most effective biography of our day, exhibiting its subject exactly as she lived and moved among us some few years ago, with her lofty virtues and her conspicuous faults, her conversation which charmed and her manner that repelled; so that she was at the same moment idolized and shunned, reverenced and ridiculed, by different sets of cultivated and considerate persons whom she met in society; and neither without obvious reasons.

"She, being dead, yet speaketh." One of the most fluent, forcible, and brilliant of talkers, she nevertheless wrote slowly and with remarkable labor; so that, but for the eminence of her conversational powers, it might have been supposed that her years of devotion to foreign languages and literature had impaired her mastery of her mother tongue. Yet this hesitancy in writing, sometimes resulting in obscurity, or even awkwardness of style, affected the manner only, and not the matter, of her essays. I doubt that any woman whose life was mainly devoted to literature has written less for the public eye than Margaret Fuller did; I believe the writings of no other woman were ever so uniformly worthy of study and preservation. Surcharged with thought, their manner may sometimes repel, but their matter can rarely or never fail to instruct. Very little that has been written by American women could be so ill spared from our literature.

These essays were, in 1846, selected by herself from all her occasional or fugitive productions, for publication in this form. She wrote very little afterward of any moment but that child of her heart, "Italy in 1848–9," which was irrecoverably lost, with herself, her husband, and child, in the shipwreck of the brig *Elizabeth*, off Fire Island, on the 19th of July, 1850. By these, therefore, with her Memoirs, and her "Woman in the Nineteenth Century," she is to be judged by those who did not know her personally; and these will amply justify her fame, though they may not seem to warrant the lofty eulogiums of her personal friends, based rather on what she said and was, than on what she did and wrote. Her "Summer on the Lakes" is an admirable book of its kind, embodying the fairest and most vivid pencilings of our noble Western prairies as they were left by the receding Indian, and as they began to be dotted by cottages, fields, and gardens, with widely-scattered flocks and herds, replacing the vanishing deer and the vanished buffalo; but its pictures of pioneer life and peculiarities are not so full, minute, and attractive as those of Mrs. Kirkland; and, while the book will continue to be read with pleasure by the judicious few, I presume it will never be reprinted.

Her "Italy" cannot so easily be spared. Knowing intimately and sympathizing thoroughly with Mazzini and the other Republican leaders in the great movement of 1848, her work would have presented that band of heroes more justly and worthily than any thing that has been printed. It would have been the completest refutation ever given to the motley crew of sham republicans, priestly calumniators, and pimps of despotism, who have striven most unscrupulously, and, alas! not unsuccessfully, to cover the last army of martyrs to the cause of Liberty and Progress with ignominy and reproach, as victims of their own boundless incapacity or criminal ambition. Of Italy's lost struggle for liberty and light, she might not merely say, with the Grattan of Ireland's kindred effort, half a century earlier, "I stood by its cradle; I followed its hearse"—she might fairly claim to have been a portion of its incitement, its animation, its informing soul. She bore more than a woman's part in its conflicts and its perils; and the bombs of that ruthless army which a false and traitorous Government impelled against the ramparts of Republican Rome, could have stilled no voice more eloquent in its exposures, no heart more lofty in its defiance, of the villainy which so wantonly drowned in blood the hopes, while crushing the dearest rights, of a people, than those of Margaret Fuller. Her last and greatest work perished irrecoverably in the wreck which closed her earthly career; but some idea of its fire and force may be gathered from passages of her letters from Italy, in 1848–9, preserved and presented in her Memoirs.

Her "Woman in the Nineteenth Century" will cease to be read only when it shall have been outgrown; and that, I apprehend, will not be very soon. Others may have perceived as clearly the injustice to Woman so firmly imbedded in our present social polity and ideas, and so slowly and with difficulty dislodged piecemeal from our laws; but rarely has there appeared a woman so qualified by thought, by culture, by position, by fearlessness, to discuss the subject thoroughly, and present the truth in its amplest and justest proportions. That some of her ideas are exposed to criticism, may be freely conceded without detracting from the merit and value of the work. Frank, original, earnest, and suggestive, this book gave an initial impulse to very much of the thought and action in this direction which have since been elicited, and its influence is even now beginning to be felt in the education of women as lecturers, physicians, etc., and in the earnest and increasing demand that they shall be admitted to equal opportunities with men in colleges and other kindred schools of preparation for efficiency and honor in the most coveted walks of professional life. And when the time shall have come, as come it must, wherein Woman shall be called calmly and authoritatively to decide for herself the proper limits of her own sphere, and to judge whether the ballot is too rude and perilous a weapon to be intrusted to her delicate hands, the expositions and the counsels of Margaret Fuller will be consulted and considered, not more deferentially, but far more widely, than they have hitherto been.

The volume herewith presented will attract a larger number of readers, and perhaps be less cherished by the few, than any other of her published works. We find in it less of the writer's heart and genius, but more of her study and culture, than in the others. In this she appears less as the creator than the critic, the former being the loftier, the latter the more readily appreciable vocation. Few of us are creators; all are more or less critics, and so qualified, in some degree, to appreciate and enjoy criticism. And while there are papers in this volume into the spirit of which the large number will not enter ("The Two Herberts" conspicuous among them), yet a majority of these essays, including "Modern British Poets," "The Modern Drama," "American Literature," etc., will fall not strangely on the general ear. "The Lives of the Great Composers" is the paper into which the writer has infused most of herself, and it will probably command a heartier approval than any thing else in the volume, though the essays on Longfellow's Poems, "Swedenborgianism," and "Methodism at the Fountain," cannot be slighted. And in an age when so many are learning to observe, to think, and to judge—when many feel the want of a wider knowledge of what is best in our current literature, and of more reliable standards for measuring the new works constantly appearing—I cannot believe that the world will soon be ready to dismiss to oblivion these Papers of MARGARET FULLER.

H. G.

NEW YORK, *May 1st*, 1852.

PREFACE.

In the original plan for publishing a selection from my essays in different kinds which have appeared in periodicals, I had aimed at more completeness of arrangement than has been attained in these two volumes. Selections had been made from essays on English literature, on Continental and American literature, and on Art. I had wished, beside, for a department in which to insert sketches of a miscellaneous character, in prose and verse.

It was proposed, in the critical pieces, to retain the extracts with which they were originally adorned, as this would give them far more harmony and interest for the general reader.

The translation, however, of the matter from a more crowded page to its present form has made such a difference, that I have been obliged to drop most of the extracts from several of the pieces. Moreover, in approaching the end of the first number, I found myself obliged to omit more than half the essays I had proposed on the subject of English literature, the greater part of those on Art, and those on Continental literature and of a miscellaneous kind entirely. I find, indeed, that the matter which I had supposed could be comprised in two of these numbers would fill six or eight.

Had I been earlier aware of this, I should have made a different selection, and one which would do more justice to the range and variety of subjects which have been before my mind during the ten years that, in the intervals allowed me by other engagements, I have written for the public.

To those of my friends, who have often expressed a wish that I "could find time to write," it will be a satisfaction to know that, though the last twenty months is the first period in my life when it has been permitted me to make my pen my chief means of expressing my thoughts, yet I have written enough, if what is afloat, and what lies hid in manuscript, were put together, to make a little library, quite large enough to exhaust the patience of the collector, if not of the reader. Should I do no more, I have at least sent my share of paper missives through the world.

The present selection contains some of my earliest and some of my latest expressions. I have not put dates to any of the pieces, though, in the earlier, I see much crudity, which I seem to have outgrown now, just as I hope I shall think ten years hence of what I write to-day. But I find an identity in the main views and ideas, a substantial harmony among these pieces, and I think those who have been interested in my mind at all, will take some pleasure in reading the youngest and crudest of these pieces, and will readily disown for me what I would myself disown.

Should these volumes meet with a kind reception, a more

complete selection from my miscellanies will be offered to the public in due time. Should these not seem to be objects of interest I shall take the hint, and consign the rest to the peaceful seclusion of the garret.

I regret omitting some pieces explanatory of foreign authors, that would have more interest now than when those authors become, as I hope they will, familiar friends to the youth of my country. It has been one great object of my life to introduce here the works of those great geniuses, the flower and fruit of a higher state of development, which might give the young who are soon to constitute the state, a higher standard in thought and action than would be demanded of them by their own time. I have hoped that, by being thus raised above their native sphere, they would become its instructors and the faithful stewards of its best riches, not its tools or slaves. I feel with satisfaction that I have done a good deal to extend the influence of the great minds of Germany and Italy among my compatriots. Of our English contemporaries, as yet but partially known here, I have written notices of Milnes, Landor, and Julius Hare, which I regret being obliged to omit, as these writers are yet but little known. Bailey and Tennyson have now a fair chance of circulation, therefore my notices may sleep with the occasion that gave them birth. Tennyson, especially, needs no usher. He has only to be heard to command the audience of that "melodious thunder."

Of the essays in the second volume, that on American literature is the only one, which has not, before, appeared in print. It is a very imperfect sketch ; the theme was great and difficult, the time to be spared for its consideration was brief. It is, however, written with sincere and earnest feelings, and from a mind that cares for nothing but what is permanent and essential. It should, then, have some merit, if only in the power of suggestion. A year or two hence, I hope to have more to say upon this topic, or the interests it represents, and to speak with more ripeness both as to the matter and the form.

S. M. F.

PAPERS ON LITERATURE AND ART.

A SHORT ESSAY ON CRITICS.

An essay on Criticism were a serious matter; for, though this age be emphatically critical, the writer would still find it necessary to investigate the laws of criticism as a science, to settle its conditions as an art. Essays, entitled critical, are epistles addressed to the public, through which the mind of the recluse relieves itself of its impressions. Of these the only law is, "Speak the best word that is in thee." Or they are regular articles got up to order by the literary hack writer, for the literary mart, and the only law is to make them plausible. There is not yet deliberate recognition of a standard of criticism, though we hope the always strengthening league of the republic of letters must ere long settle laws on which its Amphictyonic council may act. Meanwhile let us not venture to write on criticism, but, by classifying the critics, imply our hopes and thereby our thoughts.

First, there are the subjective class, (to make use of a convenient term, introduced by our German benefactors.) These are persons to whom writing is no sacred, no reverend employment. They are not driven to consider, not forced upon investigation by the fact, that they are deliberately giving their thoughts an independent existence, and that it may live to others when dead to them. They know no agonies of conscientious research, no timidities of self-respect. They see no ideal beyond the present hour, which makes its mood an uncertain tenure. How things affect them now they know; let the future, let the whole take care of itself. They state their impressions as they rise, of other men's spoken, written, or acted thoughts. They never dream of going out of themselves to seek the motive, to trace the law of another nature. They never dream that there are statures which cannot be measured from their point of view. They love, they like, or they hate; the book is detestable, immoral, absurd, or admirable, noble, of a most approved scope;—these statements they make with authority, as those who bear the evangel of pure taste and accurate judgment, and need be tried before no human synod. To them it seems that their present position commands the universe.

Thus the essays on the works of others, which are called criticisms, are often, in fact, mere records of impressions. To judge of their value you must know where the man was brought up, under what influences,—his nation, his church, his family even. He himself has never attempted to estimate the value of these circumstances, and find a law or raise a standard above all circumstances, permanent against all influence. He is content to be the creature of his place, and to represent it by his spoken and written word. He takes the same ground with a savage, who does not hesitate to say of the product of a civilization on which he could not stand, "It is bad," or "It is good."

The value of such comments is merely reflex. They characterize the critic. They give an idea of certain influences on a certain act of men in a certain time or place. Their absolute, essential value is nothing. The long review, the eloquent article by the man of the nineteenth century, are of no value by themselves considered, but only as samples of their kind. The writers were content to tell what they felt, to praise or to denounce without needing to convince us or themselves. They sought not the divine truths of philosophy, and she proffers them not if unsought.

Then there are the apprehensive. These can go out of themselves and enter fully into a foreign existence. They breathe its life; they live in its law; they tell what it meant, and why it so expressed its meaning. They reproduce the work of which they speak, and make it better known to us in so far as two statements are better than one. There are beautiful specimens in this kind. They are pleasing to us as bearing witness of the genial sympathies of nature. They have the ready grace of love with somewhat of the dignity of disinterested friendship. They sometimes give more pleasure than the original production of which they treat, as melodies will sometimes ring sweetlier in the echo. Besides there is a peculiar pleasure in a true response; it is the assurance of equipoise in the universe. These, if not true critics, come nearer the standard than the subjective class, and the value of their work is ideal as well as historical.

Then there are the comprehensive, who must also be apprehensive. They enter into the nature of another being and judge his work by its own law. But having done so, having ascertained his design and the degree of his success in fulfilling it, thus measuring his judgment, his energy, and skill, they do also know how to put that aim in its place, and how to estimate its relations. And this the critic can only do who perceives the analogies of the universe, and how they are regulated by an absolute, invariable principle. He can see how far that work expresses this principle, as well as how far it is excellent in its details. Sustained by a principle, such as can be girt within no rule, no formula, he can walk around the work, he can stand above it, he can uplift it, and try its weight. Finally, he is worthy to judge it.

Critics are poets cut down, says some one by way of jeer; but, in truth, they are men with the poetical temperament to apprehend, with the philosophical tendency to investigate. The maker is divine; the critic sees this divine, but brings it down to humanity by the analytic process. The critic is the historian who records the order of creation. In vain for the maker, who knows without learning it, but not in vain for the mind of his race.

The critic is beneath the maker, but is his needed friend. What tongue could speak but to an intelligent ear, and every noble work demands its critic. The richer the work, the more severe should be its critic; the larger its scope, the more comprehensive must be his power of scrutiny. The critic is not a base caviller, but the younger brother of genius. Next to invention is the power of interpreting invention; next to beauty the power of appreciating beauty.

And of making others appreciate it; for the universe is a scale of infinite gradation, and, below the very highest, every step is explanation down to the lowest. Religion, in the two modulations of poetry and music, descends through an infinity of waves to the lowest abysses of human nature. Nature is the literature and art of the divine mind; human literature and art the criticism on that; and they, too, find their criticism within their own sphere.

The critic, then, should be not merely a poet, not merely a philosopher, not merely an observer, but tempered of all three. If he criticise the poem, he must want nothing of what constitutes the poet, except the power of creating forms and speaking in music. He must have as good an eye and as fine a sense; but if he had as fine an organ for expression also, he would make the poem instead of judging it. He must be inspired by the philosopher's spirit of inquiry and need of generalization, but he must not be constrained by the hard cemented masonry of method to which philosophers are prone. And he must have the organic acuteness of the observer, with a love of ideal perfection, which forbids him to be content with mere beauty of details in the work or the comment upon the work.

There are persons who maintain, that there is no legitimate

criticism, except the reproductive; that we have only to say what the work is or is to us, never what it is not. But the moment we look for a principle, we feel the need of a criterion, of a standard; and then we say what the work is *not*, as well as what it *is*; and this is as healthy though not as grateful and gracious an operation of the mind as the other. We do not seek to degrade but to classify an object by stating what it is not. We detach the part from the whole, lest it stand between us and the whole. When we have ascertained in what degree it manifests the whole, we may safely restore it to its place, and love or admire it there ever after.

The use of criticism, in periodical writing is to sift, not to stamp a work. Yet should they not be "sieves and drainers for the use of luxurious readers," but for the use of earnest inquirers, giving voice and being to their objections, as well as stimulus to their sympathies. But the critic must not be an infallible adviser to his reader. He must not tell him what books are not worth reading, or what must be thought of them when read, but what he read in them. Wo to that coterie where some critic sits despotic, intrenched behind the infallible "We." Wo to that oracle who has infused such soft sleepiness, such a gentle dulness into his atmosphere, that when he opes his lips no dog will bark. It is this attempt at dictatorship in the reviewers, and the indolent acquiescence of their readers, that has brought them into disrepute. With such fairness did they make out their statements, with such dignity did they utter their verdicts, that the poor reader grew all too submissive. He learned his lesson with such docility, that the greater part of what will be said at any public or private meeting can be foretold by any one who has read the leading periodical works for twenty years back. Scholars sneer at and would fain dispense with them altogether; and the public, grown lazy and helpless by this constant use of props and stays, can now scarce brace itself even to get through a magazine article, but reads in the daily paper laid beside the breakfast plate a short notice of the last number of the long established and popular review, and thereupon passes its judgment and is content.

Then the partisan spirit of many of these journals has made it unsafe to rely upon them as guide-books and expurgatory indexes. They could not be content merely to stimulate and suggest thought, they have at last become powerless to supersede it.

From these causes and causes like these, the journals have lost much of their influence. There is a languid feeling about them, an inclination to suspect the justice of their verdicts, the value of their criticisms. But their golden age cannot be quite past. They afford too convenient a vehicle for the transmission of knowledge; they are too natural a feature of our time to have done all their work yet. Surely they may be redeemed from their abuses, they may be turned to their true uses. But how?

It were easy to say what they should *not* do. They should not have an object to carry or a cause to advocate, which obliges them either to reject all writings which wear the distinctive traits of individual life, or to file away what does not suit them, till the essay, made true to their design, is made false to the mind of the writer. An external consistency is thus produced, at the expense of all salient thought, all genuine emotion of life, in short, and all living influence. Their purpose may be of value, but by such means was no valuable purpose ever furthered long. There are those, who have with the best intention pursued this system of trimming and adaptation, and thought it well and best to

"Deceive their country for their country's good."

But their country cannot long be so governed. It misses the pure, the full tone of truth; it perceives that the voice is modulated to coax, to persuade, and it turns from the judicious man of the world, calculating the effect to be produced by each of his smooth sentences, to some earnest voice which is uttering thoughts, crude, rash, ill-arranged it may be, but true to one human breast, and uttered in full faith, that the God of Truth will guide them aright.

And here, it seems to me, has been the greatest mistake in the conduct of these journals. A smooth monotony has been attained, an uniformity of tone, so that from the title of a journal you can infer the tenor of all its chapters. But nature is ever various, ever new, and so should be her daughters, art and literature. We do not want merely a polite response to what we thought before, but by the freshness of thought in other minds to have new thought awakened in our own. We do not want stores of information only, but to be roused to digest these into knowledge. Able and experienced men write for us, and we would know what they think, as they think it not for us but for themselves. We would live with them, rather than be taught by them how to live; we would catch the contagion of their mental activity, rather than have them direct us how to regulate our own. In books, in reviews, in the senate, in the pulpit, we wish to meet thinking men, not schoolmasters or pleaders. We wish that they should do full justice to their own view, but also that they should be frank with us, and, if now our superiors, treat us as if we might some time rise to be their equals. It is this true manliness, this firmness in his own position, and this power of appreciating the position of others, that alone can make the critic our companion and friend. We would converse with him, secure that he will tell us all his thought, and speak as man to man. But if he adapts his work to us, if he stifles what is distinctively his, if he shows himself either arrogant or mean, or, above all, if he wants faith in the healthy action of free thought, and the safety of pure motive, we will not talk with him, for we cannot confide in him. We will go to the critic who trusts Genius and trusts us, who knows that all good writing must be spontaneous, and who will write out the bill of fare for the public as he read it for himself,—

> "Forgetting vulgar rules, with spirit free
> To judge each author by his own intent,
> Nor think one standard for all minds is meant."

Such an one will not disturb us with personalities, with sectarian prejudices, or an undue vehemence in favour of petty plans or temporary objects. Neither will he disgust us by smooth obsequious flatteries and an inexpressive, lifeless gentleness. He will be free and make free from the mechanical and distorting influences we hear complained of on every side. He will teach us to love wisely what we before loved well, for he knows the difference between censoriousness and discernment, infatuation and reverence; and while delighting in the genial melodies of Pan, can perceive. should Apollo bring his lyre into audience, that there may be strains more divine than those of his native groves.

CRITICISM ON ENGLISH LITERATURE.

A DIALOGUE.

POET. CRITIC.

POET. Approach me not, man of cold, steadfast eye and compressed lips. At thy coming nature shrouds herself in dull mist; fain would she hide her sighs and smiles, her buds and fruits even in a veil of snow. For thy unkindly breath, as it pierces her mystery, destroys its creative power. The birds draw back into their nests, the sunset hues into their clouds, when you are seen in the distance with your tablets all ready to write them into prose.

CRITIC. O my brother, my benefactor, do not thus repel me. Interpret me rather to our common mother; let her not avert her eyes from a younger child. I know I can never be dear to her as thou art, yet I am her child, nor would the fated revolutions of existence be fulfilled without my aid.

POET. How meanest thou? What have thy measurements, thy artificial divisions and classifications, to do with the natural revolutions? In all real growths there is a "give and take" of unerring accuracy; in all the acts of thy life there is falsity, for all are negative. Why do you not receive and produce in your kind, like the sunbeam and the rose? Then new light would be brought out, were it but the life of a weed, to bear witness to the healthful beatings of the divine heart. But this perpetual analysis, comparison, and classification, never add one atom to the sum of existence.

CRITIC. I understand you.

POET. Yes, that is always the way. You understand me, who never have the arrogance to pretend that I understand myself.

CRITIC. Why should you?—that is my province. I am the rock which gives you back the echo. I am the tuning-key, which harmonizes your instrument, the regulator to your watch. Who would speak, if no ear heard? nay, if no mind knew what the ear heard?

POET. I do not wish to be heard in thought but in love, to be recognised in judgment but in life. I would pour forth my melodies to the rejoicing winds. I would scatter my seed to the tender earth. I do not wish to hear in prose the meaning of my melody. I do not wish to see my seed neatly put away beneath a paper label. Answer in new pœans to the soul of our souls. Wake me to sweeter childhood by a fresher growth. At present you are but an excrescence produced by my life; depart, self-conscious Egotist, I know you not.

CRITIC. Dost thou so adore Nature, and yet deny me? Is not Art the child of Nature, Civilization of Man? As Religion into Philosophy, Poetry into Criticism, Life into Science, Love into Law, so did thy lyric in natural order transmute itself into my review.

POET. Review! Science! the very etymology speaks. What is gained by looking again at what has already been seen? What by giving a technical classification to what is already assimilated with the mental life?

CRITIC. What is gained by living at all?

POET. Beauty loving itself,—Happiness!

CRITIC. Does not this involve consciousness?

POET. Yes! consciousness of Truth manifested in the individual form.

CRITIC. Since consciousness is tolerated, how will you limit it?

Poet. By the instincts of my nature, which rejects yours as arrogant and superfluous.

Critic. And the dictate of my nature compels me to the processes which you despise, as essential to my peace. My brother (for I will not be rejected) I claim my place in the order of nature. The word descended and became flesh for two purposes, to organize itself, and to take cognizance of its organization. When the first Poet worked alone, he paused between the cantos to proclaim, "It is very good." Dividing himself among men, he made some to create, and others to proclaim the merits of what is created.

Poet. Well! if you were content with saying, "it is very good;" but you are always crying, "it is very bad," or ignorantly prescribing how it might be better. What do you know of it? Whatever is good could not be otherwise than it is. Why will you not take what suits you, and leave the rest? True communion of thought is worship, not criticism. Spirit will not flow through the sluices nor endure the locks of canals.

Critic. There is perpetual need of protestantism in every church. If the church be catholic, yet the priest is not infallible. Like yourself, I sigh for a perfectly natural state, in which the only criticism shall be tacit rejection, even as Venus glides not into the orbit of Jupiter, nor do the fishes seek to dwell in fire. But as you soar towards this as a Maker, so do I toil towards the same aim as a Seeker. Your pinions will not upbear you towards it in steady flight. I must often stop to cut away the brambles from my path. The law of my being is on me, and the ideal standard seeking to be realized in my mind bids me demand perfection from all I see. To say how far each object answers this demand is my criticism.

Poet. If one object does not satisfy you, pass on to another and say nothing.

Critic. It is not so that it would be well with me. I must

penetrate the secret of my wishes, verify the justice of my reasonings. I must examine, compare, sift, and winnow; what can bear this ordeal remains to me as pure gold. I cannot pass on till I know what I feel and why. An object that defies my utmost rigor of scrutiny is a new step on the stair I am making to the Olympian tables.

POET. I think you will not know the gods when you get there, if I may judge from the cold presumption I feel in your version of the great facts of literature.

CRITIC. Statement of a part always looks like ignorance, when compared with the whole, yet may promise the whole. Consider that a part implies the whole, as the everlasting No the everlasting Yes, and permit to exist the shadow of your light, the register of your inspiration.

As he spake the word he paused, for with it his companion vanished, and left floating on the cloud a starry banner with the inscription "AFFLATUR NUMINE." The Critic unfolded one on whose flag-staff he had been leaning. Its heavy folds of pearly gray satin slowly unfolding, gave to view the word NOTITIA, and *Causarum* would have followed, when a sudden breeze from the west caught it, those heavy folds folds fell back round the poor man, and stifled him probably,—at least he has never since been heard of.

THE TWO HERBERTS.

THE following sketch is meant merely to mark some prominent features in the minds of the two Herberts, under a form less elaborate and more reverent than that of criticism.

A mind of penetrating and creative power could not find a better subject for a masterly picture. The two figures stand as representatives of natural religion, and of that of the Son of Man, of the life of the philosophical man of the world, and the secluded, contemplative, though beneficent existence.

The present slight effort is not made with a view to the great and dramatic results so possible to the plan. It is intended chiefly as a setting to the Latin poems of Lord Herbert, which are known to few,—a year ago, seemingly, were so to none in this part of the world. The only desire in translating them has been to do so literally, as any paraphrase, or addition of words impairs their profound meaning. It is hoped that, even in their present repulsive garb, without rhyme or rhythm, stripped, too, of the majestic Roman mantle, the greatness of the thoughts, and the large lines of spiritual experience, will attract readers, who will not find time misspent in reading them many times.

George Herbert's heavenly strain is better, though far from generally, known.

There has been no attempt really to represent these persons speaking their own dialect, or in their own individual manners. The writer loves too well to hope to imitate the sprightly, fresh, and varied style of Lord Herbert, or the quaintness and keen sweets of his brother's. Neither have accessories been given, such as might easily have been taken from their works. But the thoughts imputed to them they might have spoken, only in better and more concise terms, and the facts—are facts. So let this be gently received with the rest of the modern tapestries. We can no longer weave them of the precious materials princes once furnished, but we can give, in our way, some notion of the original design.

It was an afternoon of one of the longest summer days. The sun had showered down his amplest bounties, the earth put on her richest garment to receive them. The clear heavens seemed to open themselves to the desire of mortals; the day had been long enough and bright enough to satisfy an immortal.

In a green lane leading from the town of Salisbury, in England, the noble stranger was reclining beneath a tree. His eye was bent in the direction of the town, as if upon some figure approaching or receding; but its inward turned expression showed that he was, in fact, no longer looking, but lost in thought.

"Happiness!" thus said his musing mind, "it would seem at such hours and in such places as if it not merely hovered over the earth, a poetic presence to animate our pulses and give us courage for what must be, but sometimes alighted. Such fulness of expression pervades these fields, these trees, that it excites, not rapture, but a blissful sense of peace. Yet, even were this permanent in the secluded lot, would I accept it in exchange for the bitter sweet of a wider, freer life? I could not if I would; yet, methinks, I would not if I could. But here comes George, I will argue the point with him."

He rose from his seat and went forward to meet his brother, who at this moment entered the lane.

The two forms were faithful expressions of their several lives. There was a family likeness between them, for they shared in that beauty of the noble English blood, of which, in these days.

few types remain: the Norman tempered by the Saxon, the fire of conquest by integrity, and a self-contained, inflexible habit of mind. In the times of the Sydneys and Russells, the English body was a strong and nobly-proportioned vase, in which shone a steady and powerful, if not brilliant light.

The chains of convention, an external life grown out of proportion with that of the heart and mind, have destroyed, for the most part, this dignified beauty. There is no longer, in fact, an aristocracy in England, because the saplings are too puny to represent the old oak. But that it once existed, and did stand for what is best in that nation, any collection of portraits from the sixteenth century will show.

The two men who now met had character enough to exhibit in their persons not only the stock from which they sprang, but what was special in themselves harmonized with it. There were ten years betwixt them, but the younger verged on middle age; and permanent habits, as well as tendencies of character, were stamped upon their persons.

Lord Edward Herbert was one of the handsomest men of his day, of a beauty alike stately, chivalric and intellectual. His person and features were cultivated by all the disciplines of a time when courtly graces were not insignificant, because a monarch mind informed the court, nor warlike customs, rude or mechanical, for individual nature had free play in the field, except as restrained by the laws of courtesy and honor. The steel glove became his hand, and the spur his heel; neither can we fancy him out of his place, for any place he would have made his own. But all this grace and dignity of the man of the world was in him subordinated to that of the man, for in his eye, and in the brooding sense of all his countenance, was felt the life of one who, while he deemed that his present honour lay in playing well the part assigned him by destiny, never forgot that it was but a part, and fed steadily his forces on that within that passes show.

It has been said, with a deep wisdom, that the figure we most need to see before us now is not that of a saint, martyr, sage, poet, artist, preacher, or any other whose vocation leads to a seclusion and partial use of faculty, but "a spiritual man of the world," able to comprehend all things, exclusively dedicate to none. Of this idea we need a new expression, peculiarly adapted to our time; but in the past it will be difficult to find one more adequate than the life and person of Lord Herbert.

George Herbert, like his elder brother, was tall, erect, and with the noble air of one sprung from a race whose spirit has never been broken or bartered; but his thin form contrasted with the full development which generous living, various exercise, and habits of enjoyment had given his brother. Nor had his features that range and depth of expression which tell of many-coloured experiences, and passions undergone or vanquished. The depth, for there was depth, was of feeling rather than experience. A penetrating sweetness beamed from him on the observer, who was rather raised and softened in himself than drawn to think of the being who infused this heavenly fire into his veins. Like the violet, the strong and subtle odour of his mind was arrayed at its source with such an air of meekness, that the receiver blessed rather the liberal winds of heaven than any earth-born flower for the gift.

Raphael has lifted the transfigured Saviour only a little way from the ground; but in the forms and expression of the feet, you see that, though they may walk there again, they would tread far more naturally a more delicate element. This buoyant lightness, which, by seeking, seems to tread the air, is indicated by the text: "Beautiful upon the mountains are the feet of those who come with glad tidings." And such thoughts were suggested by the gait and gesture of George Herbert, especially as he approached you. Through the faces of most men, even of geniuses, the soul shines as through a mask, or, at best, a crystal; we look behind a shield for the heart. But, with those of seraphic nature, or so filled with spirit that translation may be near, it seems to hover before or around, announcing or enfolding them like a luminous atmosphere. Such an one advances like a vision, and the eye must steady itself before a spiritual light, to recognize him as a reality.

Some such emotion was felt by Lord Herbert as he looked on his brother, who, for a moment or two, approached without observing him, but absorbed and radiant in his own happy thoughts. They had not met for long, and it seemed that George had grown from an uncertain boy, often blushing and shrinking either from himself or others, into an angelic clearness, such as the noble seeker had not elsewhere found.

But when he was seen, the embrace was eager and affectionate as that of the brother and the child.

"Let us not return at once," said Lord Herbert. "I had already waited for you long, and have seen all the beauties of the parsonage and church."

"Not many, I think, in the eyes of such a critic," said George, as they seated themselves in the spot his brother had before chosen for the extent and loveliness of prospect.

"Enough to make me envious of you, if I had not early seen enough to be envious of none. Indeed, I know not if such a feeling can gain admittance to your little paradise, for I never heard such love and reverence expressed as by your people for you."

George looked upon his brother with a pleased and open sweetness. Lord Herbert continued, with a little hesitation—"To tell the truth, I wondered a little at the boundless affection they declared. Our mother has long and often told me of your pure and beneficent life, and I know what you have done for this place and people, but, as I remember, you were of a choleric temper."

"And am so still!"

"Well, and do you not sometimes, by flashes of that, lose all you may have gained?"

"It does not often now," he replied, "find open way. My Master has been very good to me in suggestions of restraining prayer, which come into my mind at the hour of temptation."

Lord H.—Why do you not say, rather, that your own discerning mind and maturer will show you more and more the folly and wrong of such outbreaks.

George H.—Because that would not be saying all that I think. At such times I feel a higher power interposed, as much as I see that yonder tree is distinct from myself. Shall I repeat to you some poor verses in which I have told, by means of various likenesses, in an imperfect fashion, how it is with me in this matter?

Lord H.—Do so! I shall hear them gladly; for I, like you, though with less time and learning to perfect it, love the deliberate composition of the closet, and believe we can better understand one another by thoughts expressed so, than in the more glowing but hasty words of the moment.

George H.—

Prayer—the church's banquet; angel's age;
  God's breath in man returning to his birth;
The soul in paraphrase; heart in pilgrimage;
  The Christian plummet, sounding heaven and earth.

Engine against th' Almighty; sinner's tower;
  Reversed thunder; Christ's side-piercing spear;
The six-days' world transposing in an hour;
  A kind of tune, which all things hear and fear.

Softness, and peace, and joy, and love, and bliss;
  Exalted manna; gladness of the best;

Heaven in ordinary; man well drest;
The milky way; the bird of paradise;
Church bells beyond the stars heard; the soul's blood;
The land of spices; something understood.

Lord H.—(who has listened attentively, after a moment's thought.)—There is something in the spirit of your lines which pleases me, and, in general, I know not that I should differ; yet you have expressed yourself nearest to mine own knowledge and feeling, where you have left more room to consider our prayers as aspirations, rather than the gifts of grace; as—

"Heart in pilgrimage;"
"A kind of tune, which all things hear and fear."
"Something understood."

In your likenesses, you sometimes appear to quibble in a way unworthy the subject.

George H.—It is the nature of some minds, brother, to play with what they love best. Yours is of a grander and severer cast; it can only grasp and survey steadily what interests it. My walk is different, and I have always admired you in yours without expecting to keep pace with you.

Lord H.—I hear your sweet words with the more pleasure, George, that I had supposed you were now too much of the churchman to value the fruits of my thought.

George H.—God forbid that I should ever cease to reverence the mind that was, to my own, so truly that of an elder brother! I do lament that you will not accept the banner of my Master, and drink at what I have found the fountain of pure wisdom. But as I would not blot from the book of life the prophets and priests that came before Him, nor those antique sages who knew all

That Reason hath from Nature borrowed,
Or of itself, like a good housewife spun,
In laws and policy: what the stars conspire:

What willing Nature speaks; what, freed by fire:
Both th' old discoveries, and the new found seas:
The stock and surplus, cause and history,—

As I cannot resign and disparage these, because they have not what I conceive to be the pearl of all knowledge, how could I you?

Lord H.—You speak wisely, George, and, let me add, religiously. Were all churchmen as tolerant, I had never assailed the basis of their belief. Did they not insist and urge upon us their way as the one only way, not for them alone, but for all, none would wish to put stumbling-blocks before their feet.

George H.—Nay, my brother, do not misunderstand me. None, more than I, can think there is but one way to arrive finally at truth.

Lord H.—I do not misunderstand you; but, feeling that you are one who accept what you do from love of the best, and not from fear of the worst, I am as much inclined to tolerate your conclusions as you to tolerate mine.

George H.—I do not consider yours as conclusions, but only as steps to such. The progress of the mind should be from natural to revealed religion, as there must be a sky for the sun to give light through its expanse.

Lord H.—The sky is—nothing!

George H.—Except room for a sun, and such there is in you. Of your own need of such, did you not give convincing proof, when you prayed for a revelation to direct whether you should publish a book against revelation?*

* The following narration, published by Lord Herbert, in his life, has often been made use of by his opponents. It should be respected as an evidence of his integrity, being, like the rest of his memoir, a specimen of absolute truth and frankness towards himself and all other beings:—

Having many conscientious doubts whether or no to publish his book, *De Veritate*, (which was against revealed religion, on the ground that it was improbable that Heaven should deal partially with men, revealing its will to one

Lord H.—You borrow that objection from the crowd, George; but I wonder you have not looked into the matter more deeply. Is there any thing inconsistent with disbelief in a partial plan of salvation for the nations, which, by its necessarily limited working, excludes the majority of men up to our day, with belief that each individual soul, wherever born, however nurtured, may receive immediate response, in an earnest hour, from the source of truth.

George H.—But you believed the customary order of nature to be deranged in your behalf. What miraculous record does more?

Lord H.—It was at the expense of none other. A spirit asked, a spirit answered, and its voice was thunder; but, in this, there was nothing special, nothing partial wrought in my behalf, more than if I had arrived at the same conclusion by a process of reasoning.

George H.—I cannot but think, that if your mind were al-

race and nation, not to another,) "Being thus doubtful in my chamber, one fair day in the summer, my casement being opened to the south, the sun shining clear and no wind stirring, I took my book, *De Veritate*, in my hand, and kneeling on my knees, devoutly said these words:—O, thou eternal God, author of the light which now shines upon me, and giver of all inward illuminations, I do beseech thee, of thy infinite goodness, to pardon a greater request than a sinner ought to make. I am not satisfied enough whether I shall publish this book, *De Veritate*. If it be for thy glory, I beseech thee give me some sign from heaven; if not, I shall suppress it.—I had no sooner spoken these words, but a loud, though yet gentle noise came from the heavens, (for it was like nothing on earth,) which did so comfort and cheer me, that I took my petition as granted, and that I had the sign I demanded, whereupon, also, I resolved to print my book. This, how strange soever it may seem, I protest before the Eternal God, is true; neither am I any way superstitiously deceived herein, since I did not only clearly hear the noise, but in the serenest sky that ever I saw, being without all cloud, did, to my thinking, see the place from whence it came."

Lord Orford observes, with his natural sneer, "How could a man who doubted of *partial*, believe *individual revelation?*"

lowed, by the nature of your life, its free force to search, it would survey the subject in a different way, and draw inferences more legitimate from a comparison of its own experience with the gospel.

Lord H.—My brother does not think the mind is free to act in courts and camps. To me it seems that the mind takes its own course everywhere, and that, if men cannot have outward, they can always mental seclusion. None is so profoundly lonely, none so in need of constant self-support, as he who, living in the crowd, thinks an inch aside from, or in advance of it. The hermitage of such an one is still and cold; its silence unbroken to a degree of which these beautiful and fragrant solitudes give no hint. These sunny sights and sounds, promoting reverie rather than thought, are scarce more favourable to a great advance in the intellect, than the distractions of the busy street. Beside, we need the assaults of other minds to quicken our powers, so easily hushed to sleep, and call it peace. The mind takes a bias too easily, and does not examine whether from tradition or a native growth intended by the heavens.

George H.—But you are no common man. You shine, you charm, you win, and the world presses too eagerly on you to leave many hours for meditation.

Lord H.—It is a common error to believe that the most prosperous men love the world best. It may be hardest for them to leave it, because they have been made effeminate and slothful by want of that exercise which difficulty brings. But this is not the case with me; for, while the common boons of life's game have been too easily attained, to hold high value in my eyes, the goal which my secret mind, from earliest infancy, prescribed, has been high enough to task all my energies. Every year has helped to make that, and that alone, of value in my eyes; and did I believe that life, in scenes like this, would lead me to it more speedily than in my accustomed broader way, I would seek it to-morrow—nay, to-day. But is it worthy of a man to make him a cell, in which alone he can worship? Give me rather the always open temple of the universe! To me, it seems that the only course for a man is that pointed out by birth and fortune. Let him take that and pursue it with clear eyes and head erect, secure that it must point at last to those truths which are central to us, wherever we stand; and if my road, leading through the busy crowd of men, amid the clang and bustle of conflicting interests and passions, detain me longer than would the still path through the groves, the chosen haunt of contemplation, yet I incline to think that progress so, though slower, is surer. Owing no safety, no clearness to my position, but so far as it is attained to mine own effort, encountering what temptations, doubts and lures may beset a man, what I do possess is more surely mine, and less a prey to contingencies. It is a well-tempered wine that has been carried over many seas, and escaped many shipwrecks.

George H.—I can the less gainsay you, my lord and brother, that your course would have been mine could I have chosen.

Lord H.—Yes; I remember thy verse:—

> Whereas my birth and spirits rather took
> The way that takes the town;
> Thou didst betray me to a lingering book,
> And wrap me in a gown.

It was not my fault, George, that it so chanced.

George H.—I have long learnt to feel that it noway chanced; that thus, and no other, was it well for me. But how I view these matters you are, or may be well aware, through a little book I have writ. Of you I would fain learn more than can be shown me by the display of your skill in controversy in your printed works, or the rumors of your feats at arms, or success with the circles of fair ladies, which reach even this quiet nook. Rather let us, in this hour of intimate converse, such as we have not had for years, and may not have again, draw near in what is nearest; and do you, my dear Lord, vouchsafe your friend and brother some clear tokens as to that goal you say has from childhood been mentally prescribed you, and the way you have taken to gain it.

Lord H.—I will do this willingly, and the rather that I have with me a leaf, in which I have lately recorded what appeared to me in glimpse or flash in my young years, and now shines upon my life with steady ray. I brought it, with some thought that I might impart it to you, which confidence I have not shown to any yet; though if, as I purpose, some memoir of my life and times should fall from my pen, these poems may be interwoven there as cause and comment for all I felt, and knew, and was. The first contains my thought of the beginning and progress of life:—

(*From the Latin of Lord Herbert.*)

LIFE.

First, the life stirred within the genial seed,
Seeking its properties, whence plastic power
Was born. Chaos, with lively juice pervading,
External form in its recess restraining,
While the conspiring causes might accede,
And full creation safely be essayed.

Next, movement was in the maternal field;
Fermenting spirit puts on tender limbs,
And, earnest, now prepares, of wondrous fabric,
The powers of sense, a dwelling not too mean for mind contriving
That, sliding from its heaven, it may put on
These faculties, and, prophesying future fate,
Correct the slothful weight (of matter,) nor uselessly be manifested.

A third stage, now, scene truly great contains
The solemn feast of heaven, the theatre of earth,
Kindred and species, varied forms of things

Are here discerned,—and, from its own impulse,
It is permitted to the soul to circle,
Hither and thither rove, that it may see
Laws and eternal covenants of its world,
And stars returning in assiduous course,
The causes and the bonds of life to learn,
And from afar foresee the highest will.
How he to admirable harmony
Tempers the various motions of the world,
And Father, Lord, Guardian, and Builder-up,
And Deity on every side is styled.
Next, from this knowledge the fourth stage proceeds:
Cleansing away its stains, mind daily grows more pure,
Enriched with various learning, strong in virtue,
Extends its powers, and breathes sublimer air:
A secret spur is felt within the inmost heart,
That he who will, may emerge from this perishable state,
And a happier is sought
By ambitious rites, consecrations, religious worship,
And a new hope succeeds, conscious of a better fate,
Clinging to things above, expanding through all the heavens,
And the Divine descends to meet a holy love,
And unequivocal token is given of celestial life.
That, as a good servant, I shall receive my reward;
Or, if worthy, enter as a son, into the goods of my father,
God himself is my surety. When I shall put off this life,
Confident in a better, free in my own will,
He himself is my surety, that a fifth, yet higher state shall ensue,
And a sixth, and all, in fine, that my heart shall know how to ask.

CONJECTURES CONCERNING THE HEAVENLY LIFE.

Purified in my whole genius, I congratulate myself
Secure of fate, while neither am I downcast by any terrors,
Nor store up secret griefs in my heart,
But pass my days cheerfully in the midst of mishaps,
Despite the evils which engird the earth,
Seeking the way above the stars with ardent virtue.
I have received, beforehand, the first fruits of heavenly life—

I now seek the later, sustained by divine love,
Through which, conquering at once the scoffs of a gloomy destiny,
I leave the barbarous company of a frantic age,
Breathing out for the last time the infernal air—breathing in the supernal,
I enfold myself wholly in these sacred flames,
And, sustained by them, ascend the highest dome,
And far and wide survey the wonders of a new sphere,
And see well-known spirits, now beautiful in their proper light,
And the choirs of the higher powers, and blessed beings
With whom I desire to mingle fires and sacred bonds—
Passing from joy to joy the heaven of all,
What has been given to ourselves, or sanctioned by a common vow.
God, in the meantime, accumulating his rewards,
May at once increase our honour and illustrate his own love.
Nor heavens shall be wanting to heavens, nor numberless ages to life,
Nor new joys to these ages, such as an
Eternity shall not diminish, nor the infinite bring to an end.
Nor, more than all, shall the fair favour of the Divine be wanting—
Constantly increasing these joys, varied in admirable modes,
And making each state yield only to one yet happier,
And what we never even knew how to hope, is given to us—
Nor is aught kept back except what only the One can conceive,
And what in their own nature are by far most perfect
In us, at least, appear embellished,
Since the sleeping minds which heaven prepares from the beginning—
Only our labor and industry can vivify,
Polishing them with learning and with morals,
That they may return all fair, bearing back a dowry to heaven,
When, by use of our free will, we put to rout those ills
Which heaven has neither dispelled, nor will hereafter dispel.
Thus through us is magnified the glory of God,
And our glory, too, shall resound throughout the heavens,
And what are the due rewards of virtue, finally
Must render the Father himself more happy than his wont.
Whence still more ample grace shall be showered upon us,
Each and all yielding to our prayer,
For, if *liberty* be dear, it is permitted
To roam through the loveliest regions obvious to innumerable heavens,
And gather, as we pass, the delights of each,

If *fixed contemplation* be chosen rather in the mind,
All the mysteries of the high regions shall be laid open to us,
And the joy will be to know the methods of God,—
Then it may be permitted to act upon earth, to have a care
Of the weal of men, and to bestow just laws.
If we are more delighted with celestial *love*,
We are dissolved into flames which glide about and excite one another
Mutually, embraced in sacred ardours,
Spring upwards, enfolded together in firmest bonds,
In parts and wholes, mingling by turns,
And the ardour of the Divine kindles (in them) still new ardours,
It will make us happy to praise God, while he commands us,
The angelic choir, singing together with sweet modulation,
Sounds through heaven, publishing our joys,
And beauteous spectacles are put forth, hour by hour,
And, as it were, the whole fabric of heaven becomes a theatre,
Till the divine energy pervades the whole sweep of the world,
And chisels out from it new forms,
Adorned with new faculties, of larger powers.
Our forms, too, may then be renewed—
Assume new forms and senses, till our
Joys again rise up consummate.
If trusting thus, I shall have put off this mortal weed,
Why may not then still greater things be disclosed?

George H.—(who, during his brother's reading, has listened, with head bowed down, leaned on his arm, looks up after a few moments' silence)—Pardon, my lord, if I have not fit words to answer you. The flood of your thought has swept over me like music, and like that, for the time, at least, it fills and satisfies. I am conscious of many feelings which are not touched upon there,—of the depths of love and sorrow made known to men, through One whom you as yet know not. But of these I will not speak now, except to ask, borne on this strong pinion, have you never faltered till you felt the need of a friend? strong in this clear vision, have you never sighed for a more homefelt assurance to your faith? steady in your demand of what the soul requires, have you never known fear lest you want purity to receive the boon if granted ?

Lord H.—I do not count those weak moments, George ; they are not my true life.

George H.—It suffices that you know them, for, in time, I doubt not that every conviction which a human being needs, to be reconciled to the Parent of all, will be granted to a nature so ample, so open, and so aspiring. Let me answer in a strain which bespeaks my heart as truly, if not as nobly as yours answers to your great mind,—

My joy, my life, my crown!
My heart was meaning all the day
Somewhat it fain would say;
And still it runneth, muttering, up and down,
With only this—*my joy, my life, my crown.*

Yet slight not these few words;
If truly said, they may take part
Among the best in art.
The fineness which a hymn or psalm affords,
Is, when the soul unto the lines accords.

He who craves all the mind
And all the soul, and strength and time;
If the words only rhyme,
Justly complains, that somewhat is behind
To make his verse or write a hymn in kind.

Whereas, if the heart be moved,
Although the verse be somewhat scant,
God doth supply the want—
As when the heart says, sighing to be approved,
"Oh, could I love!" and stops; God writeth, *loved.*

Lord H.—I cannot say to you truly that my mind replies to this, although I discern a beauty in it. You will say I lack humility to understand yours.

George H.—I will say nothing, but leave you to time and the care of a greater than I. We have exchanged our verse, let us now change our subject too, and walk homeward; for I trust you, this night, intend to make my roof happy in your presence, and the sun is sinking.

Lord H.—Yes, you know I am there to be introduced to my new sister, whom I hope to love, and win from her a sisterly regard in turn.

George H.—You, none can fail to regard; and for her, even as you love me, you must her, for we are one.

Lord H.—(smiling)—Indeed; two years wed, and say that.

George H.—Will your lordship doubt it? From your muse I took my first lesson.

* * * * * *

With a look, it seem'd denied
All earthly powers but hers, yet so
As if to her breath he did owe
This borrow'd life, he thus replied—

And shall our love, so far beyond
That low and dying appetite,
And which so chaste desires unite,
Not hold in an eternal bond?

O no, belov'd! I am most sure
Those virtuous habits we acquire,
As being with the soul entire,
Must with it evermore endure.

Else should our souls in vain elect;
And vainer yet were heaven's laws
When to an everlasting cause
They gave a perishing effect.

Lord H.—(sighing)—You recall a happy season, when my thoughts were as delicate of hue, and of as heavenly a perfume as the flowers of May.

George H.—Have those flowers borne no fruit?

Lord H.—My experience of the world and men had made me believe that they did not indeed bloom in vain, but that the fruit would be ripened in some future sphere of our existence. What my own marriage was you know,—a family arrangement made for me in my childhood. Such obligations as such a marriage could imply, I have fulfilled, and it has not failed to bring me some benefits of good-will and esteem, and far more, in the happiness of being a parent. But my observation of the ties formed, by those whose choice was left free, has not taught me that a higher happiness than mine was the destined portion of men. They are too immature to form permanent relations; all that they do seems experiment, and mostly fails for the present. Thus I had postponed all hopes except of fleeting joys or ideal pictures. Will you tell me that you are possessed already of so much more?

George H.—I am indeed united in a bond, whose reality I cannot doubt, with one whose thoughts, affections, and objects every way correspond with mine, and in whose life I see a purpose so pure that, if we are ever separated, the fault must be mine. I believe God, in his exceeding grace, gave us to one another, for we met almost at a glance, without doubt before, jar or repentance after, the vow which bound our lives together.

Lord H.—Then there is indeed one circumstance of your lot I could wish to share with you. (After some moments' silence on both sides)—They told me at the house, that, with all your engagements, you go twice a-week to Salisbury. How is that? How can you leave your business and your happy home, so much and often?

George H.—I go to hear the music; the great solemn church music. This is, at once, the luxury and the necessity of my life. I know not how it is with others, but, with me, there is a frequent drooping of the wings, a smouldering of the inward fires, a languor, almost a loathing of corporeal existence. Of this visible diurnal sphere I am, by turns, the master, the interpreter, and the victim; an ever burning lamp, to warm again the embers of the altar; a skiff, that cannot be becalmed, to bear me again on the ocean of hope; an elixir, that fills the dullest fibre with ethereal energy; such, music is to me. It stands in relation to speech, even to the speech of poets, as the angelic choir, who, in their subtler being, may inform the space around us, unseen but felt, do to men, even to prophetic men. It answers to the soul's presage, and, in its fluent life, embodies all I yet know how to desire. As all the thoughts and hopes of human souls are blended by the organ to a stream of prayer and praise, I tune at it my separate breast, and return to my little home, cheered and ready for my day's work, as the lark does to her nest after her morning visit to the sun.

Lord H.—The ancients held that the spheres made music to those who had risen into a state which enabled them to hear it. Pythagoras, who prepared different kinds of melody to guide and expand the differing natures of his pupils, needed himself to hear none on instruments made by human art, for the universal harmony which comprehends all these was audible to him. Man feels in all his higher moments, the need of traversing a subtler element, of a winged existence. Artists have recognised wings as the symbol of the state next above ours; but they have not been able so to attach them to the forms of gods and angels as to make them agree with the anatomy of the human frame. Perhaps music gives this instruction, and supplies the deficiency. Although I see that I do not feel it as habitually or as profoundly as you do, I have experienced such impressions from it.

George H.—That is truly what I mean. It introduces me into that winged nature, and not as by way of supplement, but of inevitable transition. All that has budded in me, bursts into bloom, under this influence. As I sit in our noble cathedral, in itself one of the holiest thoughts ever embodied by the power of man, the great tides of song come rushing through its aisles; they pervade all the space, and my soul within it, perfuming me like incense, bearing me on like the wind, and on and on to regions of unutterable joy, and freedom, and certainty. As their triumph rises, I rise with them, and learn to comprehend by living them, till at last a calm rapture seizes me, and holds me poised. The same life you have attained in your description of the celestial choirs. It is the music of the soul, when centred in the will of God, thrilled by the love, expanded by the energy, with which it is fulfilled through all the ranges of active life. From such hours, I return through these green lanes, to hear the same tones from the slightest flower, to long for a life of purity and praise, such as is manifested by the flowers.

At this moment they reached the door, and there paused to look back. George Herbert bent upon the scene a half-abstracted look, yet which had a celestial tearfulness in it, a pensiveness beyond joy. His brother looked on *him*, and, beneath that fading twilight, it seemed to him a farewell look. It was so. Soon George Herbert soared into the purer state, for which his soul had long been ready, though not impatient.

The brothers met no more; but they had enjoyed together one hour of true friendship, when mind drew near to mind by the light of faith, and heart mingled with heart in the atmosphere of Divine love. It was a great boon to be granted two mortals.

THE PROSE WORKS OF MILTON.

WITH A BIOGRAPHICAL INTRODUCTION, BY R. W. GRISWOLD.

THE noble lines of Wordsworth, quoted by Mr. Griswold on his title-page, would be the best and a sufficient advertisement of each reprint:

"Milton! thou shouldst be living at this hour.
Return to us again,
And give us manners, virtue, freedom, power.
Thy soul was like a Star, and dwelt apart;
Thou hadst a voice whose sound was like the Sea:
Pure as the naked Heavens, majestic, free:
So didst thou travel on life's common way
In cheerful Godliness, and yet thy heart
The lowliest duties on herself did lay."

One should have climbed to as high a point as Wordsworth to be able to review Milton, or even to view in part his high places. From the hill-top we still strain our eyes looking up to the mountain-peak—

"Itself Earth's Rosy Star."

We rejoice to see that there is again a call for an edition of Milton's Prose Works. There could not be a surer sign that there is still pure blood in the nation than a call for these. The print and paper are tolerably good; if not worthy of the matter, yet they are, we suppose, as good as can be afforded and make the book cheap enough for general circulation. We wish there had been three volumes, instead of two clumsy ones, with that detestably narrow inner margin of which we have heretofore complained. But we trust the work is in such a shape that it will lie on the table of all poor students who are ever to be scholars, and be the good angel, the Ithuriel warner of many a youth at the parting of the ways. Who chooses that way which the foot of Milton never forsook, will find in him a never failing authority for the indissoluble union between permanent strength and purity. May many, born and bred amid the corruptions of a false world till the heart is on the verge of a desolate scepticism and the good genius preparing to fly, be led to recall him and make him at home forever by such passages as we have read this beautiful bright September morning, in the 'Apology for Smectymnuus.' We chanced happily upon them, as we were pondering some sad narrations of daily life, and others who need the same consolation, will no doubt detect them in a short intercourse with the volumes.

Mr. Griswold thus closes his "Biographical Introduction:"—

"On Sunday, the eighth day of November, 1674, one month before completing his sixty-sixth year, JOHN MILTON died. He was the greatest of all human beings: the noblest and the ennobler of mankind. He has steadily grown in the world's reverence, and his fame will still increase with the lapse of ages."

The absolute of this superlative pleases us, even if we do believe that there are four or five names on the scroll of history which may be placed beside that of Milton. We love hero-worship, where the hero is, indeed, worthy the honors of a demi-god. And, if Milton be not absolutely the greatest of human beings, it is hard to name one who combines so many features of God's own image, ideal grandeur, a life of spotless virtue, heroic endeavour and constancy, with such richness of gifts.

We cannot speak worthily of the books before us. They have been, as they will be, our friends and teachers, but to express with any justice what they are to us, or our idea of what they are to the world at large—to make any estimate of the vast fund of pure gold they contain and allow for the residuum of local and partial judgment and human frailty—to examine the bearings of various essays on the past and present with even that degree of thought and justice of which we are capable, would be a work of months. It would be to us a careful, a solemn, a sacred task, and not in anywise to be undertaken in the columns of a daily paper. Beside, who can think of Milton without the feeling which he himself expresses ?—

"He who would not be frustrate of his hope to write well hereafter in laudable things, ought himself to be a true poem; that is, a composition and pattern of the best and honorablest things; not presuming to sing high praises of heroic men, or famous cities, unless he have in himself the experience and the practice of all that which is praiseworthy."

We shall, then, content ourselves with stating three reasons which at this moment occur to us why these Essays of Milton deserve to be sought and studied beyond any other volumes of English prose:

1st. He draws us to a central point whither converge the rays of sacred and profane, ancient and modern Literature. Those who sit at his feet obtain every hour glimpses in all directions. The constant perception of principles, richness in illustrations and fullness of knowledge, make him the greatest Master we have in the way of giving clues and impulses. His plan tempts even very timid students to hope they may thread the mighty maze of the Past. This fullness of knowledge only a genius masculine and divine like his could animate. He says, in a letter to Diodati, written as late as his thirtieth year: "It is well known, and you well know, that I am naturally slow in writing and adverse to write." Indeed his passion for acquisition preceded long and far outwent, in the first part of his prime, the need of creation or expression, and, probably, no era less grand and fervent than his own could have made him still more the genius than the scholar. But he was fortunate in an epoch fitted to develop him to his full stature—an epoch rich alike in thought, action and passion, in great results and still greater beginnings. There was fire enough to bring the immense materials he had collected into a state of fusion. Still his original bias infects the pupil, and this Master makes us thirst for Learning no less than for Life.

2d. He affords the highest exercise at once to the poetic and reflective faculties. Before us move sublime presences, the types of whole regions of creation: God, man, and elementary spirits in multitudinous glory are present to our consciousness. But meanwhile every detail is grasped and examined, and strong daily interests mark out for us a wide and plain path on the earth—a wide and plain path, but one in which it requires the most varied and strenuous application of our energies to follow the rapid and vigorous course of our guide. No one can read the Essays without feeling that the glow which follows is no mere nervous exaltation, no result of electricity from another mind under which he could remain passive, but a thorough and wholesome animation of his own powers. We seek to know, to act, and to be what is possible to Man.

3d. Mr. Griswold justly and wisely observes:—"Milton is more emphatically *American* than any author who has lived in the United States." He is so because in him is expressed so much of the primitive vitality of that thought from which America is born, though at present disposed to forswear her lineage in so many ways. He is the purity of Puritanism. He understood the nature of liberty, of justice—what is required for the unimpeded action of conscience—what constitutes true marriage, and the scope of a manly education. He is one of the Fathers of this Age, of that new Idea which agitates the sleep of Europe, and of which America, if awake to the design of Heaven and her own duty, would become the principal exponent. But the Father is still far beyond the understanding of his child.

His ideas of marriage, as expressed in the treatises on Divorce, are high and pure. He aims at a marriage of souls. If he incline too much to the prerogative of his own sex, it was from that mannishness, almost the same with boorishness, that is evident in men of the greatest and richest natures, who have never known the refining influence of happy, mutual love, as the best women evince narrowness and poverty under the same privation. In every line we see how much Milton required the benefit of "the thousand decencies that daily flow" from such a relation, and how greatly he would have been the gainer by it, both as man and as genius. In his mind lay originally the fairest ideal of woman; to see it realized would have "finished his education." *His* commonwealth could only have grown from the perfecting of individual men. The private means to such an end he rather hints than states in the short essay to Education. They are such as we are gradually learning to prize. Healthful diet, varied bodily exercises, to which we no longer need give the martial aim he proposed, fit the mind for studies which are by him arranged in a large, plastic and natural method.

Among the prophetic features of his system we may mention the place given to Agriculture and Music:

> "The next step would be to the authors on agriculture—Cato, Varro and Columella—for the matter is most easy; and if the language be difficult so much the better; it is not a difficulty above their years. And here will be an occasion of inciting, and enabling them hereafter to improve the tillage of their country, to recover their bad soil, and to remedy the waste that is made of good; for this was one of Hercules' praises."

How wise, too, his directions as to interspersing the study with travel and personal observation of important objects. We must have methods of our own, but the hints we might borrow from this short essay of Milton's are endless.

Then of music—

"The interim may, both with profit and delight, be taken up in recreating and composing their travailed spirits with the solemn and divine harmonies of music heard or learned; either whilst the skillful organist plies his grave and fancied descant in lofty fugues, or the whole symphony with artful and unimaginable touches adorn and grace the well-studied chords of some choice composer; sometimes the lute or soft organ-stop waiting on elegant voices, either to religious, martial, or civil ditties; which, if wise men and prophets be not extremely out, have a great power over disposition and manners to smoothe and make them gentle from rustic harshness and distempered passions."

He does not mention here the higher offices of music, but that they had been fulfilled to him is evident in the whole texture of his mind and his page. The organ was his instrument, and there is not a strain of its peculiar music that may not somewhere be traced in his verse or prose. Here, too, he was prophetical of our age, of which Music is the great and growing art, making deeper revelations than any other mode of expression now adopted by the soul.

After these scanty remarks upon the glories of this sun-like mind, let us look for a moment on the clouds which hung about its earthly course. Let us take some hints from his letters:—

"It is often a subject of sorrowful reflection to me, that those with whom I have been either fortuitously or legally associated by contiguity of place or some tie of little moment, are continually at hand to infest my home, to stun me with their noise and waste me with vexation, while those who are endeared to me by the closest sympathy of manners, of tastes and pursuits, are almost all withheld from my embrace either by death or an insuperable distance of place; and have for the most part been so rapidly hurried from my sight, that my prospects seem continually solitary, and my heart perpetually desolate."

The last letter in the volume ends thus:

"What you term policy, and which I wish that you had rather called patriotic piety, has, if I may so say, almost left me, who was charmed with so sweet a sound, without a country. * * * I will conclude after first begging you, if there be any errors in the diction or the punctuation, to impute it to the boy who wrote this, who is quite ignorant of Latin, and to whom I was, with no little vexation, *obliged to dictate not the words, but, one by one, the letters of which they were composed.*"

The account of the gradual increase of his blindness is interesting, physiologically as well as otherwise :—

"It is now, I think, about ten years (1654) since I perceived my vision to grow weak and dull; and, at the same time, I was troubled with pain in my kidneys and bowels, accompanied with flatulency. In the morning, if I began to read, as was my custom, my eyes instantly ached intensely, but were refreshed after a little corporeal exercise. The candle which I looked at seemed as if it were encircled by a rainbow. Not long after the sight in the left part of the left eye (which I lost some years before the other) became quite obscured, and prevented me from discerning any object on that side. The sight in my other eye has now been gradually and sensibly vanishing away for about three years; some months before it had entirely perished, though I stood motionless, every thing which I looked at seemed in motion to and fro. A stiff cloudy vapor seemed to have settled on my forehead and temples, which usually occasions a sort of somnolent pressure upon my eyes, and particularly from dinner till evening. So that I often recollect what is said of the poet Phineas in the Argonautics:

'A stupor deep his cloudy temples bound,
And when he waked he seemed as whirling round,
Or in a feeble trance he speechless lay.'

I ought not to omit that, while I had any sight left, as soon as I lay down on my bed, and turned on either side, a flood of light used to gush from my closed eyelids. Then, as my sight became daily more impaired, the colors became more faint, and were emitted with a certain crackling sound; but, at present, every species of illumination being, as it were, extinguished, there is diffused around me nothing but darkness, or darkness mingled and streaked with an ashy brown. Yet the darkness in which I am perpetually immersed seems always, both by night and day, to approach nearer to a white than black; and when the eye is rolling in its socket, it admits a little particle of light as through a chink. And though your physician may kindle a small ray of hope, yet I make up my mind to the malady as quite incurable; and I often reflect, that as the wise man admonishes, days of darkness are destined to each of us. The darkness which I experience, less oppressive than that of the tomb, is, owing to the singular goodness of the Deity, passed amid the pursuits of literature and the cheering salutations of friendship. But if, as it is written, man shall not live by bread alone, but by every word that proceedeth from the mouth of God why may not any one acquiesce in the privation of his sight, when God has so amply furnished his mind and his conscience with eyes? While He so tenderly provides for me, while He so graciously leads me by the hand and conducts me on the way, I will, since it is His pleasure, rather rejoice than repine at being blind. And my dear Philura, whatever may be the event, I wish you adieu with no less courage and composure than if I had the eyes of a lynx."

Though the organist was wrapped in utter darkness, 'only mingled and streaked with an ashy brown,' still the organ pealed forth its perpetual, sublime Te Deum! Shall we, sitting in the open sun-light, dare tune our humble pipes to any other strain? Thou may'st thank Him, Milton, for, but for this misfortune, thou hadst been a benefactor to the great and strong only, but now to the multitude and suffering also thy voice comes, bidding them 'bate no jot of heart or hope,' with archangelic power and melody.

THE LIFE OF SIR JAMES MACKINTOSH.

BY HIS SON; ROBERT JAMES MACKINTOSH.

"Biography is by nature the most universally profitable, universally pleasant of all things; especially biography of distinguished individuals." [Opinion of the sagacious Hofrath Henshrecke, as quoted in Sartor Resartus.]

If the biography of a distinguished individual be thus especially pleasant a matter, how most of all pleasant is it when a child is found worthy to erect the monument with which the world esteems his father worthy to be honoured! We see that it is no part of the plan of the universe to make nature or talent hereditary. The education of circumstances supersedes that of system, unlooked for influences disturb the natural action of the parent's character on that of the child; and all who have made even a few observations of this sort, must feel that, here as elsewhere, planting and watering had best be done for duty or love's sake, without any sanguine hopes as to the increase. From mistaken notions of freedom, or an ill-directed fondness for experimentalizing, the son is often seen to disregard the precepts or example of his father; and it is a matter of surprise if the scion is found to bear fruit of a similar, not to say equal flavor, with the parent tree.

How opposed all this is to our natural wishes and expectations, (i. e., to our ideal of a state of perfection,) is evident from the pleasure we feel when family relations preserve their harmony, and the father becomes to the son a master and a model—a reverend teacher and a favourite study. Such a happy state of things makes the biography before us very attractive. It is in itself good, though, probably not as interesting or impressive as one who could have painted the subject from somewhat a greater distance might have made it. The affections of the writer are nowhere obtruded upon us. The feeling shown towards his amiable and accomplished father is every where reverential and tender, nowhere blind or exaggerated. Sir James is always, when possible, permitted to speak for himself; and we are not teased by attempts to heighten or alter the natural effect of his thoughts and opinions. The impressions he produced on different minds are given us unmutilated and unqualified. The youthful errors, and the one great defect which had power to prevent so rich a piece of creation from blooming into all that love or admiration could have wished, are neither dissembled nor excused. Perhaps here Mr. Mackintosh kept in mind his father's admirable remark upon Mrs. Opie's Memoir of her husband. "One passage I object to; where she makes an excuse for not exposing his faults. She ought either to have been absolutely silent, or, with an intrepid confidence in the character of her husband, to have stated faults, which she was sure would not have been dust in the balance, placed in the scale opposite to his merits."

Indeed, the defect here was not to be hidden, since it sapped the noblest undertakings and baffled the highest aspirations of the gentle and generous critic; but we might have been annoyed by awkward attempts to gloss it over, which would have prevented our enjoying in full confidence the record of so many virtues and remarkable attainments. To these discerning and calm justice is done; more, as the son and friend felt, was not needed. And, upon the whole, if filial delicacy has prevented the Life of Sir J. M. from making so brilliant and entertaining a book as it might be in the hands of one who felt at liberty to analyze more deeply and eulogize more eloquently, our knowledge of it as history is probably more correct, and of greater permanent value.

The recollections of childhood are scanty. We see, indeed,

an extraordinary boy, but get little light as to what helped to make him what he was. Generally we know, that if there be anything of talent in a boy, a Scotch mist has wonderful power to draw it out. Add to this, that he lived much in solitude, and on the banks of a beautiful lake. To such means of intellectual developement many a Swiss and many a Highlander has done no visible, or at least so far as this world knoweth, no immortal honour; but there be hardy striplings, who expand their energies in chasing the deer and the chamois, and act out the impulse, poetic or otherwise, as it rises; while the little Jamie was fed on books, and taught how thought and feeling may be hoarded and put out at interest while he had plenty of time and means for hoarding. Yet is the precocity natural to a boy of genius wher his attention is so little dissipated, and the sphere of exercising his childish energies so limited, very undesirable. For precocity some great price is always demanded sooner or later in life. Nature intended the years of childhood to be spent in perceiving and playing, not in reflecting and acting; and when her processes are hurried or disturbed, she is sure to exact a penalty. Bacon paid by moral perversion for his premature intellectual developement. Mozart gave half a life for a first half all science and soul. Mackintosh brought out so wonderfully his powers of acquisition at the expense of those of creation, to say nothing of the usual fine of delicate health. How much he lived *out* of books we know not, but he tells us of little else. The details of his best plaything—the boy-club at which he exercised himself, as the every-day boy rides the great horse, or the young Indian tries his father's bow, are interesting. At an early age he went to Aberdeen, where he came under the instruction of a Dr. Dunbar, who, if he did not impart much positive knowledge, seems to have been successful in breathing into his pupil that strong desire of knowing and doing, which is of more value than any thing one can receive from another. Here too, was he happy in that friendship with Robert Hall, which probably did more for his mind, than all the teachings of all his youthful years. They were eighteen and nineteen years of age, an age when the mind is hoping every thing—fearing nothing; a time when perfect freedom of intercourse is possible; for then no community of interests is exacted between two noble natures, except that of aims which may be carried forward into infinity. How beautiful, how purely intellectual, this friendship was, may be best felt from reading the two letters Sir James wrote many years after to Robert Hall upon his recovery from derangement. In these exquisite letters, a subject which would seem almost too delicate for an angel's touch, is in nowise profaned; and the most elevated, as well as the most consoling view is taken with the confidence of one who had seen into the very depths of Hall's nature. There is no pity, no flattery—no ill-advised application of the wise counsels of calm hours and untried spirits, but that noble and sincere faith, which might have created beneath the ribs of death what it expected to find there. The trust of one who had tried the kernel, and knew that the tree was an oak; and, though shattered by lightning, could not lose its royalty of nature.

From the scene of metaphysical and religious discussions, which gave such a bias to his mind and character, Sir James went to lead a life of great animal and mental excitement in Edinburgh. Here he first tourneyed with the world, and came off from the lists, not inglorious if not altogether victorious. Already he had loved once; but this seems, like his after-attachments, not to have been very deep; and as he ingenuously confesses, declined on his side, without any particular reason, except, indeed, that his character was, at that time growing; which is reason enough. A man so intellectual, so versatile, and so easily moved as he, was formed to enjoy and need society, both in and out of the domestic circle, but not to be the slave of the Passions, nor yet their master. Perhaps it may be doubted whether any man can become the master of the passions of others without having some time gone through the apprenticeship, i. e. the slavery to his own. Sir James never had power to electrify at will a large body of men—he had not stored up within the dangerous materials for the "lightning of the mind"—and every way there was more of the Apollo than the Jupiter about him.

At Edinburgh he made many friends, acquired and evaporated many prejudices, learned much, and talked more. Here was confirmed that love, which, degenerating into a need, of society, took from him the power of bearing the seclusion and solitary effort, which would have enabled him to win permanent glory and confer permanent benefits.

Then came his London life, rather a bright page, but of not more happy portent. Compare it with the London experiment of the poet Crabbe, made known to us not long since by the pen of his son. Do we not see here a comment on the hackneyed text, "Sweet are the uses of adversity," and find reason to admire the impartiality always in the long run to be observed in the distribution of human lots? To view the thing superficially, Crabbe, ill-educated, seemingly fit for no sphere, certainly unable to find any for which he thought himself fit, labouring on poetry, which the most thinking public (of booksellers) would not buy, reduced to his last fourpence, and apparently for ever separated from his Myra, was a less prosperous person than Mackintosh, on whose wit and learning so many brilliant circles daily feasted, whose budding genius mature statesmen delighted to honour, the husband of that excellent woman he has so beautifully described, and the not unsuccessful antagonist of that Burke on whom Crabbe had been a dependant. Yet look more deeply into the matter, and you see Crabbe ripening energy of purpose, and power of patient endurance, into an even heroic strength; nor is there anywhere a finer monument of the dignity to which the human soul can rise independent of circumstances, than the letter which he wrote to Burke from that fit of depression which could never become abject; a letter alike honourable to the writer and him to whom it was addressed. In that trial, Crabbe, not found wanting, tested his powers to bear and to act—he ascertained what he would do, and it was done—Mackintosh, squandering at every step the treasures which he had never been forced to count, divided in his wishes, imperfect in his efforts, wanting to himself, though so far above the herd, might well have been glad to leave his flowery paths for those through which Crabbe was led over a stony soil, and beneath a parching sun, but still—upwards. Had it been so, what a noble work might we have had instead of the Vindiciæ Gallicæ! A bright star was that, but we might have had a sun.

Yet had the publication of the Vindiciæ been followed by Sir James's getting into parliament, and becoming the English great man, the mover of the day, the minister to the hour, it had been much; and we should not have been forward to express regret, even though we might deem his natural vocation to be for literature and philosophy. Freedom has so often been obliged to retreat into garrison in England, that the honor of being one of her sentinels there is sufficient for a life. But here again a broken thread—a beginning not followed up. He goes to India, and after that he was always to act with divided soul, and his life could be nothing better than a fragment; a splendid fragment indeed, but one on which it is impossible to look without sorrowful thoughts of the whole that might have been erected from materials such as centuries may not again bring together.

The mind of man acknowledges two classes of benefactors—those who suggest thoughts and plans, and those who develope and fit for use those already suggested. We are more ready to be grateful to the latter, whose labours are more easily appreciated by their contemporaries; while the other, smaller class, really comprises intellects of the higher order, gifted with a rapidity and fertility of conception too great to be wholly brought out in the compass of a short human life. As their heirs and pupils bring into use more and more of the wealth they bequeathed to the world in unwrought ore, they are elevated by posterity from the rank which their own day assigned them of visionaries and obscure thinkers, to be revered almost as the Demigods of literature and science. Notwithstanding the hours of gloom and bitter tears by which such lives are defaced, they are happy to a degree, which those who are born to minister to the moment can never comprehend. For theirs are hours of "deep and uncommunicable joy," hours when the oracle within boldly predicts the time when that which is divine in them, and which they now to all appearance are breathing out in vain, shall become needful as vital air to myriads of immortal spirit.

But Sir James Mackintosh belonged strictly to neither of these classes. Much he learned—thought much—collected much treasure; but the greater part of it was buried with him. Many a prize, hung on high in the intellectual firmament, he could discern with eyes carefully purged from the films of ignorance and grossness; he could discern the steps even by which he might have mounted to the possession of any one which he had resolutely chosen and perseveringly sought—but this he did not. And though many a pillar and many a stone remain to tell where he dwelt and how he strove, we seek in vain for the temple of perfect workmanship with which Nature meant so skilful an architect should have adorned her Earth.

Sir James was an excellent man; a man of many thoughts—of varied knowledge—of liberal views—almost a great man; but he did NOT become a great man, when he might by more earnestness of purpose; he knew this, and could not be happy. This want of earnestness of purpose, which prevented the goodly tree

4

from bearing goodly fruit in due season, may be attributed in a great measure to these two causes.

First, the want of systematic training in early life. Much has been well-written and much ill-spoken to prove that minds of great native energy will help themselves, that the best attainments are made from inward impulse, and that outward discipline is likely to impair both grace and strength. Here is some truth—more error. Native energy *will* effect wonders, unaided by school or college. The best attainments *are* made from inward impulse, but it does not follow that outward discipline of any liberality will impair grace or strength; and it is impossible for any mind fully and harmoniously to ascertain its own wants, without being made to resound from some strong outward pressure. Crabbe helped himself, and formed his peculiar faculties to great perfection; but Coleridge was well tasked—and not without much hard work could Southey become as "erudite as natural." The flower of Byron's genius expanded with little care of the gardener; but the greatest observer, the deepest thinker, and as the greatest artist, necessarily the warmest admirer of Nature of our time (we refer to Goethe), grew into grace and strength beneath the rules and systems of a disciplinarian father. Genius *will* live and thrive without training, but it does not the less reward the watering-pot and pruning-knife. Let the mind take its own course, and it is apt to fix too exclusively on a pursuit or set of pursuits to which it will devote itself till there is not strength for others, till the mind stands in the relation to a well-balanced mind, that the body of the blacksmith does to that of the gladiator. We are not in favor of a stiff, artificial balance of character, of learning by the hour, and dividing the attention by rule and line; but the young should be so variously called out and disciplined, that they may be sure that it is a genuine vocation, and not an accidental bias, which decides the course on reaching maturity.

Sir James Mackintosh read and talked through his early

youth; had he been induced to reproduce in writing and bear more severe mental drudgery, great deeds would have been easy to him in after-days. He acquired such a habit of receiving from books and reproducing only a small part of what he received, and this, too, in slight and daily efforts, that the stimulus of others' thoughts became necessary for his comfort to an enervating degree. Books cease to be food, and become no better than cigars, or gin and water, when indulged in to excess after a certain period. It is distressing to see half the hours of such a man as Sir James Mackintosh for so many years consumed in reading of a desultory, though always interesting nature. We remember no diary that could in this respect vie with his, unless it be Lady M. W. Montague's after she retired from the world. For *her* it was very suitable, but we cannot excuse it in *him*, even beneath the burning Indian sky. We cannot help wishing he had been provided, as Mirabeau always was, with a literary taster and crammer; or that, at least, he might have felt that a man who means to think and write a great deal, must, after six and twenty, learn to read with his fingers. But nothing can be more luxuriously indolent than his style of reading. Reading aloud too, every evening, was not the thing for a man whom Nature had provided with so many tasks. That his apprenticeship had not been sufficiently severe, he himself felt and sometimes laments. However, the copious journals of his reading are most entertaining, full of penetrating remarks and delicate critical touches. What his friend Lord Jeffrey mentions, "firmness of mind," is remarkable here. Here, carelessly dashed off in a diary, are the best criticisms on Madame de Staël that we have ever seen. She had that stimulating kind of talent which it is hardly possible for any one to criticise calmly who has felt its influence. And, as her pictures of life are such as to excite our hidden sympathies, a very detailed criticism upon her resembles a personal confession, while she is that sort of writer whom it is very easy to praise or blame in general terms. Sir James has seized the effect produced upon her works by the difference between her ideal and real character. This is one great secret of her eloquence; to this mournful tone, which vibrates through all her brilliancy, most hearts respond without liking to own it. Here Sir James drew near to her; his feminine refinement of thought enabled him to appreciate hers, while a less impassioned temperament enabled him coolly to criticise her dazzling intuitions.

How much is comprehended in these few words upon Priestley.

"I have just read Priestley's Life of himself. It is an honest, plain, and somewhat dry account of a well-spent life. But I never read such a narrative, however written, without feeling my mind softened and bettered, at least for a time. Priestley was a good man, though *his life was too busy to leave him leisure for that refinement and ardor of moral sentiment, which have been felt by men of less blameless life.* Frankness and disinterestedness in the avowal of his opinion were his point of honor. In other respects his morality was more useful than brilliant. But the virtue of the sentimental moralist is so over-precarious and ostentatious, that he can seldom be entitled to look down with contempt on the steady, though homely morals of the household."

And those upon Mirabeau, to whom it is so very difficult for a good man to do justice. There is something of even Socratic beauty in the following:

"The letters of this extraordinary man are all full of the highest flights of virtuous sentiment, amidst the grossest obscenities and the constant violation of the most sacred duties. Yet these declarations of sentiment were not insincere. They were only useless, and perhaps pernicious, as they concealed from him that depravity which he could scarcely otherwise have endured.

"A fair recital of his conduct must always have the air of invective. Yet his mind had originally grand capabilities. It had many irregular sketches of high virtue, and he must have had many moments of the noblest moral enthusiasm."

We say Socratic beauty, for we know no one since the Greek, who seems to have so great a love for the beautiful in human nature with such a pity—(a pity how unlike the blindness of weak charity or hypocritical tenderness)—for the odious traits which are sometimes so closely allied with it. Sir James, allowing for all that was perverting in Mirabeau's position acting upon elements so fraught with good and ill, saw him as he was, no demon, but a miserable man become savage and diseased from circumstances.

We should like to enrich this article with the highly finished miniature pictures of Fox, Windham, and Francis Xavier; but here is little room, and we will content ourselves with these striking remarks upon the Hindoo character.

"The Rajpoots are the representatives of Hinduism. In them are seen all the qualities of the Hindu race, unmitigated by foreign mixture, exerted with their original energy, and displayed in the strongest light. They exhibit the genuine form of a Hindu community, formed of the most discordant materials, and combining the most extraordinary contrasts of moral nature, unconquerable adherence to native opinions and usages, with servile submission to any foreign yoke or unbelieving priesthood, ready to suffer martyrdom for the most petty observances of their professed faith; a superstition which inspires the resolution to inflict or to suffer the most atrocious barbarities, without cultivating any natural sentiment or enforcing any social duty; all the stages in the progress of society brought together in one nation, from some abject castes more brutal than the savages of New Zealand, to the polish of manners and refinement of character conspicuous in the upper ranks; attachment to kindred and to home, with no friendship, and no love of country; good temper and gentle disposition; little active cruelty, except when stimulated by superstition; but little sensibility, little compassion, scarcely any disposition to relieve suffering or relieve wrong done to themselves or others. Timidity, with its natural attendants, falsehood and meanness, in the ordinary relations of human life, joined with a capability of becoming excited to courage in the field, to military enthusiasm, to heroic self-devotion. Abstemiousness in some respects more rigorous than that of a western hermit, in a life of intoxication; austerities and self-tortures almost incredible, practised by those who otherwise wallow in gross sensuality, childish levity, barefaced falsehood, no faith, no constancy, no shame, no belief in the existence of justice."

But to return. Sir James's uncommon talents for conversation proved no less detrimental to his glory as an author or as a statesman, than the want of early discipline. Evanescent as are the triumphs, unsatisfactory as are the results of this sort of power, they are too intoxicating to be despised by any but minds of the greatest strength. Madame de Staël remarks: "Say what you will, men of genius must naturally be good talkers; the full mind delights to vent itself in every way." Undoubtedly the great author, whether of plans or books, will not be likely to say uninteresting things; and unless early habits of seclusion have deprived him of readiness, and made it difficult for him to come near other minds in the usual ways, he will probably talk well. But the most eloquent talkers cannot always converse even pleasingly; of this Madame de Staël herself was a striking instance. To take up a subject and harangue upon it, as was her wont, requires the same habits of mind with writing; to *converse*, as could Sir J. Mackintosh, supposes habits quite dissimilar. The ready tact to apprehend the mood of your companions and their capacity for receiving what you can bestow, the skill to touch upon a variety of subjects with that lightness, grace, and rapidity, which constantly excite and never exhaust the attention, the love for sparkling sallies, the playfulness and variety, which make a man brilliant and attractive in conversation, are the reverse of the love of method, the earnestness of concentration, and the onward march of thought, which are required by the higher kinds of writing. The butterfly is no less active than the eagle; his wings of gauze move not less swiftly than those stronger pinions, he loses no moment, but visits every flower in the garden, and exults in the sunlight which he enriches: meanwhile the noble, but not more beautiful, winged one is soaring steadily upward to contemplate the source of light from the highest fields of ether. Add to this, that writing seems dry work, and but a languid way of transmitting thought to one accustomed to the electric excitement of personal intercourse; as on the other hand, conversation is generally too aimless and superficial to suit one, whose mental training has been severe and independent of immediate action from other intellects.

Every kind of power is admirable, and indefinitely useful; if a man be born to talk, and can be satisfied to bring out his thoughts in conversation only or chiefly, let him. Sir James did so much in this way, stimulated so many young, enchanted and refined so many mature minds, blessed daily so many warm hearts; as a husband and a father, he appears so amiable, probably so much more so than he would if his ambition had glowed with greater intensity; what he *did* write, was so excellent, and so calculated to promote the best kind of culture, that if he could have been satisfied, we might; but he could not; we find himself in his journals perpetually lamenting that his life was one of "projects and inactivity." For even achievements like his will seem mere idleness to one who has the capacity of achieving and doing so much more. Man can never come up to his ideal standard; it is the nature of the immortal spirit to raise that standard higher and higher as it goes from strength to strength, still upward and onward. Accordingly the wisest and greatest men are ever the most modest. Yet he who feels that if he is not what he would, he "has done what he could," is not without a serene self-complacency, (how remote from self-sufficiency!) the want of which embittered Sir James's latter years. Four great tasks presented themselves to him in the course of his life, which, perhaps, no man was better able to have performed. Nature seems to have intended him for a philosopher; since, to singular delicacy and precision of observation, he added such a tendency to generalization. In metaphysics he would have explored far, and his reports would have claimed our confidence; since his candour and love of truth would have made it impossible for him to become the slave of system. He himself, and those who knew him best, believed this to be his forte. Had he left this aside, and devoted himself exclusively to politics, he would have been, if not of the first class of statesmen, one of the first in the second class.

He went to India, and that large piece taken out of the best part of his life made this also impossible. Had he then devoted his leisure hours to researches on Indian antiquities, how much might he have done in that vast field, where so small a portion of the harvest is yet gathered in. Nobody was better qualified to disregard the common prejudices with respect to the representations of the Hindoos, to find a clue which should guide him through the mighty maze of Indian theology, and remove the world of rubbish, beneath which forms radiant in truth and beauty lie concealed. His fondness for the history of opinion would here have had full scope, and he might have cast a blaze of light upon a most interesting portion of the annals of mankind. This "fair occasion," too, he let slip, and returned to Europe, broken in health and spirits, and weakened, as any man must be, who has passed so many years in occupations which called for only so small a portion of his powers.

Did he then fix his attention on that other noble aim which rose before him, and labour to become for ever illustrious as the historian of his country? No! Man may escape from every foe and every difficulty, except what are within—himself. Sir James, as formerly, worked with a divided heart and will; and Fame substituted a meaner coronal for the amaranthine wreath she had destined for his brow. Greatness was not thrust upon him and he wanted earnestness of purpose to achieve it for himself.

Let us now turn from the sorrowful contemplation of his *one* fault, to the many endearing or splendid qualities intimately connected with, or possibly fostered by this very fault. For so it is, "what makes our virtues thrive openly, will also, if we be not watchful, make our faults thrive in secret;" and vice versa. Let us admire his varied knowledge, his refinement of thought, which was such that only his truly philosophic turn could have prevented it from degenerating into sophistry ; his devotion, even more tender than enthusiastic, to the highest interests of humanity ; that beautiful fairness of mind, in which he was unequalled, a fairness which evidenced equal modesty, generosity, and pure attachment to truth ; a fairness which made him more sensible to every one's merits, and more ready to perceive the excuses for every one's defects than his own ; a fairness not to be disturbed by party prejudice or personal injury ; a fairness in which nobody, except Sir W. Scott, who was never deeply tried as he was, can compare with him. In what other journal shall we find an entry like the following, the sincerity of which no one can doubt :—

"—— has, I think, a distaste for me, which I believe to be natural to the family. I think the worse of nobody for such a feeling; indeed, I often feel a distaste for myself; I am sure I should not esteem my own character in another person. It is more likely that I should have disrespectable or disagreeable qualities than that —— should have an unreasonable antipathy."

The letter to Mr. Sharpe on the changes in his own opinions, exhibits this trait to a remarkable degree.

It has been said that had he been less ready to confess his own mistakes of judgment, and less careful to respect the intentions of others, more arrogant in his pretensions and less gentle towards his opponents, he would have enjoyed greater influence, and been saved from many slights and disappointments. Here, at least, is no room for regret.

We have not, of course, attempted any thing like a comprehensive criticism upon the Life. The range of Sir James's connexions and pursuits being so wide, and the history of his mind being identical with that of the great political movement of his day, a volume would not give more than verge enough for all the thoughts it naturally suggests. If these few reflections excite the attention of some readers and are acceptable to others, as sympathy, they will attain their legitimate object.

MODERN BRITISH POETS.

"Poets—dwell on earth,
To clothe whate'er the soul admires and loves,
With language and with numbers."

AKENSIDE.

NINE muses were enough for one Greece, and nine poets are enough for one country, even in the nineteenth century. And these nine are "a sacred nine," who, if not quite equal to Shakspeare, Spenser, and Milton, are fairly initiated masters of the wand and spell; and whose least moving incantation should have silenced that blasphemer, who dared to say, in the pages of Blackwood, that "all men, women, and children, are poets, saving only—those who write verses."

First—There is CAMPBELL—a poet; simply a poet—no philosopher. His forte is strong conception, a style free and bold; occasionally a passage is ill-finished, but the lights and shades are so happily distributed, the touch so masterly and vigorous, with such tact at knowing where to stop, that we must *look for* the faults in order to *see* them. There is little, if any, originality of thought; no profound meaning; no esoteric charm, which you cannot make your own on a first reading; yet we have all probably read Campbell many times. It is his *manner* which we admire; and in him we enjoy what most minds enjoy most, not new thoughts, new feelings, but recognition of

"What oft was thought, but ne'er so well expressed."

Thus, in Campbell's best productions we are satisfied, not stimulated. "The Mariners of England" is just what it should be ;—for we find free, deep tones, from the seaman's breast, chorded into harmony by an artist happy enough to feel nature—wise enough to follow nature. "Lochiel" is what it should be, a wild, breezy symphony, from the romantic Highlands. There are, in fact, flat lines and tame passages in "Lochiel ;" but I should never have discovered them, if I had not chanced to hear that noble composition recited by a dull schoolboy. The idealizing tendency in the reader, stimulated by the poet's real magnetic power, would prevent their being perceived in a solitary perusal, and a *bright* schoolboy would have been sufficiently inspired by the general grandeur of the piece ; to have known how to sink such lines as

> "Welcome be Cumberland's steed to the shock,
> Let him dash his proud foam like a wave on the rock ;"

or,

> "Draw, dotard, around thy old, wavering sight;"

and a few other imperfections in favour of

> "Proud bird of the mountain, thy plume shall be torn,"

and other striking passages.

As for the sweet tale of "Wyoming," the expression of the dying Gertrude's lips is not more "bland, more beautiful," than the music of the lay in which she is embalmed. It were difficult to read this poem, so holy in its purity and tenderness, so deliciously soft and soothing in its coloring, without feeling better and happier.

The feeling of Campbell towards women is refined and deep. To him they are not angels—not, in the common sense, heroines ; but of a "perfect woman nobly planned," he has a better idea than most men, or even poets. Witness one of his poems, which has never received its meed of fame ; I allude to Theodric. Who can be insensible to the charms of Constance, the matron counterpart to Gertrude's girlhood ?

"To know her well,
Prolonged, exalted, bound enchantment's spell;
For with affections warm, intense, refined,
She mixed such calm and holy strength of mind,
That, like Heaven's image in the smiling brook,
Celestial peace was pictured in her look;
Her's was the brow in trials unperplexed,
That cheered the sad and tranquillized the vexed;
She studied not the meanest to eclipse,
And yet the wisest listened to her lips;
She sang not, knew not Music's magic skill,
But yet her voice had tones that swayed the will."

* * * * * *

"To paint that being to a grovelling mind
Were like portraying pictures to the blind.
'Twas needful even infectiously to feel
Her temper's fond, and firm, and gladsome zeal,
To share existence with her, and to gain
Sparks from her love's electrifying chain,
Of that pure pride, which, lessening to her breast
Life's ills, gave all its joys a treble zest,
Before the mind completely understood
That mighty truth—how happy are the good!
Even when her light forsook him, it bequeathed
Ennobling sorrow; and her memory breathed
A sweetness that survived her living days,
As odorous scents outlast the censer's blaze.
Or if a trouble dimmed their golden joy,
'Twas outward dross and not infused alloy;
Their home knew but affection's look and speech,
A little Heaven beyond dissension's reach.
But midst her kindred there was strife and gall;
Save one congenial sister, they were all
Such foils to her bright intellect and grace,
As if she had engrossed the virtue of her race,
Her nature strove th' unnatural feuds to heal,
Her wisdom made the weak to her appeal;
And though the wounds she cured were soon unclosed,
Unwearied still her kindness interposed."

The stanzas addressed to John Kemble I have never heard admired to the fulness of my feeling. Can any thing be finer than this?

> " A majesty possessed
> His transport's most impetuous tone;
> And to each passion of his breast
> The graces gave their zone."

or,

> " Who forgets that white discrowned head,
> Those bursts of reason's half-extinguished glare,
> Those tears upon Cordelia's bosom shed
> In doubt more touching than despair,
> If 'twas reality he felt?"

or,

> " Fair as some classic dome,
> Robust and richly graced,
> Your Kemble's spirit was the home
> Of genius and of taste.—
> Taste like the silent dial's power,
> That, when supernal light is given,
> Can measure inspiration's hour
> And tell its height in Heaven.
> At once ennobled and correct,
> His mind surveyed the tragic page;
> And what the actor could effect,
> The scholar could presage."

These stanzas are in Campbell's best style. Had he possessed as much lyric flow as force, his odes might have vied with those of Collins. But, though soaring upward on a strong pinion, his flights are never prolonged, and in this province, which earnestness and justness of sentiment, simplicity of imagery, and a picturesque turn in expression, seem to have marked out as his own, he is surpassed by Shelley, Coleridge, and Wordsworth, from their greater power of continuous self-impulse.

I do not know where to class Campbell as a poet. What he has done seems to be by snatches, and his poems might have been published under the title of "Leisure Hours, or Recreations of a Great Man." They seem like fragments, not very heedfully stricken off from the bed of a rich quarry; for, with all their individual finish, there is no trace of a fixed purpose to be discerned in them. They appear to be merely occasional effusions, like natural popular poetry; but, as they are written by an accomplished man in these modern days of design and system, we are prompted to look for an aim, a prevading purpose. We shall not find it. Campbell has given us much delight; if he has not directly stimulated our thoughts, he has done so much to refine our tastes, that we must respectfully tender the poetic garland.

And thou, ANACREON MOORE, sweet warbler of Erin! What an ecstasy of sensation must thy poetic life have been! Certainly the dancing of the blood never before inspired so many verses. Moore's poetry is to literature, what the compositions of Rossini are to music. It is the hey-day of animal existence, embellished by a brilliant fancy, and ardent though superficial affections. The giddy flush of youthful impulse empurples the most pensive strains of his patriotism, throbs in his most delicate touches of pathos, and is felt as much in Tara's Halls as in the description of the Harem. His muse is light of step and free of air, yet not vulgarly free; she is not a little excited, but it is with quaffing the purest and most sparkling champagne. There is no temperance, no chastened harmony in her grief or in her joy. His melodies are metrically perfect; they absolutely set themselves to music, and talk of spring, and the most voluptuous breath of the blossom-laden western breeze, and the wildest notes of the just returning birds. For his poetic embodying of a particular stage of human existence, and his scintillating wit, will Moore chiefly be remembered. He has been boon-companion and toast-master to the youth of his day. This could not last. When he ceased to be young, and to warble his own verses, their fascination in a great measure disappeared. Many are now not more attractive than dead flowers in a close room. Anacreon cannot really charm when his hair is gray; there is a time for all things, and the gayest youth loves not the Epicurean old man. Yet he, too, is a poet; and his works will not be suffered to go out of print, though they are, even now, little read. Of course his reputation as a prose writer is another matter, and apart from our present purpose.

The poetry of WALTER SCOTT has been superseded by his prose, yet it fills no unimportant niche in the literary history of the last half century, and may be read, at least once in life, with great pleasure. "Marmion," "The Lay of the Last Minstrel," &c., cannot, indeed, be companions of those Sabbath hours of which the weariest, dreariest life need not be destitute, for their bearing is not upon the true life of man, his immortal life. Coleridge felt this so deeply, that in a lately published work (Letters, Conversations, &c., of S. T. Coleridge) he is recorded to have said, "not twenty lines of Scott's poetry will ever reach posterity; it has relation to nothing." This is altogether too harsh, and proves that the philosopher is subject to narrowness and partial views, from his peculiar mode of looking at an object, equally with the mere man of taste. These poems are chiefly remarkable for presenting pictures of particular epochs, and, considered in that light, truly admirable. Much poetry has come down to us, thus far, whose interest is almost exclusively of the same nature; in which, at least, moral conflict does not constitute the prominent interest.

To one who has read Scott's novels first, and looks in his poems for the same dramatic interest, the rich humor, the tragic force, the highly wrought yet flowing dialogue, and the countless minutiæ in the finish of character, they must bring disappointment. For their excellence consists in graphic descriptions of architecture and natural scenery, a happy choice of subject, and effective grouping of slightly sketched characters, combined with steady march and great simplicity of narrative. Here and there sentiments are introduced, always just and gracefully worded, but without that delicacy of shading, fine and harmonious as Nature's workmanship in the rose-leaf, which delights us in his prose works. It is, indeed, astonishing that he should lose so much by a constraint so lightly worn ; for his facility of versification is wonderful, his numbers seem almost to have coined themselves, and you cannot detect any thing like searching for a word to tag a verse withal. Yet certain it is, we receive no adequate idea of the exuberance and versatility of his genius, or his great knowledge of the human heart, from his poetry. His lore is there as profusely displayed, his good sense and tact as admirable, as in his prose works ; and, if only on account of their fidelity of description, these poems are invaluable, and must always hold a place in English literature. They are interesting too, as giving a more complete idea of the character and habits of one of our greatest and best men, than his remarkable modesty would permit the public to obtain more directly. His modes of life, his personal feelings, are no where so detailed, as in the epistles perfixed to the cantos of Marmion. These bring us close to his side, and leading us with him through the rural and romantic scenes he loved, talk with us by the way of all the rich associations of which he was master. His dogs are with him ; he surveys these dumb friends with the eye of a sportsman and a philosopher, and omits nothing in the description of them which could interest either. An old castle frowns upon the road ; he bids its story live before you with all the animation of a drama and the fidelity of a chronicle. Are topics of the day introduced ? He states his opinions with firmness and composure, expresses his admiration with energy, and, where he dissents from those he addresses, does so with unaffected candor and cordial benignity. Good and great man! More and more imposing as nearer seen; thou art like that product of a superhuman intellect, that stately temple, which rears its head in the clouds, yet must be studied through and through, for months and years, to be appreciated in all its grandeur.

Nothing surprises me more in Scott's poetry, than that a person of so strong imagination should see every thing so in detail as he does. Nothing interferes with his faculty of observation. No minor part is sacrificed to give effect to the whole; no peculiar light cast on the picture: you only see through a wonderfully far-seeing and accurately observing pair of eyes, and all this when he has so decided a taste for the picturesque. Take, as a specimen, the opening description in Marmion.

THE CASTLE.

"Day set on Norham's castled steep,
And Tweed's fair river, broad and deep,
And Cheviot's mountains lone;
The battled towers, the donjon keep,
The loophole grates, where captives weep,
The flanking walls that round it sweep,
In yellow lustre shone;—
The warriors on the turrets high,
Moving athwart the evening sky,
Seemed forms of giant height;
Their armor, as it caught the rays,
Flashed back again the western blaze,
In lines of dazzling light.
St. George's banner, broad and gay,
Now faded, as the fading ray
Less bright, and less, was flung;
The evening gale had scarce the power
To wave it on the donjon tower,
So heavily it hung.

The scouts had parted on their search,
  The castle gates were barred,
Above the gloomy portal arch,
Timing his footsteps to a march,
  The warden kept his guard,
Low humming, as he passed along,
Some ancient border gathering song."

How picturesque, yet how minute! Not even Wordsworth, devoted as he is to nature, and to visible as well as invisible truth, can compare with Scott in fidelity of description. Not even Crabbe, that least imaginative of poets, can compare with him for accuracy of touch and truth of colouring. Scott's faculties being nicely balanced, never disturbed one another; we perceive this even more distinctly in his poetry than in his prose, perhaps because less excited while reading it.

I have said that Crabbe was the least imaginative of poets. He has *no* imagination in the commonly received sense of the term; there is nothing of creation in his works; nay, I dare affirm, in opposition to that refined critic, Sir James Mackintosh, that there was no touch of an idealizing tendency in his mind; yet he is a poet; he is so through his calm but deep and steady sympathy with all that is human; he is so by his distinguished power of observation; he is so by his graphic skill. No literature boasts an author more individual than Crabbe. He is unique. Moore described him well.

"Grand from the truth that reigns o'er all,
The unshrinking truth that lets her light
Through life's low, dark, interior fall,
Opening the whole severely bright.
Yet softening, as she frowns along,
O'er scenes which angels weep to see,
Where truth herself half veils the wrong
  In pity of the misery."

I could never enter into the state of a mind which could support viewing life and human nature as Crabbe's did, softened by no cool shadow, gladdened by no rose-light. I wish Sir Walter Scott, when expressing his admiration for the poetry of Crabbe, had told us more distinctly the nature of the impressions he received from it. Sir Walter, while he observes with equal accuracy, is sure to detect something comic or something lovely, some pretty dalliance of light and shade in the "low, dark interior" of the most outwardly desolate hovel. Cowper saw the follies and vices of mankind as clearly, but his Christian love is an ever softly-murmuring under-current, which relieves the rude sounds of the upper world. Crabbe in his view of the human mind may be compared with Cowper or Scott, as the anatomist, in his view of the human form, may be compared with the painter or sculptor. Unshrinking, he tears apart that glorious fabric which has been called "the crown of creation;" he sees its beauty and its strength with calm approval, its weaknesses, its liability to disease, with stern pity or cold indignation. His nicely dissected or undraped virtues are scarcely more attractive than vices, and, with profound knowledge of the passions, not one ray of passionate enthusiasm casts a glow over the dramatic recitative of his poems.

Crabbe has the true spirit of the man of science; he seeks truth alone, content to take all parts of God's creations as they are, if he may but get a distinct idea of the laws which govern them. He sees human nature as only a human being could see it, but he describes it like a spirit which has never known human longings; yet in no unfriendly temper—far from it; but with a strange bleak fidelity, unbiassed either by impatience or tenderness.

The poor and humble owe him much, for he has made them known to the upper classes, not as they ought to be, but as they really are; and in so doing, in distinctly portraying the evils of their condition, he has opened the way to amelioration. He is the poet of the lower classes, though probably rather valuable to them as an interpreter than agreeable as a household friend. They like something more stimulating, they would prefer gin or rum to lemonade. Indeed, that class of readers rarely like to find themselves in print ; they want something romantic, something which takes them out of their sphere ; and high sounding words, such as they are not in the habit of using, have peculiar charms for them. That is a high stage of culture in which simplicity is appreciated.

The same cold tints pervade Crabbe's descriptions of natural scenery. We can conceive that his eye was educated at the sea-side. An east-wind blows, his colours are sharp and decided, and the glitter which falls upon land and wave has no warmth.

It is difficult to do Crabbe justice, both because the subject is so large a one, and because tempted to discuss it rather in admiration than in love.

I turn to one whom I love still more than I admire ; the gentle, the gifted, the ill-fated Shelley.

Let not prejudice deny him a place among the great ones of the day. The youth of Shelley was unfortunate. He committed many errors ; what else could be expected from one so precocious ? No one begins life so early who is not at some period forced to retrace his steps, and those precepts which are learned so happily from a mother's lips, must be paid for by the heart's best blood when bought from the stern teacher, Experience. Poor Shelley ! Thou wert the warmest of philanthropists, yet doomed to live at variance with thy country and thy time. Full of the spirit of genuine Christianity, yet ranking thyself among unbelievers, because in early life thou hadst been bewildered by seeing it perverted, sinking beneath those precious gifts which should have made a world thine own, intoxicated with thy lyric enthusiasm and thick-coming fancies, adoring Nature as a goddess, yet misinterpreting her oracles, cut off from life just as thou wert beginning to read it aright; O, most musical, most melancholy singer; who that has a soul to feel genius, a heart to grieve over misguided nobleness, can forbear watering the profuse blossoms of thy too early closed spring with tears of sympathy, of love, and (if we may dare it for one so superior in intellect) of pity?

Although the struggles of Shelley's mind destroyed that serenity of tone which is essential to the finest poetry, and his tenderness has not always that elevation of hope which should hallow it; although in no one of his productions is there sufficient unity of purpose and regulation of parts to entitle it to unlimited admiration, yet they all abound with passages of infinite beauty, and in two particulars, he surpasses any poet of the day.

First, in fertility of Fancy. Here his riches, from want of arrangement, sometimes fail to give pleasure, yet we cannot but perceive that they are priceless riches. In this respect parts of his "Adonais," "Marianne's Dream," and "Medusa," are not to be excelled, except in Shakspeare.

Second, in sympathy with Nature. To her lightest tones his being gave an echo; truly she *spoke* to him, and it is this which gives unequalled melody to his versification; I say unequalled, for I do not think either Moore or Coleridge can here vie with him, though each is in his way a master of the lyre. The rush, the flow, the delicacy of vibration, in Shelley's verse, can only be paralleled by the waterfall, the rivulet, the notes of the bird and of the insect world. This is a sort of excellence not frequently to be expected now, when men listen less zealously than of old to the mystic whispers of Nature; when little is understood that is not told in set phrases, and when even poets write more frequently in curtained and carpeted rooms, than "among thickets of odoriferous blossoming trees and flowery glades," as Shelley did.

It were "a curious piece of work enough," to run a parallel between the Skylark of Shelley and that of Wordsworth, and thus illustrate mental processes so similar in dissimilitude. The mood of mind, the ideas, are not unlike in the two. Hear Wordsworth.

"*Up with me, up with me, into the clouds,*" *etc.*

"Lift me, guide me, till I find
The spot which seems so to thy mind,
I have walked through wildernesses dreary,
And to-day my heart is weary,
Had I now the wings of a Fairy
Up to thee would I fly;
There is madness about thee, and joy divine
In that song of thine:

Joyous as morning, thou art laughing and scorning;
And though little troubled with sloth,
Drunken Lark, thou would'st be loth
To be such a traveller as I!
Happy, happy liver,
With a soul as strong as a mountain river,
Pouring out praise to the Almighty Giver,
Joy and jollity be with us both."

Hear Shelley.

Hail to thee, blithe spirit!
Bird thou never wert,
That from heaven or near it,
Pourest thy full heart
In *profuse strains of unpremeditated art.*

Higher still and higher,
From the earth thou springest,
Like a cloud of fire
The blue deep thou wingest,
And singing still dost soar, and soaring ever singest.

In the golden lightning
Of the sunken sun,

O'er which clouds are bright'ning,
Thou dost float and run
Like an unbodied joy, whose race is just begun.

The pale purple even
Melts around thy flight;
Like a star of heaven,
In the broad daylight,
Thou art unseen, but yet I hear thy shrill delight.

Keen as are the arrows
Of that silver sphere,
Whose intense lamp narrows
In the white dawn clear,
Until we hardly see, we feel that it is there.

All the earth and air
With thy voice is loud,
As, when night is bare,
From one lonely cloud
The moon rains out her beams, and heaven is overflowed.

What thou art we know not;
What is most like thee?
From rainbow clouds there flow not
Drops so bright to see,
As from thy presence showers a rain of melody.

Like a poet hidden
In the light of thought,
Singing hymns unbidden,
Till the world is wrought
To sympathy with hopes and fears it heeded not.

Like a high-born maiden
In a palace tower,
Soothing her love-laden
Soul in secret hour,
With music sweet as love which overflows her bower.

Like a glow-worm golden
In a dell of dew

Scattering unbeholden
  Its aerial hue
Among the flowers and grass which screen it from the view

Like a rose embowered
  In its own green leaves,
By warm winds deflowered,
  Till the scent it gives
Makes faint with too much sweet, those heavy-winged thieves.

Sound of vernal showers
  On the twinkling grass,
Rain-awakened flowers,
  All that ever was
Joyous, and clear, and fresh, thy music doth surpass.

Teach us, sprite or bird,
  What sweet thoughts are thine:
I have never heard
  Praise of love or wine
That panted forth a flood of rapture so divine.

Chorus hymeneal,
  Or triumphant chaunt,
Matched with thine would be all
  But an empty vaunt—
A thing wherein we feel there is some hidden want.

What objects are the fountains
  Of thy happy strain?
What fields, or waves, or mountains?
  What shapes of sky or plain?
What love of thine own kind? what ignorance of pain?

With thy clear keen joyance
  Languor cannot be;
Shadow of annoyance
  Never came near thee:
Thou lovest; but ne'er knew love's sad satiety."

I do not like to omit a word of it: but it is taking too much room. Should we not say from the samples before us that Shelley, in melody and exuberance cf fancy, was incalculably superior to Wordsworth? But mark their *inferences.*

Shelley.

"Teach me half the gladness
That thy brain must know,
Such harmonious madness
From my lips would flow
The world should listen, then, as I am listening now."

Wordsworth.

"What though my course be rugged and uneven,
To prickly moors and dusty ways confined,
Yet, hearing thee and others of thy kind
As full of gladness and as free of heaven,
I o'er the earth will go plodding on
By myself, cheerfully, till the day is done."

If Wordsworth have superiority then, it consists in greater maturity and dignity of sentiment.

While reading Shelley, we must surrender ourselves without reserve to the magnetic power of genius; we must not expect to be satisfied, but rest content with being stimulated. He alone who can resign his soul in unquestioning simplicity to the descant of the nightingale or the absorption of the sea-side, may hope to receive from the mind of a Shelley the suggestions which, to those who know how to receive, he can so liberally impart.

I cannot leave Shelley without quoting two or three stanzas, in which he speaks of himself, and which are full of his peculiar beauties and peculiar faults.

"A frail form,
A phantom among men, companionless,
As the last cloud of an expiring storm,
Whose thunder is its knell; he, as I guess,
Had gazed on Nature's naked loveliness
Actaeon-like, and now he fled astray

With feeble steps o'er the world's wilderness,
And his own thoughts, along that rugged way,
Pursued like raging hounds their father and their prey.
A pard-like Spirit, beautiful and swift—
A love in desolation masked; a power
Girt round with weakness; it can scarce uplift
The weight of the superincumbent hour;
It is a dying lamp, a falling shower,
A breaking billow; even whilst we speak
Is it not broken? On the withering flower
The killing sun smiles brightly; on a cheek
The life can burn in blood, even while the heart may break.

His head was bound with pansies overblown,
And faded violets, white, and pied, and blue;
And a light spear, topped with a cypress cone,
Round whose rude shaft dark ivy-tresses grew
Yet dripping with the forest's noon-day dew,
Vibrated as the ever-beating heart
Shook the weak hand that grasped it; of that crew
He came the last, neglected and apart;
A herd-abandoned deer, struck by the hunter's dart."

Shelley is no longer "neglected," but I believe his works have never been republished in this country, and therefore these extracts may be new to most readers.

Byron naturally in our hall of imagery takes place next his friend. Both are noble poetic shapes, both mournful in their beauty. The radiant gentleness of Shelley's brow and eye delight us, but there are marks of suffering on that delicate cheek and about that sweet mouth; while a sorrowful indignation curls too strongly the lip, lightens too fiercely in the eye, of Byron.

The unfortunate Byron, (*unfortunate* I call him, because "mind and destiny are but two names for one idea,") has long been at rest; the adoration and the hatred of which he was the object, are both dying out. His poems have done their work; a strong personal interest no longer gives them a factitious charm, and they are beginning to find their proper level. Their value is two-fold—immortal and eternal, as records of thoughts and feelings which must be immortally and eternally interesting to the mind of individual man; historical, because they are the most complete chronicle of a particular set of impulses in the public mind.

How much of the first sort of value the poems of Byron possess, posterity must decide, and the verdict can only be ascertained by degrees; I, for one, should say not much. There are many beautiful pictures; infinite wit, but too local and temporary in its range to be greatly prized beyond his own time; little originality; but much vigor, both of thought and expression; with a deep, even a passionate love of the beautiful and grand. I have often thought, in relation to him, of Wordsworth's description of

> "A youth to whom was given
> So much of Earth, so much of Heaven,
> And such impetuous blood."
>
> * * * * *
>
> "Whatever in those climes he found,
> Irregular in sight or sound,
> Did to his mind impart
> A kindred impulse, seemed allied
> To his own powers, and justified
> The workings of his heart.
>
> Nor less to feed voluptuous thought,
> The beauteous forms of nature wrought,
> Fair trees and lovely flowers;
> The breezes their own languor lent,
> The stars had feelings which they sent
> Into those gorgeous bowers.
>
> And in his worst pursuits, I ween,
> That sometimes there did intervene
> Pure hopes of high intent;

> For passions linked to forms so fair
> And stately, needs must have their share
> Of noble sentiment."

It is worthy of remark that Byron's moral perversion never paralyzed or obscured his intellectual powers, though it might lower their aims. With regard to the plan and style of his works, he showed strong good sense and clear judgment. The man who indulged such narrowing egotism, such irrational scorn, would prune and polish without mercy the stanzas in which he uttered them; and this bewildered Idealist was a very bigot in behoof of the commonsensical satirist, the almost peevish Realist —Pope.

Historically these poems are valuable as records of that strange malady, that sickness of the soul, which has, in our day, cankered so visibly the rose of youth. It is common to speak of the Byronic mood as morbid, false, and foolish; it is the two former, and, if it could be avoided, would most assuredly be the latter also. But how can it always be avoided? Like as a fever rages in the blood before we are aware, even so creeps upon the soul this disease, offspring of a moral malaria, an influence impalpable till we feel its results within ourselves. Since skilful physicians are not always at hand, would it not be better to purify the atmosphere than to rail at the patient? Those who have passed through this process seem to have wondrous little pity for those who are still struggling with its horrors, and very little care to aid them. Yet if it be disease, does it not claim pity, and would it not be well to try some other remedy than hard knocks for its cure? What though these sick youths do mourn and lament somewhat wearisomely, and we feel vexed, on bright May mornings, to have them try to persuade us that this beautiful green earth, with all its flowers and bird-notes, is no better than a vast hospital? Consider, it is a relief to the delirious to rave audibly, and few, like Professor Teufelsdrock, have strength to keep a whole Satanic school in the soul from spouting aloud. What says the benign Uhland ?

> " If our first lays too piteous have been,
>   And you have feared our tears would never cease,
> If we too gloomily life's prose have seen,
>   Nor suffered Man nor Mouse to dwell in peace,
> Yet pardon us for our youth's take. The vine
> Must weep from her crushed grapes the generous wine;
> Not without pain the precious beverage flows;
> Thus joy and power may yet spring from the woes
> Which have so wearied every long-tasked ear;" &c.

There is no getting rid of the epidemic of the season, however annoying and useless it may seem. You cannot cough down an influenza ; it will cough you down.

Why young people will just now profess themselves so very miserable, for no better reason than that assigned by the poet to some " inquiring friends,"

> "Nought do I mourn I e'er possessed,
> I grieve that I cannot be blessed ;"

I have here no room to explain. Enough that there has for some time prevailed a sickliness of feeling, whose highest water-mark may be found in the writings of Byron. He is the " power man" (as the Germans call him, meaning perhaps the *power-loom* !) who has woven into one tissue all those myriad threads, tear-stained and dull-gray, with which the malignant spiders of speculation had filled the machine shop of society, and by so doing has, though I admit, unintentionally, conferred benefits upon us incalculable for a long time to come. He has lived through this experience for us, and shown us that the natural fruits of indulgence in such a temper are dissonance, cynicism, irritability, and all uncharitableness. Accordingly, since his time the evil has lessened. With this warning before them, let the young examine that world, which seems at times so deformed by evils and endless contradictions,

> "Control them and subdue, transmute, bereave
> Of their bad influence, and the good receive."

Grief loses half its charm when we find that others have endured the same to a higher degree, and lived through it. Nor do I believe that the misanthropy of Byron ever made a single misanthrope; that his scepticism, so uneasy and sorrowful beneath its thin mask of levity, ever made a single sceptic. I know those whom it has cured of their yet half-developed errors. I believe it has cured thousands.

As supplying materials for the history of opinion, then, Byron's poems will be valuable. And as a poet, I believe posterity will assign him no obscure place, though he will probably be classed far beneath some who have exercised a less obvious or immediate influence on their own times; beneath the noble Three of whom I am yet to speak, whose merits are immortal, because their tendencies are towards immortality, and all whose influence must be a growing influence; beneath Southey, Coleridge, and Wordsworth.

Before proceeding to discuss these last, for which there is hardly room in the present paper, I would be allowed to conclude this division of my subject with a fine passage in which Shelley speaks of Byron. I wish to quote it, because it is of kindred strain with what Walter Scott and Rogers (in his "Italy") have written about their much abused compeer. It is well for us to see great men judging so gently, and excusing so generously, faults from which they themselves are entirely free; faults at which men of less genius, and less purity too, found it so easy and pleasant to rail. I quote it in preference to any thing from Scott and Rogers, because I presume it to be less generally known.

In apostrophizing Venice, Shelley says,

"Perish! let there only be
Floating o'er thy hearthless sea,
As the garment of thy sky
Clothes the world immortally,
One remembrance more sublime
Than the tattered pall of Time,
Which scarce hides thy visage wan;
That a tempest-cleaving swan
Of the songs of Albion,
Driven from his ancestral streams
By the might of evil dreams,
Found a nest in thee; and Ocean
Welcomed him with such emotion
That its joy grew his, and sprung
From his lips like music flung
O'er a mighty thunder-fit
Chastening terror;—What though yet
Poesy's unfailing river,
Which through Albion winds for ever
Lashing with melodious wave
Many a sacred poet's grave,
Mourn its latest nursling fled!
What though thou, with all thy dead,
Scarce can for this fame repay
Aught thine own;—oh, rather say
Though thy sins and slaveries foul
Overcloud a sun-like soul!
As the ghost of Homer clings
Round Scamander's wasting springs;
As divinest Shakspeare's might
Fills Avon and the world with light;
Like omniscient power, which he
Imaged 'mid mortality:
As the love from Petrarch's urn
Yet amid yon hills doth burn,
A quenchless lamp by which the heart
Sees things unearthly; so thou art,
Mighty spirit; so shall be
The city that did refuge thee."

In earlier days the greatest poets addressed themselves more to the passions or heart-emotions of their fellow-men than to their thoughts or mind-emotions. The passions were then in their natural state, and held their natural places in the character. They were not made sickly by a false refinement, or stimulated to a diseased and incessantly craving state. Men loved and hated to excess, perhaps; but there was nothing factitious in their love or hatred. The tone of poetry, even when employed on the most tragic subjects, might waken in the hearer's heart a chord of joy; for in such natural sorrow there was a healthful life, an energy which told of healing yet to come and the endless riches of love and hope.

How different is its tone in Faust and Manfred; how false to simple nature, yet how true to the time! As the mechanism of society has become more complex, and must be regulated more by combined efforts, desire after individuality brings him who manifests it into a state of conflict with society. This is felt from a passion, whether it be love or ambition, which seeks to make its own world independent of trivial daily circumstances, and struggles long against the lessons of experience, which tell it that such singleness of effort and of possession cannot be, consistently with that grand maxim of the day, *the greatest happiness of the greatest number*. Not until equally enlightened and humble, can the human being learn that individuality of character is not necessarily combined with individuality of possession, but depends alone on the zealous observance of truth. Few can be wise enough to realize with Schiller, that "to be truly immortal one must live in the whole." The mind struggles long, before it can resolve on sacrificing any thing of its impulsive nature to the requisitions of the time. And while it struggles it mourns, and these lamentations compose the popular poetry. Men do not now look in poetry for a serene world, amid whose vocal groves and green meads they may refresh themselves after the heat of action, and in paradisaical quiet listen to the tales of other days. No! dissatisfied and represt, they want to be made to weep, because, in so doing, they feel themselves in some sense free.

All this conflict and apparently bootless fretting and wailing mark a transition-state—a state of gradual revolution, in which men try all things, seeking what they hold fast, and feel that it is good. But there are some, the pilot-minds of the age, who cannot submit to pass all their lives in experimentalizing. They cannot consent to drift across the waves in the hope of finding *somewhere* a haven and a home; but, seeing the blue sky over them, and believing that God's love is every where, try to make the best of that spot on which they have been placed, and, not unfrequently, by the aid of spiritual assistance, more benign than that of Faust's Lemures, win from the raging billows large territories, whose sands they can convert into Eden bowers, tenanted by lovely and majestic shapes.

Such are Southey, Coleridge, and Wordsworth. They could not be satisfied, like Byron, with embodying the peculiar wit or peculiar sufferings of the times; nor like Scott, with depicting an era which has said its say and produced its fruit: nor like Campbell, with occasionally giving a voice and a permanent being to some brilliant moment or fair scene. Not of nobler nature, not more richly endowed than Shelley, they were not doomed to misguided efforts and baffled strivings; much less could they, like Moore, consider poetry merely as the harmonious expression of transient sensations. To them Poetry was, must be, the expression of what is eternal in man's nature, through illustrations drawn from his temporal state; a representation in letters of fire, on life's dark curtain, of that which lies beyond; philosophy dressed in the robes of Taste and Imagination; the voice of Nature and of God, humanized by being echoed back from the understanding hearts of Priests and Seers! Of course this could not be the popular poetry of the day. Being eminently the product of reflection and experience, it could only be appreciated by those who had thought and felt to some depth. I confess that it is not the best possible poetry, since so exclusively adapted to the meditative few. In Shakspeare, or Homer, there is for minds of every grade as much as they are competent to receive, the shallow or careless find there amusement; minds of a higher order, meaning which enlightens and beauty which enchants them.

This fault which I have admitted, this want of universality is not surprising, since it was necessary for these three poets to stand apart from the tide of opinion, and disregard the popular tastes, in order to attain firmness, depth, or permanent beauty. And they being, as I have said, the pilot-minds of their time, their works enjoy a growing, though not a rapidly growing, popularity.

Coleridge, in particular, is now very much read, nor, notwithstanding his was but occasional homage to the shrine of poesy, was he the least valuable votary of the three, since, if he has done least, if his works form a less perfect whole, and are therefore less satisfactory than those of the other two, he is far more suggestive, more filled with the divine magnetism of intuition, than they.

The muse of Southey is a beautiful statue of crystal, in whose bosom burns an immortal flame. We hardly admire, as they deserve, the perfection of the finish, and the elegance of the contours, because our attention is so fixed on the radiance which glows through them.

Thus Southey is remarkable for the fidelity, and still more for the grace, of his descriptions; for his elegant manner of expressing sentiments noble, delicate, and consistent in their tone; for his imagination, but, more than all, for his expansive and fervent piety.

In his fidelity of description there is nothing of the minute accuracy of Scott. Southey takes no pleasure in making little dots and marks; his style is free and bold, yet always true, sometimes elaborately true, to nature. Indeed, if he has a fault, it is that he elaborates too much. He himself has said that poetry should be "thoroughly erudite, thoroughly animated, and thoroughly natural." His poetry cannot always boast of the two last essentials. Even in his most brilliant passages there is nothing of the heat of inspiration, nothing of that celestial fire which makes us feel that the author has, by intensifying the action of his mind, raised himself to communion with superior intelligences. It is where he is most calm that he is most beautiful; and, accordingly, he is more excellent in the expression of sentiment than in narration. Scarce any writer presents to us a sentiment with such a tearful depth of expression; but though it is a tearful depth, those tears were shed long since, and Faith and Love have hallowed them. You nowhere are made to feel the bitterness, the vehemence of present emotion; but the phœnix born from passion is seen hovering over the ashes of what was once combined with it. Southey is particularly exquisite in painting those sentiments which arise from the parental and filial relation: whether the daughter looks back from her heavenly lover, and the opening bowers of bliss, still tenderly solicitous for her father, whom she, in the true language of woman's heart, recommends to favour, as

"That wretched, persecuted, *poor good* man;"

or the father, as in "Thalaba," shows a faith in the benignity and holiness of his lost daughter, which the lover, who had given up for her so high a destiny, wanted;—or, as in "Roderick," the miserable, sinful child wanders back to relieve himself from the load of pollution at the feet of a sainted mother; always—always he speaks from a full, a sanctified soul, in tones of thrilling melody.

The imagination of Southey is marked by similar traits; there is no flash, no scintillation about it, but a steady light as of day itself. As specimens of his best manner, I would mention the last stage of Thalaba's journey to the Domdaniel Caves, and, in the "Curse of Kehama," the sea-palace of Baly, "The Glendoveer," and "The Ship of Heaven." As Southey's poems are not very generally read, I will extract the two latter:

"THE SHIP OF HEAVEN.

"THE ship of heaven, instinct with thought displayed
Its living sail and glides along the sky,
On either side, in wavy tide,
The clouds of morn along its path divide;
The winds that swept in wild career on high,
Before its presence check their charmed force;
The winds that, loitering, lagged along their course
Around the living bark enamored play,
Swell underneath the sail, and sing before its way.

"That bark in shape was like the furrowed shell
Wherein the sea-nymphs to their parent king,
On festal days their duteous offerings bring;
Its hue? go watch the last green light
Ere evening yields the western sky to night,
Or fix upon the sun thy strenuous sight
Till thou hast reached its orb of chrysolite.
The sail, from end to end displayed,
Bent, like a rainbow, o'er the maid;
An angel's head with visual eye,
Through trackless space directs its chosen way;
Nor aid of wing, nor foot nor fin,
Requires to voyage o'er the obedient sky.
Smooth as the swan when not a breeze at even
Disturbs the surface of the silver stream,
Through air and sunshine sails the ship of heaven."

Southey professes to have borrowed the description of the Glendoveer from an old and forgotten book. He has given the prose extract in a note to the "Curse of Kehama," and I think no one can compare the two without feeling that the true alchymy has been at work there. His poetry is a new and life-giving element to the very striking thoughts he borrowed. Charcoal and diamonds are not more unlike in their effect upon the observer.

"THE GLENDOVEER.

" Of human form divine was he,
The immortal youth of heaven who floated by,
Even such as that divinest form shall be
In those blest stages of our mortal race,
When no infirmity,
Low thought, nor base desire, nor wasting care
Deface the semblance of our heavenly sire—
The wings of eagle or of cherubim
Had seemed unworthy him;
Angelic power and dignity and grace
Were in his glorious pennons; from the neck
Down to the ankle reached their swelling web
Richer than robes of Tyrian dye, that deck
Imperial majesty:
Their color, like the winter's moonless sky
When all the stars of midnight's canopy
Shine forth; or like the azure deep at noon,
Reflecting back to heaven a brighter blue,
Such was their tint when closed, but when outspread,
The permeating light
Shed through their substance thin a varying hue;
Now bright as when the rose,
Beauteous as fragrant, gives to scent and sight
A like delight, now like the juice that flows
From Douro's generous vine,
Or ruby when with deepest red it glows;
Or as the morning clouds refulgent shine
When at forthcoming of the lord of day,
The orient, like a shrine,
Kindles as it receives the rising ray,
And heralding his way

Proclaims the presence of the power divine—
Thus glorious were the wings
Of that celestial spirit, as he went
Disporting through his native element—
Nor these alone
The gorgeous beauties that they gave to view;
Through the broad membrane branched a pliant bone,
Spreading like fibres from their parent stem;
Its vines like interwoven silver shone;
Or as the chaster hue
Of pearls that grace some sultan's diadem.
Now with slow stroke and strong, behold him smite
The buoyant air, and now in gentler flight
On motionless wing expanded, shoot along."

All Southey's works are instinct, and replete with the experiences of piety, from that fine picture of natural religion, Joan of Arc's confession of faith, to that as noble sermon as ever was preached upon Christianity, the penitence of Roderic the Goth. This last is the most original and elevated in its design of all Southey's poems. In "Thalaba" and "Joan of Arc," he had illustrated the power of faith; in "Madoc" contrasted religion under a pure and simple form with the hydra ugliness of superstition. In "Kehama" he has exhibited virtue struggling against the most dreadful inflictions with heavenly fortitude, and made manifest to us the angel-guards who love to wait on innocence and goodness. But in Roderic the design has even a higher scope, is more difficult of execution; and, so far as I know, unique. The temptations which beset a single soul have been a frequent subject, and one sure of sympathy if treated with any power. Breathlessly we watch the conflict, with heartfelt anguish mourn defeat, or with heart-expanding triumph hail a conquest. But, where there *has* been defeat, to lead us back with the fallen one through the thorny and desolate paths of repentance to purification, to win not only our pity, but our sympathy, for one crushed and degraded by his own sin; and finally, through his faithful though secret efforts to redeem the past, secure to him, justly blighted and world-forsaken as he is, not only our sorrowing love, but our respect;—*this* Southey alone has done, perhaps alone could do. As a scene of unrivalled excellence, both for its meaning and its manner, I would mention that of Florinda's return with "Roderic," (who is disguised as a monk, and whom she does not know,) to her father; when after such a strife of heart-rending words and heart-broken tears, they, exhausted, seat themselves on the bank of the little stream, and watch together the quiet moon. Never has Christianity spoken in accents of more penetrating tenderness since the promise was given to thɔm that be weary and heavy-laden.

Of Coleridge I shall say little. Few minds are capable of fathoming his by their own sympathies, and he has left us no adequate manifestation of himself as a poet by which to judge him. For his dramas, I consider them complete failures, and more like visions than dramas. For a metaphysical mind like his to attempt that walk, was scarcely more judicious than it would be for a blind man to essay painting the bay of Naples. Many of his smaller pieces are perfect in their way, indeed no writer could excel him in depicting a single mood of mind, as Dejection, for instance. Could Shakspeare have surpassed these lines?

"A grief without a pang, void, dark, and drear
A stifled, drowsy, unimpassioned grief,
Which finds no natural outlet, no relief,
In word, or sigh, or tear.
  O Lady, in this wan and heartless mood,
To other thoughts by yonder throstle wooed,
All this long eve, so balmy and serene,
  Have I been gazing on the western sky
And its peculiar tint of yellow green:
  And still I gaze—and with how blank an eye!
And those thin clouds above, in flakes and bars,
That give away their motion to the stars;

Those stars, that glide behind them or between,
Now sparkling, now bedimmed, but always seen;
Yon crescent moon, as fixed as if it grew
In its own cloudless, starless lake of blue;
I see them all, so excellently fair,
I see, not feel, how beautiful they are!
My genial spirits fail,
And what can these avail
To lift the smothering weight from off my breast?
It were a vain endeavour,
Though I should gaze for ever
On that green light that lingers in the West,
I may not hope from outward forms to win
The passion and the life whose fountains are within."

Give Coleridge a canvass, and he will paint a single mood as if his colors were made of the mind's own atoms. Here he is very unlike Southey. There is nothing of the spectator about Coleridge; he is all life; not impassioned, not vehement, but searching, intellectual life, which seems "listening through the frame" to its own pulses.

I have little more to say at present except to express a great, though not fanatical veneration for Coleridge, and a conviction that the benefits conferred by him on this and future ages are as yet incalculable. Every mind will praise him for what it can best receive from him. He can suggest to an infinite degree; he can *in*form, but he cannot *re*form and renovate. To the unprepared he is nothing, to the prepared, every thing. Of him may be said what he said of Nature,

"We receive but what we give,
In kind though not in measure."

I was once requested, by a very sensible and excellent personage to explain what is meant by "Christabel" and "The Ancient Mariner." I declined the task. I had not then seen Coleridge's answer to a question of similar tenor from Mrs. Barbauld, or I should have referred to that as an expression, not altogether unintelligible, of the discrepancy which must ever exist between those minds which are commonly styled *rational*, (as the received definition of *common* sense is insensibility to *uncommon* sense,) and that of Coleridge. As to myself, if I understand nothing beyond the execution of those "singularly wild and original poems," I could not tell my gratitude for the degree of refinement which Taste has received from them. To those who cannot understand the voice of Nature or Poetry, unless it speak in apothegms, and tag each story with a moral, I have nothing to say. My own greatest obligation to Coleridge I have already mentioned. It is for his suggestive power that I thank him.

Wordsworth! beloved friend and venerated teacher; it is more easy and perhaps as profitable to speak of thee. It is less difficult to interpret thee, since no *acquired nature*, but merely a theory, severs thee from my mind.

Classification on such a subject is rarely satisfactory, yet I will attempt to define in that way the impressions produced by Wordsworth on myself. I esteem his characteristics to be—of Spirit,

Perfect simplicity,
Perfect truth,
Perfect love.

Of mind or talent,

Calmness,
Penetration,
Power of Analysis.

Of manner,

Energetic greatness,
Pathetic tendernesss,
Mild, persuasive eloquence.

The time has gone by when groundlings could laugh with impunity at "Peter Bell" and the "Idiot Mother." Almost every line of Wordsworth has been quoted and requoted ; every feeling echoed back, and every drop of that " cup of still and serious thought" drunk up by some " spirit profound ;" enough to satisfy the giver.

Wordsworth is emphatically the friend and teacher of mature years. Youth, in whose bosom " the stately passions burn, ' is little disposed to drink with him from the

" urn
Of lowly pleasure."

He has not an idealizing tendency, if by this be meant the desire of creating from materials supplied by our minds, and by the world in which they abide for a season, a new and more beautiful world. It is the aspiration of a noble nature animated by genius, it is allied with the resolve for self-perfection ; and few, without some of its influence, can bring to blossom the bud of any virtue. It is fruitful in illusions, but those illusions have heavenly truth interwoven with their temporary errors. But the mind of Wordsworth, like that of the man of science, finds enough of beauty in the real present world. He delights in penetrating the designs of God, rather than in sketching designs of his own. Generally speaking, minds in which the faculty of observation is so prominent, have little enthusiasm, little dignity of sentiment. That is, indeed, an intellect of the first order, which can see the great in the little, and dignify the petty operations of Nature, by tracing through them her most sublime principles. Wordsworth scrutinizes man and nature with the exact and searching eye of a Cervantes, a Fielding, or a Richter, but without any love for that humorous wit which cannot obtain its needful food unaided by such scrutiny ; while dissection merely for curiosity's sake is his horror. He has the delicacy of perception, the universality of feeling which distinguish Shakspeare and the three or four other poets of the first class, and might have taken rank with them had he been equally gifted with versatility of talent. Many might reply, " in wanting this last he wants the better half." To this I cannot agree. Talent, or facility in making use of thought, is dependent, in a great measure, on education and circumstance; while thought itself is immortal as the soul from which it radiates. Wherever we perceive a profound thought, however imperfectly expressed, we offer a higher homage than we can to commonplace thoughts, however beautiful, or if expressed with all that grace of art which it is often most easy for ordinary minds to acquire. There is a suggestive and stimulating power in original thought which cannot be gauged by the first sensation or temporary effect it produces. The circles grow wider and wider as the impulse is propagated through the deep waters of eternity. An exhibition of talent causes immediate delight; almost all of us can enjoy seeing a thing well done; not all of us can enjoy being roused to do and dare for ourselves. Yet when the mind *is* roused to penetrate the secret meaning of each human effort, a higher pleasure and a greater benefit may be derived from the rude but masterly sketch, than from the elaborately finished miniature. In the former case our creative powers are taxed to supply what is wanting, while in the latter our tastes are refined by admiring what another has created. Now, since I esteem Wordsworth as superior in originality and philosophic unity of thought, to the other poets I have been discussing, I give him the highest place, though they may be superior to *him* either in melody, brilliancy of fancy, dramatic power, or general versatility of talent. Yet I do not place him on a par with those who combine those minor excellencies with originality and philosophic unity of thought. He is not a Shakspeare, but he is the greatest poet of the day; and this is more remarkable, as he is, par excellence, a didactic poet.

I have paid him the most flattering tribute in saying that there is not a line of his which has not been quoted and requoted.

Men have found such a response to their lightest as well as their deepest feelings, such beautiful morality with such lucid philosophy, that every thinking mind has, consciously or unconsciously, appropriated something from Wordsworth. Those who have never read his poems have imbibed some part of their spirit from the public or private discourse of his happy pupils; and it is, as yet, impossible to estimate duly the effect which the balm of his meditations has had in allaying the fever of the public heart, as exhibited in the writings of Byron and Shelley.

But, as I said before, he is not for youth, he is too tranquil. His early years were passed in listening to, his mature years in interpreting, the oracles of Nature; and though in pity and in love he sympathizes with the conflicts of life, it is not by mingling his tears with the sufferer's, but by the consolations of patient faith, that he would heal their griefs.

The sonnet on Tranquillity, to be found in the present little volume, exhibits him true to his old love and natural religion.

"Tranquillity! the solemn aim wert thou
In heathen schools of philosophic lore;
Heart-stricken by stern destiny of yore,
The tragic muse thee served with thoughtful vow;
And what of hope Elysium could allow
Was fondly seized by Sculpture, to restore
Peace to the mourner's soul; but he who wore
The crown of thorns around his bleeding brow,
Warmed our sad being with his glorious light;
Then arts which still had drawn a softening grace
From shadowy fountains of the Infinite,
Communed with that idea face to face;
And move around it now as planets run,
Each in its orbit round the central sun."

The doctrine of tranquillity does not suit the impetuous blood of the young, yet some there are, who, with pulses of temperate and even though warm and lively beat, are able to prize such poetry from their earliest days. One young person in particular I knew, very like his own description of

> "Those whose hearts every hour run wild,
> But never yet did go astray;"

who had read nothing but Wordsworth, and had by him been plentifully fed. I do not mean that she never skimmed novels nor dipped into periodicals; but she never, properly speaking, read, i. e. comprehended and reflected on any other book. But as all knowledge has been taught by Professor Jacotot from the Telemachus of Fenelon, so was she taught the secrets of the universe from Wordsworth's poems. He pointed out to her how

> "The primal duties shine aloft like stars,
> The charities that soothe, and heal, and bless,
> Are scattered at the feet of Man—like flowers."

He read her lectures about the daisy, the robin red-breast, and the waterfall. He taught her to study Nature and *feel* God's presence; to enjoy and prize human sympathies without needing the stimulus of human passions; to love beauty with a faith which enabled her to perceive it amid seeming ugliness, to hope goodness so as to create it. And she was a very pretty specimen of Wordsworthianism; so sincere, so simple, so animated and so equable, so hopeful and so calm. She was confiding as an infant, and so may remain till her latest day, for she has no touch of idolatry; and her trustfulness is not in any chosen person or persons, but in the goodness of God, who will always protect those who are true to themselves and sincere towards others.

But the young, in general, are idolaters. They will have their private chapels of ease in the great temple of nature; they will ornament, according to fancy, their favorite shrines; and ah! too frequently look with aversion or contempt upon all others. Till this ceases to be so, till they can feel the general beauty of design, and live content to be immortal in the grand whole, they cannot really love Wordsworth; nor can to them "the simplest flower" bring "thoughts that lie too deep for tears." Happy his pupils; they are gentle, they are calm, and they must always be progressing in our knowledge; for, to a mind which can sympathize with his, no hour, no scene can possibly be barren.

The contents of the lately published little volume* accord perfectly, in essentials, with those of the preceding four. The sonnets are like those he has previously written—equally unfinished as sonnets, equally full of meaning as poems. If it be the case with all his poems, that scarcely one forms a perfect whole by itself, but is valuable as a leaf out of his mind, it is peculiarly so with his sonnets. I presume he only makes use of this difficult mode of writing because it is a concise one for the expression of a single thought or a single mood. I know not that one of his sonnets is polished and wrought to a point, as this most artistical of all poems should be; but neither do I know one which does not contain something we would not willingly lose. As the beautiful sonnet which I shall give presently, whose import is so wide and yet so easily understood, contains in the motto, what Messer Petrarca would have said in the two concluding lines.

(Miss not the occasion; by the forelock take
That subtle power, the never-halting time,
Lest a mere moment's putting off should make
Mischance almost as heavy as a crime)—
"Wait, prithee, wait! this answer Lesbia threw
Forth to her dove, and took no further heed;
Her eyes were busy, while her fingers flew
Across the harp, with soul-engrossing speed;
But from that bondage when her thoughts were freed,
She rose, and toward the shut casement drew,
Whence the poor, unregarded favourite, true
To old affections, had been heard to plead
With flapping wing for entrance—What a shriek

* Yarrow Revisited, and other poems.

Forced from that voice so lately tuned to a strain
Of harmony!—a shriek of terror, pain,
And self-reproach!—for from aloft a kite
Pounced, and the dove, which from its ruthless beak
She could not rescue, perished in her sight!"

Even the Sonnet upon Sonnets, so perfect in the details, is not perfect as a whole.

However, I am not so fastidious as some persons about the dress of a thought. These sonnets are so replete with sweetness and spirit, that we can excuse their want of symmetry; and probably should not feel it, except from comparison with more highly-finished works of the same kind. One more let me extract, which should be laid to heart:

"Desponding father! mark this altered bough
So beautiful of late, with sunshine warmed,
Or moist with dews; what more unsightly now,
Its blossom shrivelled, and its fruit, if formed,
Invisible! yet Spring her genial brow
Knits not o'er that discolouring and decay
As false to expectation. Nor fret thou
At like unlovely process in the May
Of human life; a stripling's graces blow,
Fade and are shed, that from their timely fall
(Misdeem it not a cankerous change) may grow
Rich mellow bearings that for thanks shall call;
In all men sinful is it to be slow
To hope—in parents sinful above all."

"Yarrow Revisited" is a beautiful reverie. It ought to be read as such, for it has no determined aim. These are fine verses.

"And what for this frail world were all
That mortals do or suffer,
Did no responsive harp, no pen,
Memorial tribute offer?
Yea, what were mighty Nature's self?
Her features, could they win us,
Unhelped by the poetic voice
That hourly speaks within us?

"Nor deem that localized romance
Plays false with our affections;
Unsanctifies our tears—made sport
For fanciful dejections;
Ah, no! the visions of the past
Sustain the heart in feeling
Life as she is—our changeful life,
With friends and kindred dealing."

and this stanza,

"Eternal blessings on the Muse,
And her divine employment!
The blameless Muse, who trains her sons
For hope and calm enjoyment;
Albeit sickness, lingering yet,
Has o'er their pillow brooded;
And care waylay their steps—a sprite
Not easily eluded."

reminds us of what Scott says in his farewell to the Harp of the North:

"Much have I owed thy strains, on life's long way,
Through secret woes the world has never known,
When on the weary night dawned wearier day,
And bitter was the grief devoured alone,
That I o'erlive such woes, Enchantress, is thine own."

"The Egyptian Maid" is distinguished by a soft visionary style of painting, and a stealthy alluring movement, like the rippling of advancing waters, which, I do not remember elsewhere in Wordsworth's writings.

"The Armenian Lady's love" is a fine balled. The following verses are admirable for delicacy of sentiment and musical sweetness.

"Judge both fugitives with knowledge;
In those old romantic days
Mighty were the soul's commandments
To support, restrain, or raise.

Foes might hang upon their path, snakes rustle near,
But nothing from their inward selves had they to fear.

"Thought infirm ne'er came between them,
Whether printing desert sands
With accordant steps, or gathering
Forest fruit with social hands;
Or whispering like two reeds that in the cold moonbeam
Bend with the breeze their heads beside a crystal stream."

The Evening Voluntaries are very beautiful in manner, and full of suggestions. The second is worth extracting as a forcible exhibition of one of Wordsworth's leading opinions.

"Not in the lucid intervals of life
That come but as a curse to party strife;
Not in some hour when pleasure with a sigh
Of languor, puts his rosy garland by;
Not in the breathing times of that poor slave
Who daily piles up wealth in Mammon's cave,
Is nature felt, or can be; nor do words
Which practised talent readily affords
Prove that her hands have touched responsive chords.
Nor has her gentle beauty power to move
With genuine rapture and with fervent love
The soul of genius, if he dares to take
Life's rule from passion craved for passion's sake,
Untaught that meekness is the cherished bent
Of all the truly great and all the innocent;
But who is innocent? By grace divine,
Not otherwise, O Nature! we are thine,
Through good and evil thine, or just degree
Of rational and manly sympathy,
To all that earth from pensive hearts is stealing,
And heaven is now to gladdened eyes revealing,
Add every charm the universe can show
Through every change its aspects undergo,
Care may be respited, but not repealed;
No perfect cure grows on that bounded field,

Vain is the pleasure, a false calm the peace,
If he through whom alone our conflicts cease,
Our virtuous hopes without relapse advance,
Come not to speed the soul's deliverance;
To the distempered intellect refuse
His gracious help, or give what we abuse."

But nothing in this volume better deserves attention than "Lines suggested by a Portrait from the pencil of F. Stone," and "Stanzas on the Power of Sound." The first for a refinement and justness of thought rarely surpassed, and the second for a lyric flow, a swelling inspiration, and a width of range, which Wordsworth has never equalled, except in the "Ode on the Intimations of Immortality," and the noble ode, or rather hymn, to Duty. It should be read entire, and I shall not quote a line. By a singular naiveté the poet has prefixed to these stanzas a table of contents. This distrust of his reader seems to prove that he had risen above his usual level.

What more to the purpose can we say about Wordsworth, except—read him. Like his beloved Nature, to be known he must be loved. His thoughts may be transfused, but never adequately interpreted. Verily,

"To paint *his* being to a grovelling mind,
Were like describing pictures to the blind.

But no one, in whose bosom there yet lives a spark of nature or feeling, need despair of some time sympathizing with him; since one of the most brilliantly factitious writers of the day, one I should have singled out as seven-fold shielded against his gentle influence, has paid him so feeling a tribute:

"How must thy lone and lofty soul have gone
Exulting on its way, beyond the loud
Self-taunting mockery of the scoffers grown
Tethered and dulled to Nature, in the crowd!
Earth has no nobler, no more moral sight
Than a Great Poet, whom the world disowns,

But stills not, neither angers; from his height
As from a star, float forth his sphere-like tones;
He wits not whether the vexed herd may hear
The music wafted to the reverent ear;
And far man's wrath, or scorn, or heed above,
Smiles down the calm disdain of his majestic love!"
[*From Stanzas addressed by Bulwer to Wordsworth.*]

Read him, then, in your leisure hours, and when you walk into the summer fields you shall find the sky more blue, the flowers more fair, the birds more musical, your minds more awake, and your hearts more tender, for having held communion with him.

I have not troubled myself to point out the occasional affectations of Southey, the frequent obscurity of Coleridge, or the diffuseness of Wordsworth. I should fear to be treated like the critic mentioned in the story Addison quotes from Boccalini, whom Apollo rewarded for his labours by presenting him with a bushel of chaff from which all the wheat had been winnowed. For myself I think that where there is such beauty and strength, we can afford to be silent about slight defects; and that we refine our tastes more effectually by venerating the grand and lovely, than by detecting the little and mean.

THE MODERN DRAMA.*

A TRAGEDY in five acts!—what student of poetry,—(for, admire, O Posterity, the strange fact, these days of book-craft produce not only inspired singers, and enchanted listeners, but students of poetry,)—what student in this strange sort, I say, has not felt his eye rivetted to this title, as it were written in letters of fire? has not heard it whispered in his secret breast?—In this form alone canst thou express thy thought in the liveliness of life, this success alone should satisfy thy ambition!

Were all these ardours caught from a genuine fire, such as, in favouring eras, led the master geniuses by their successive efforts to perfect this form, till it afforded the greatest advantages in the smallest space, we should be glad to warm and cheer us at a very small blaze. But it is not so. The drama, at least the English drama of our day, shows a reflected light, not a spreading fire. It is not because the touch of genius has roused genius to production, but because the admiration of genius has made talent ambitious, that the harvest is still so abundant.

This is not an observation to which there are no exceptions, some we shall proceed to specify, but those who have, with any care, watched this ambition in their own minds, or analyzed its

* The Patrician's Daughter, a tragedy, in five acts, by J. Westland Marston: London: C. Mitchel, Red Lion Court, Fleet Street, 1841.

Athelwold, a tragedy in five acts, by W. Smith, Esq.; William Blackwood and Sons. London and Edinburgh, 1842.

Strafford, a tragedy, by John Sterling. London; Edward Moxon, Dover Street, 1843.

results in the works of others, cannot but feel that the drama is not a growth native to this age, and that the numerous grafts produce little fruit, worthy the toil they cost.

'Tis indeed, hard to believe that the drama, once invented, should cease to be a habitual and healthy expression of the mind. It satisfies so fully the wants both of sense and soul, supplying both deep and light excitements, simple, comprehensive, and various, adapted either to great national and religious subjects, or to the private woes of any human breast. The space and the time occupied, the vehicle of expression, fit it equally for the entertainment of an evening, or the closet theme of meditative years. Ædipus, Macbeth, Wallenstein, chain us for the hour, lead us through the age.

Who would not covet this mirror, which, like that of the old wizards, not only reflects, but reproduces the whole range of forms, this key, which unlocks the realms of speculation at the hour when the lights are boldest and the shadows most suggestive, this goblet, whose single sparkling draught is locked from common air by walls of glittering ice? An artful wild, where nature finds no bound to her fertility, while art steadily draws to a whole its linked chain.

Were it in man's power by choosing the best, to attain the best in any particular kind, we would not blame the young poet, if he always chose the drama.

But by the same law of faery which ordains that wishes shall be granted unavailingly to the wisher, no form of art will succeed with him to whom it is the object of deliberate choice. It must grow from his nature in a certain position, as it first did from the general mind in a certain position, and be no garment taken from the shining store to be worn at a banquet, but a real body gradually woven and assimilated from the earth and sky which environed the poet in his youthful years. He may learn from the old Greek or Hindoo, but he must speak in his mother-tongue.

It was a melancholy praise bestowed on the German Iphigenia, that it was an echo of the Greek mind. O give us something rather than Greece more Grecian, so new, so universal, so individual!

An "After Muse," an appendix period must come to every kind of greatness. It is the criticism of the grandchild upon the inheritance bequeathed by his ancestors. It writes madrigals and sonnets, it makes Brutus wigs, and covers old chairs with damask patch-work, yet happy those who have no affection towards such virtue and entertain their friends with a pipe cut from their own grove, rather than display an ivory lute handed down from the old time, whose sweetness we want the skill to draw forth.

The drama cannot die out: it is too naturally born of certain periods of national development. It is a stream that will sink in one place, only to rise to light in another. As it has appeared successively in Hindostan, Greece, (Rome we cannot count,) England, Spain, France, Italy, Germany, so has it yet to appear in New Holland, New Zealand, and among ourselves, when we too shall be made new by a sunrise of our own, when our population shall have settled into a homogeneous, national life, and we have attained vigour to walk in our own way, make our own world, and leave off copying Europe.

At present our attempts are, for the most part, feebler than those of the British "After Muse," for our play-wrights are not from youth so fancy-fed by the crumbs that fall from the tables of the lords of literature, and having no relish for the berries of our own woods, the roots of our own fields, they are meagre, and their works bodiless; yet, as they are pupils of the British school, their works need not be classed apart, and I shall mention one or two of the most note-worthy by-and by.

England boasts one Shakspeare—ah! that alone was more than the share of any one kingdom,—such a king! There Apollo himself tended sheep, and there is not a blade of the field but glows with a peculiar light. At times we are tempted to think him the only genius earth has ever known, so beyond compare is he, when looked at as the myriad-minded; then he seems to sit at the head of the stream of thought, a lone god beside his urn; the minds of others, lower down, feed the current to a greater width, but they come not near him. Happily, in the constructive power, in sweep of soul, others may be named beside him: he is not always all alone.

Historically, such isolation was not possible. Such a being implies a long ancestry, a longer posterity. We discern immortal vigour in the stem that rose to this height.

But his children should not hope to walk in his steps. Prospero gave Miranda a sceptre, not his wand. His genius is too great for his followers, they dwindle in its shadow. They see objects so early with his eyes, they can hardly learn to use their own. "They seek to produce from themselves, but they only reproduce him."

He is the cause why so much of England's intellect tends towards the drama, a cause why it so often fails. His works bring despair to genius, they are the bait and the snare of talent.

The impetus he has given, the lustre with which he dazzles, are a chief cause of the dramatic efforts, one cause of failure, but not the only one, for it seems probable that European life tends to new languages, and for a while neglecting this form of representation, would explore the realms of sound and sight, to make to itself other organs, which must for a time supersede the drama.

There is, perhaps, a correspondence between the successions of literary vegetation with those of the earth's surface, where, if you burn or cut down an ancient wood, the next offering of the soil will not be in the same kind, but raspberries and purple flowers will succeed the oak, poplars the pine. Thus, beneath the roots of the drama, lay seeds of the historic novel, the romantic epic, which were to take its place to the reader, and for the scene, the oratorios, the opera, and ballet.

Music is the great art of the time. Its dominion is constantly widening, its powers are more profoundly recognized. In the forms it has already evolved, it is equal to representing any subject, can address the entire range of thoughts and emotions. These forms have not yet attained their completeness, and already we discern many others hovering in the vast distances of the Tone-world.

The opera is in this inferior to the drama, that it produces its effects by the double method of dialogue and song. So easy seems it to excite a feeling, and by the orchestral accompaniments to sustain it to the end, that we have not the intellectual exhilaration which accompanies a severer enjoyment. For the same reasons, nothing can surpass the mere luxury of a fine opera.

The oratorio, so great, so perfect in itself, is limited in its subjects; and these, though they must be of the graver class, do not properly admit of tragedy. Minds cannot dwell on special griefs and seeming partial fates, when circling the universe on the wings of the great chorus, sharing the will of the Divine, catching the sense of humanity.

Thus much, as has been given, we demand from music yet another method, simpler and more comprehensive than these. In instrumental music this is given by the symphony, but we want another that shall admit the voice, too, and permit the association of the spectacle.

The ballet seems capable of an infinite perfection. There is no boundary here to the powers of design and expression, if only fit artists can be formed mentally and practically. What could not a vigorous imagination do, if it had delicate Ariels to enact its plans, with that facility and completeness which pantomine permits? There is reason to think we shall see the language of the eye, of gesture and attitude carried to a perfection, body made pliant to the inspirations of spirit, as it can hardly be where spoken words are admitted to eke out deficiencies. From our America we hope some form entirely new, not yet to be predicted, while, though the desire for dramatic representation exists, as it always must where there is any vigorous life, the habit of borrowing is so pervasive, that in the lately peopled prairies of the West, where civilization is but five years old, we find the young people acting plays, indeed, and "on successive nights to overflowing audiences,"—but what? Some drama, ready made to hand by the fortunes of Boon, or the defeats of Black Hawk? Not at all, but—Tamerlane and the like—Bombastes Furioso, and King Cambyses vein to the "storekeepers" and labourers of republican America.

In this connection let me mention the drama of Metamora, a favourite on the boards in our cities, which, if it have no other merit, yields something that belongs to this region, Forrest having studied for this part the Indian gait and expression with some success. He is naturally adapted to the part by the strength and dignity of his person and outline.

To return to Britain.

The stage was full of life, after the drama began to decline, and the actors, whom Shakspeare should have had to represent his parts, were born, after his departure, from the dignity given to the profession by the existence of such occasion for it. And again, out of the existence of such actors rose hosts of playwrights, who wrote not to embody the spirit of life, in forms shifting and interwoven in the space of a spectacle, but to give room for display of the powers of such and such actors. A little higher stood those, who excelled in invention of plots, pregnant crises, or brilliant point of dialogue, but both degraded the drama, Sheridan scarcely less than Cibber; and Garrick and the Kembles, while they lighted up the edifice, left slow fire for its destruction.

A partial stigma rests, as it has always rested, on the profession of the actor. At first flash, we marvel why. Why do not men bow in reverence before those, who hold the mirror up to nature, and not to common nature, but to her most exalted, profound, and impassioned hours?

Some have imputed this to an association with the trickeries and coarse illusions of the scene, with pasteboard swords and crowns, mock-thunder and tinfoil moonshine. But in what profession are not mummeries practised, and ludicrous accessories interposed? Are the big wig of the barrister, the pen behind the ear of the merchant, so reverend in our eyes?

Some say that it is because we pay the actor for amusing us; but we pay other men for all kinds of service, without feeling them degraded thereby. And is he, who has administered an exhilarating draught to my mind, in less pleasing associations there, than he who has administered a febrifuge to the body?

Again, that the strong excitements of the scene and its motley life dispose to low and sensual habits.

But the instances, where all such temptations have been resisted, are so many, compared with the number engaged, that every one must feel that here, as elsewhere, the temptation is determined by the man.

Why is it then that to the profession, which numbers in its ranks Shakspeare and Moliere, which is dignified by such figures as Siddons, Talma, and Macready, respect is less willingly conceded than applause? Why is not discrimination used here as elsewhere? Is it the same thing to act the "Lady in Comus," and the Lady in "She stoops to Conquer," Hamlet, Prince of Denmark, and Sir Lucius O'Trigger? Is not the actor, according to his sphere, a great artist or a poor buffoon, just as a lawyer may become a chancellor of the three kingdoms, or a base pettifogger ?

Prejudice on this score, must be the remnant of a barbarism which saw minstrels the pensioned guests at barons' tables, and murdered Correggio beneath a sack of copper. As man better understands that his positive existence is only effigy of the ideal, and that nothing is useful or honourable which does not advance the reign of Beauty, Art and Artists rank constantly higher, as one with Religion. Let Artists also know their calling, let the Actor live and die a Roman Actor,* more than Raphael shall be

* We may be permitted to copy, in this connection, the fine plea of Massinger's "Roman Actor."

PARIS. If desire of honor was the base
On which the building of the Roman empire
Was raised up to this height; if, to inflame
The noble youth, with an ambitious heat,
To endure the posts of danger, nay, of death,
To be thought worthy the triumphal wreath,
By glorious undertakings, may deserve
Reward, or favor from the commonwealth;
Actors may put in for as large a share,
As all the sects of the philosophers:
They with cold precepts (perhaps seldom read)
Deliver what an honorable thing
The active virtue is: but does that fire
The blood, or swell the veins with emulation,
To be both good and great, equal to that
Which is presented on our theatres ?
Let a good actor, in a lofty scene,
Show great Alcides, honored in the sweat
Of his twelve labors; or a bold Camillus,
Forbidding Rome to be redeemed with gold
From the insulting Gauls, or Scipio,
After his victories, imposing tribute
On conquered Carthage; if done to the life,

elected Cardinals, and of a purer church; and it shall be ere long remembered as dream and fable, that the representative of "*my Cid*" could not rest in consecrated ground.

As if they saw their dangers, and their glories,
And did partake with them in their rewards,
All that have any spark of Roman in them,
The slothful arts laid by, contend to be
Like those they see presented.

SECOND SENATOR. He has put
The consuls to their whisper.

PARIS. But 'tis urged
That we corrupt youth, and traduce superiors.
When do we bring a vice upon the stage,
That does go off unpunished? Do we teach,
By the success of wicked undertakings,
Others to tread in their forbidden steps?
We show no arts of Lydian panderism,
Corinthian poisons, Persian flatteries,
But mulcted so in the conclusion, that
Even those spectators, that were so inclined,
Go home changed men. And for traducing such
That are above us, publishing to the world
Their secret crimes, we are as innocent
As such as are born dumb. When we present
An heir, that does conspire against the life
Of his dear parent, numbering every hour
He lives, as tedious to him; if there be
Among the auditors one, whose conscience tells him
He is of the same mould,—WE CANNOT HELP IT.
Or, bringing on the stage a loose adulteress,
That does maintain the riotous expense
Of her licentious paramour, yet suffers
The lawful pledges of a former bed
To starve the while for hunger; if a matron,
However great in fortune, birth, or titles,
Cry out, 'Tis writ for me!—WE CANNOT HELP IT.
Or, when a covetous man's expressed, whose wealth

In Germany these questions have already been fairly weighed, and those who read the sketches of her great actors, as given by Tieck, know that there, at least, they took with the best minds of their age and country their proper place.

And who, that reads Joanna Baillie's address to Mrs. Siddons, but feels that the fate, which placed his birth in another age from her, has robbed him of full sense of a kind of greatness whose absence none other can entirely supply.

* * * * * *

The impassioned changes of thy beauteous face,
Thy arms impetuous tost, thy robe's wide flow,
And the dark tempest gathered on thy brow,
What time thy flashing eye and lip of scorn
Down to the dust thy mimic foes have borne;
Remorseful musings sunk to deep dejection,
The fixed and yearning looks of strong affection;

Arithmetic cannot number, and whose lordships
A falcon in one day cannot fly over;
Yet he so sordid in his mind, so griping
As not to afford himself the necessaries
To maintain life, if a patrician,
(Though honored with a consulship) find himself
Touched to the quick in this,—WE CANNOT HELP IT.
Or, when we show a judge that is corrupt,
And will give up his sentence, as he favors
The person, not the cause; saving the guilty
If of his faction, and as oft condemning
The innocent, out of particular spleen;
If any in this reverend assembly,
Nay, even yourself, my lord, that are the image
Of absent Cæsar, feel something in your bosom
That puts you in remembrance of things past,
Or things intended,—'TIS NOT IN US TO HELP IT.
I have said, my lord, and now, as you find cause,
Or censure us, or free us with applause.

The actioned turmoil of a bosom rending,
Where pity, love, and honor, are contending;
* * * * * *
Thy varied accents, rapid, fitful, slow,
Loud rage, and fear's snatch'd whisper, quick and low,
The burst of stifled love, the wail of grief,
And tones of high command, full, solemn, brief;
The change of voice and emphasis that threw
Light on obscurity, and brought to view
Distinctions nice, when grave or comic mood,
Or mingled humors, terse and new, elude
Common perception, as earth's smallest things
To size and form the vesting hoar-frost brings.
* * * * * * *
* * * Thy light * * * *
* from the mental world can never fade,
Till all, who've seen thee, in the grave are laid.
Thy graceful form still moves in nightly dreams
And what thou wert to the rapt sleeper seems,
While feverish fancy oft doth fondly trace
Within her curtained couch thy wondrous face;
Yea, and to many a wight, bereft and lone,
In musing hours, though all to thee unknown,
Soothing his early course of good and ill,
With all thy potent charm thou actest still.

Perhaps the effect produced by Mrs. Siddons is still more vividly shown in the character of Jane de Montfort, which seems modelled from her. We have no such lotus cup to drink. Mademoiselle Rachel indeed seems to possess as much electric force as Mrs. Siddons, but not the same imposing individuality. The Kembles and Talma were cast in the royal mint to commemorate the victories of genius. That Mrs. Siddons even added somewhat of congenial glory to Shakspeare's own conceptions, those who compare the engravings of her in Lady Macbeth and Catherine of Arragon, with the picture drawn in their own minds from acquaintance with these beings in the original, cannot doubt; the sun is reflected with new glory in the majestic river.

Yet, under all these disadvantages there have risen up often, in England, and even in our own country, actors who gave a reason for the continued existence of the theatre, who sustained the ill-educated, flimsy troop, which commonly fills it, and provoked both the poet and the playwright to turn their powers in that direction.

The plays written for them, though no genuine dramas, are not without value as spectacle, and the opportunity, however lame, gives freer play to the actor's powers, than would the simple recitation, by which some have thought any attempt at acting whole plays should be superseded. And under the starring system it is certainly less painful, on the whole, to see a play of Knowles's than one of Shakspeare's; for the former, with its frigid diction, unnatural dialogue, and academic figures, affords scope for the actor to produce striking effects, and to show a knowledge of the passions, while all the various beauties of Shakspeare are traduced by the puppets who should repeat them, and the being closer to nature, brings no one figure into such bold relief as is desirable when there is only one actor. Virginius, the Hunchback, Metamora, are plays quite good enough for the stage at present; and they are such as those who attend the representations of plays will be very likely to write.

Another class of dramas are those written by the scholars and thinkers, whose tastes have been formed, and whose ambition kindled, by acquaintance with the genuine English dramatists. These again may be divided into two sorts. One, those who have some idea to bring out, which craves a form more lively than the essay, more compact than the narrative, and who therefore adopt (if Hibernicism may be permitted) the dialogued monologue to very good purpose. Such are Festus, Paracelsus, Coleridge's Remorse, Shelley's Cenci; Miss Baillie's plays, though meant for action, and with studied attempts to vary them by the lighter shades of common nature, which, from her want of lively power, have no effect, except to break up the interest, and Byron's are of the same class; they have no present life, no action, no slight natural touches, no delicate lines, as of one who paints his portrait from the fact; their interest is poetic, nature apprehended in her spirit; philosophic, actions traced back to their causes; but not dramatic, nature reproduced in actual presence. This, as a form for the closet, is a very good one, and well fitted to the genius of our time. Whenever the writers of such fail, it is because they have the stage in view, instead of considering the *dramatis personæ* merely as names for classes of thoughts. Somewhere betwixt these and the mere acting plays stand such as Maturin's Bertram, Talfourd's Ion, and (now before me) Longfellow's Spanish Student. Bertram is a good acting play, that is, it gives a good opportunity to one actor, and its painting, though coarse, is effective. Ion, also, can be acted, though its principal merit is in the nobleness of design, and in details it is too elaborate for the scene. Still it does move and melt, and it is honorable to us that a piece constructed on so high a *motive*, whose tragedy is so much nobler than the customary forms of passion, can act on audiences long unfamiliar with such religion. The Spanish Student might also be acted, though with no great effect, for there is little movement in the piece, or development of character; its chief merit is in the graceful expression of single thoughts or fancies; as here,

All the means of action
The shapeless masses, the materials,
Lie every where about us. What we need
Is the celestial fire to change the flint
Into transparent crystal, bright and clear.
That fire is genius! The rude peasant sits
At evening in his smoky cot, and draws
With charcoal uncouth figures on the wall.
The son of genius comes, foot-sore with travel,
And begs a shelter from the inclement night.

He takes the charcoal from the peasant's hand,
And by the magic of his touch at once
Transfigured, all its hidden virtues shine,
And in the eyes of the astonished clown,
It gleams a diamond. Even thus transformed,
Rude popular traditions and old tales
Shine as immortal poems, at the touch
Of some poor houseless, homeless, wandering bard,
Who had but a night's lodging for his pains.
But there are brighter dreams than those of fame,
Which are the dreams of love! Out of the heart
Rises the bright ideal of these dreams,
As from some woodland fount a spirit rises
And sinks again into its silent deeps,
Ere the enamoured knight can touch her robe!
'T is this ideal, that the soul of man,
Like the enamoured knight beside the fountain,
Waits for upon the margin of life's stream;
Waits to behold her rise from the dark waters
Clad in a mortal shape! Alas! how many
Must wait in vain! The stream flows evermore,
But from its silent deeps no spirit rises.

Or here,

I will forget her! All dear recollections
Pressed in my heart, like flowers within a book,
Shall be torn out, and scattered to the winds;
I will forget her! But perhaps hereafter,
When she shall learn how heartless is the world,
A voice within her will repeat my name,
And she will say, 'He was indeed my friend.'

Passages like these would give great pleasure in the chaste and carefully-shaded recitation of Macready or Miss Tree. The style of the play is, throughout, elegant and simple. Neither the plot nor characters can boast any originality, but the one is woven with skill and taste, the others very well drawn, for so slight handling.

We had purposed in this place to notice some of the modern

French plays, which hold about the same relation to the true drama, but this task must wait a more convenient season.

One of the plays at the head of this notice also comes in here, The Patrician's Daughter, which, though a failure as a tragedy, from an improbability in the plot, and a want of power to touch the secret springs of passion, yet has the merits of genteel comedy in the unstrained and flowing dialogue, and dignity in the conception of character. A piece like this pleases, if only by the atmosphere of intellect and refinement it breathes.

But a third class, of higher interest, is the historical, such as may well have been suggested to one whose youth was familiar with Shakspeare's Julius Cæsar, and Kings of England. Who that wears in his breast an English heart, and has feeling to appreciate the capabilities of the historic drama, but must burn with desire to use the occasions offered in profusion by the chronicles of England and kindred nations, to adorn the inherited halls with one tapestry more. It is difficult to say why such an attempt should fail, yet it does fail, and each effort in this kind shows plainly that the historic novel, not the historic drama, is the form appropriate to the genius of our day. Yet these failures come so near success, the spent arrows show so bold and strong a hand in the marksman, that we would not, for much, be without them.

First and highest in this list comes Philip Van Artevelde, of which we can say that it bears new fruit on the twentieth reading. At first it fell rather coldly on the mind, coming as it did, not as the flower of full flushed being, but with the air of an experiment made to verify a theory. It came with wrinkled critic's brow, consciously antagonistic to a tendency of the age, and we looked on it with cold critic's eye, unapt to weep or glow at its bidding. But, on closer acquaintance, we see that this way of looking, though induced by the author, is quite unjust. It is really a noble work that teaches us, a genuine growth that makes us grow, a reflex of nature from the calm depths of a large soul.

The grave and comprehensive character of the ripened man, of him whom fire, and light, and earth have tempered to an intelligent delegate of humanity, has never been more justly felt, rarely more life-like painted, than by this author. The Flemish blood and the fiery soul are both understood. Philip stands among his compatriots the man mature, not premature or alien. He is what they should be, his life the reconciling word of his age and nation, the thinking head of an unintelligent and easily distempered body, a true king. The accessories are all in keeping, saplings of the same wood. The eating, drinking, quarrelling citizens, the petulant sister, the pure and lovely bride, the sorrowful and stained, but deep-souled mistress, the monk, much a priest, but more a man, all belong to him and all require him. We cannot think of any part of this piece without its centre, and this fact proclaims it a great work of art. It is great, the conception of the swelling tide of fortune, on which this figure is upborne serenely eminent, of the sinking of that tide with the same face rising from the depths, veiled with the same cloud as the heavens, in its sadness calmer yet. Too wise and rich a nature he, too intelligent of the teachings of earth and heaven to be a stoic, but too comprehensive, too poetic, to be swayed, though he might be moved, by chance or passion. Some one called him Philip the Imperturbable, but his greatness is, that he is *not* imperturbable, only, as the author announces, " not passion's slave." The gods would not be gods, if they were ignorant, or impassive; they must be able to see all that men see, only from a higher point of view.

Such pictures make us willing to live in the widest sense, to bear all that may be borne, for we see that virgin gold may be fit to adorn a scabbard, but the good blade is made of tempered steel.

Justice has not been done by the critics to the admirable conduct of the Second Part, because our imaginations were at first so struck by the full length picture of the hero in the conquering days of the First Part, and it was painful to see its majesty veiled with crape, its towering strength sink to ruins in the second. Then there are more grand and full passages in the First which can be detached and recollected ; as,

> We have not time to mourn; the worse for us,
> He that lacks time to mourn lacks time to mend;
> Eternity mourns that. 'T is an ill cure
> For life's worst ills, to have no time to feel them.
> Where sorrow's held intrusive and turned out,
> There wisdom will not enter, nor true power,
> Nor aught that dignifies humanity.

That beginning,

> To bring a cloud upon the summer day,

or this famous one,

> Nor do I now despond, &c.

or the fine scene between Clara, Van Artevelde, and Father John, where she describes the death scene at Sesenheim's, beginning,

> Much hast thou merited, my sister dear.

The second part must be taken as a whole, the dark cloud widening and blackening as it advances, while ghastly flashes of presage come more and more frequent as the daylight diminishes. But there is far more fervor of genius than in the First, showing a mind less possessing, more possessed by, the subject, and finer touches of nature. Van Artevelde's dignity overpowers us more, as he himself feels it less ; as in the acceptance of Father John's reproof.

> VAN ARTEVELDE.
> Father John!
> Though peradventure fallen in your esteem,
> I humbly ask your blessing, as a man,
> That having passed for more in your repute
> Than he could justify, should be content,
> Not with his state, but with the judgment true

That to the lowly level of his state
Brings down his reputation.

FATHER JOHN.

Oh, my son!
High as you stand, I will not strain my eyes
To see how higher still you stood before.
God's blessing be upon you. Fare you well.
[*Exit.*

ARTEVELDE.

The old man weeps.

But he reverts at once to the topic of his thought,

Should England play me false, &c.

as he always does, for a mind so great, so high, that it cannot fail to look over and around any one object, any especial emotion, returns to its habitual mood with an ease of which shallow and excitable natures cannot conceive. Thus his reflection, after he has wooed Elena, is not that of heartlessness, but of a deep heart.

How little flattering is a woman's love!

And is in keeping with

I know my course
And be it armies, cities, people, priests,
That quarrel with my love, wise men or fools,
Friends, foes, or factions, they may swear their oaths,
And make their murmur; rave, and fret, and fear,
Suspect, admonish; they but waste their rage,
Their wits, their words, their counsel; here I stand
Upon the deep foundations of my faith,
To this fair outcast plighted; and the storm
That princes from their palaces shakes out,
Though it should turn and head me, should not strain
The seeming silken texture of this tie.

And not less with

Pain and grief
Are transitory things no less than joy;

And though they leave us not the men we were,
Yet they do leave us.

With the admirable passages that follow.

The delicate touches, with which Elena is made to depict her own character, move us more than Artevelde's most beautiful description of Adriana.

I have been much unfortunate, my lord,
I would not love again.

Shakspeare could not mend the collocation of those words.

When he is absent I am full of thought,
And fruitful in expression inwardly,
And fresh, and free, and cordial, is the flow
Of my ideal and unheard discourse,
Calling him in my heart endearing names,
Familiarly fearless. But alas!
No sooner is he present than my thoughts
Are breathless and bewitched, and stunted so
In force and freedom, that I ask myself
Whether I think at all, or feel, or live,
So senseless am I.

Would that I were merry!
Mirth have I valued not before; but now
What would I give to be the laughing front
Of gay imaginations ever bright,
And sparkling fantasies! Oh, all I have,
Which is not nothing, though I prize it not;
My understanding soul, my brooding sense,
My passionate fancy, and the gift of gifts
Dearest to woman, which deflowering Time,
Slow ravisher, from clenchedest fingers wrings,
My corporal beauty would I barter now
For such an antic and exulting spirit
As lives in lively women.

Your grave, and wise,
And melancholy men, if they have souls,

As commonly they have, susceptible
Of all impressions, lavish most their love
Upon the blithe and sportive, and on such
As yield their want, and chase their sad excess,
With jocund salutations, nimble talk,
And buoyant bearing.

All herself is in the line,

Which is not nothing, though I prize it not.

And in her song,

Down lay in a nook my lady's brach.

This song I have heard quoted, and applied in such a way as to show that the profound meaning, so simply expressed, has sometimes been understood.

See with what a strain of reflection Van Artevelde greets the news that makes sure his overthrow.

It is strange, yet true,
That doubtful knowledge travels with a speed
Miraculous, which certain cannot match;
I know not why, when this or that has chanced,
The smoke should come before the flash; yet 't is so.

The creative power of a soul of genius, is shown by bringing out the poetic sweetness of Van Artevelde, more and more, as the scene assumes a gloomier hue. The melancholy music of his speech penetrates the heart more and more up to the close.

The gibbous moon was in a wan decline,
And all was silent as a sick man's chamber,
Mixing its small beginnings with the dregs
Of the pale moonshine, and a few faint stars,
The cold uncomfortable daylight dawned;
And the white tents, topping a low-ground fog,
Showed like a fleet becalmed.

At the close of the vision:

And midmost in the eddy and the whirl,
My own face saw I, which was pale and calm
As death could make it,—then the vision passed,

And I perceived the river and the bridge,
The mottled sky, and horizontal moon,
The distant camp and all things as they were.

* * * * * *

Elena, think not that I stand in need
Of false encouragement; I have my strength,
Which, though it lie not in the sanguine mood,
Will answer my occasions. To yourself,
Though to none other, I at times present
The gloomiest thoughts that gloomy truths inspire,
Because I love you. But I need no prop!
Nor could I find it in a tinsel show
Of prosperous surmise. Before the world
I wear a cheerful aspect, not so false
As for your lover's solace you put on;
Nor in my closet does the oil run low,
Or the light flicker.

ELENA.

Lo, now! you are angry
Because I try to cheer you.

VAN ARTEVELDE.

No, my love,
Not angry; that I never was with you;
But as I deal not falsely with my own,
So would I wish the heart of her I love,
To be both true and brave; nor self-beguiled,
Nor putting on disguises for my sake,
As though I faltered. I have anxious hours;
As who in like extremities has not?
But I have something stable here within,
Which bears their weight.

In the last scenes:

CECILE.

She will be better soon, my lord.

VAN ARTEVELDE.

Say worse;
'T is better for her to be thus bereft.
One other kiss on that bewitching brow,

Pale hemisphere of charms. Unhappy girl!
The curse of beauty was upon thy birth,
Nor love bestowed a blessing. Fare thee well!

How clear his voice sounds at the very last.

The rumor ran that I was hurt to death,
And then they staggered. Lo! we're flying all!
Mount, mount, old man; at least let one be saved!
Roosdyk! Vauclaire! the gallant and the kind!
Who shall inscribe your merits on your tombs!
May mine tell nothing to the world but this:
That never did that prince or leader live,
Who had more loyal or more loving friends!
Let it be written that fidelity
Could go no farther. Mount, old friend, and fly!

VAN RYK.

With you, my lord, not else. A fear-struck throng,
Comes rushing from Mount Dorre. Sir, cross the bridge.

ARTEVELDE.

The bridge! my soul abhors—but cross it thou;
And take this token to my love, Van Ryk;
Fly, for my sake in hers, and take her hence!
It is my last command. See her conveyed
To Ghent by Olsen, or what safer road
Thy prudence shall descry. This do, Van Ryk.
Lo! now they pour upon us like a flood!—
Thou that didst never disobey me yet—
This last good office render me. Begone!
Fly whilst the way is free.

What commanding sweetness in the utterance of the name, Van Ryk, and what a weight of tragedy in the broken sentence which speaks of the fatal bridge. These are the things that actors rarely give us, the very passages to which it would be their vocation to do justice; saying out those tones we divine from the order of the words.

Yet Talma's *Pas encore* set itself to music in the mind of the hearer; and *Zara, you weep*, was so spoken as to melt the whole French nation into that one moment.

Elena's sob of anguish:

> Arouse yourself, sweet lady: fly with me,
> I pray you hear; it was his last command
> That I should take you hence to Ghent by Olsen.
>
> ELENA.
>
> I cannot go on foot.
>
> VAN RYK.
>
> No, lady, no,
> You shall not need; horses are close at hand,
> Let me but take you hence. I pray you come.
>
> ELENA.
>
> Take *him* then too.
>
> VAN RYK.
>
> The enemy is near,
> In hot pursuit; we cannot take the body.
>
> ELENA.
>
> The body! Oh!

In this place Miss Kemble alone would have had force of passion to represent her, who

> Flung that long funereal note
> Into the upper sky?

Though her acting was not refined enough by intellect and culture for the more delicate lineaments of the character. She also would have given its expression to the unintelligent, broken-hearted,

> I cannot go on foot.

The body—yes, that temple could be so deserted by its god, that men could call it so! That form so instinct with rich gifts, that baseness and sloth seemed mere names in its atmosphere, could lie on the earth as unable to vindicate its rights, as any other clod. The exclamation of Elena, better bespoke the tragedy of this fact, than any eulogium of a common observer, though that of Burgundy is fitly worded.

Dire rebel though he was,
Yet with a noble nature and great gifts
Was he endowed: courage, discretion, wit,
An equal temper and an ample soul,
Rock-bound and fortified against assaults
Of transitory passion, but below
Built on a surging subterraneous fire,
That stirred and lifted him to high attempts,
So prompt and capable, and yet so calm;
He nothing lacked in sovereignty but the right,
Nothing in soldiership except good fortune.

That *was* the grandeur of the character, that its calmness had nothing to do with slowness of blood, but was "built on a surging subterranean fire."

Its magnanimity is shown with a fine simplicity. To blame one's self is easy, to condemn one's own changes and declensions of character and life painful, but inevitable to a deep mind. But to bear well the blame of a lesser nature, unequal to seeing what the fault grows from, is not easy; to take blame as Van Artevelde does, so quietly, indifferent from whence truth comes, so it be truth, is a trait seen in the greatest only.

ELENA.

Too anxious, Artevelde,
And too impatient are you grown of late;
You used to be so calm and even-minded,
That nothing ruffled you.

ARTEVELDE.

I stand reproved;
'T is time and circumstance that tries us all;
And they that temperately take their start,
And keep their souls indifferently sedate,
Through much of good and evil at the last,
May find the weakness of their hearts thus tried.
My cause appears more precious than it did
In its triumphant days.

I have ventured to be the more lavish of extracts that, although the publication of Philip Van Artevelde at once placed Mr. Taylor in the second rank of English poets, a high meed of glory, when we remember who compose the first, we seldom now hear the poem mentioned, or a line quoted from it, though it is a work which might, from all considerations, well make a part of habitual reading, and habitual thought. Mr. Taylor has since published another dramatic poem, "Edwin the Fair," whose excellencies, though considerable, are not of the same commanding character with those of its predecessor. He was less fortunate in his subject. There is no great and noble figure in the foreground on which to concentrate the interest, from which to distribute the lights. Neither is the spirit of an era seized with the same power. The figures are modern English under Saxon names, and affect us like a Boston face, tricked out in the appurtenances of Goethe's Faust. Such a character as Dunstan's should be subordinated in a drama; its interest is that of intellectual analysis, mere feelings it revolts. The main character of the piece should attract the feelings, and we should be led to analysis, to understand, not to excuse its life.

There are, however, fine passages, as profound, refined, and expressed with the same unstrained force and purity, as those in Philip Van Artevelde.

Athelwold, another of the tragedies at the head of this notice, takes up some of the same characters a few years later. Without poetic depth, or boldness of conception, it yet boasts many beauties from the free talent, and noble feelings of the author. Athelwold is the best sketch in it, and the chief interest consists in his obstinate rejection of Elfrida, whose tardy penitence could no way cancel the wrong, her baseness of nature did his faith. This is worked up with the more art, that there is justice in her plea, but love, shocked from its infinity, could not stop short of despair. Here deep feeling rises to poetry.

Dunstan and Edgar are well drawn sketches, but show not the subtle touches of a life-like treatment.

This, we should think, as well as the Patrician's Daughter, might be a good acting play.

We come now to the work which affords the most interesting theme for this notice, from its novelty, its merits, and its subject, which is taken from that portion of English history with which we are most closely bound, the time preceding the Commonwealth.

Its author, Mr. Sterling, has many admirers among us, drawn to him by his productions, both in prose and verse, which for a time enriched the pages of Blackwood. Some of these have been collected into a small volume, which has been republished in this country.

These smaller pieces are of very unequal merit; but the best among them are distinguished by vigor of conception and touch, by manliness and modesty of feeling, by a depth of experience, rare in these days of babbling criticism and speculation. His verse does not flow or soar with the highest lyrical inspiration, neither does he enrich us by a large stock of original images, but for grasp and picturesque presentation of his subject, for frequent bold and forceful passages, and the constantly fresh breath of character, we know few that could be named with him. The Sexton's Daughter is the longest and best known, but not the best of the minor poems. It has, however, in a high degree, the merits we have mentioned. The yew tree makes a fine centre to the whole picture. The tale is told in too many words, the homely verse becomes garrulous, but the strong, pure feeling of natural relations endears them all.

His Aphrodite is fitly painted, and we should have dreamed it so from all his verse.

* * * * *

The high immortal queen from heaven,
  The calm Olympian face;

Eyes pure from human tear or smile,
  Yet ruling all on earth,
And limbs whose garb of golden air
  Was Dawn's primeval birth.

With tones like music of a lyre,
  Continuous, piercing, low,
The sovran lips began to speak,
  Spoke on in liquid flow,
It seemed the distant ocean's voice,
  Brought near and shaped to speech,
But breathing with a sense beyond
  What words of man may reach.

Weak child! Not I the puny power
  Thy wish would have me be,
A roseleaf floating with the wind
  Upon a summer sea.
If such thou need'st, go range the fields,
And hunt the gilded fly,
And when it mounts above thy head,
  Then lay thee down and die.

The spells which rule in earth and stars,
  Each mightiest thought that lives,
Are stronger than the kiss a child
  In sudden fancy gives.
They cannot change, or fail, or fade,
  Nor deign o'er aught to sway,
Too weak to suffer and to strive,
  And tired while still 't is day.

And thou with better wisdom learn
  The ancient lore to scan,
Which tells that first in Ocean's breast
  Thy rule o'er all began;
And know that not in breathless noon
  Upon the glassy main,
The power was born that taught the world
  To hail her endless reign.

The winds were loud, the waves were high,
  In drear eclipse the sun
Was crouched within the caves of heaven,
  And light had scarce begun;
The Earth's green front lay drowned below,
  And Death and Chaos fought
O'er all the tumult vast of things
  Not yet to severance brought.

'T was then that spoke the fateful voice,
  And 'mid the huge uproar,
Above the dark I sprang to life,
  A good unhoped before.
My tresses waved along the sky,
  And stars leapt out around,
And earth beneath my feet arose,
  And hid the pale profound.

A lamp amid the night, a feast
  That ends the strife of war,
To wearied mariners a port,
  To fainting limbs a car,
To exiled men the friendly roof,
  To mourning hearts the lay,
To him who long has roamed by night
  The sudden dawn of day.

All these are mine, and mine the bliss
  That visits breasts in woe,
And fills with wine the cup that once
  With tears was made to flow.
Nor question thou the help that comes
  From Aphrodite's hand;
For madness dogs the bard who doubts
  Whate'er the gods command.

Alfred the Harper has the same strong picture and noble beat of wing. One line we have heard so repeated by a voice, that could give it its full meaning, that we should be very grateful to the poet for that alone.

Still lives the song though Regnar dies.

Dædalus we must quote.

DÆDALUS.

1.

Wail for Dædalus all that is fairest!
All that is tuneful in air or wave!
Shapes, whose beauty is truest and rarest,
Haunt with your lamps and spells his grave!

2.

Statues, bend your heads in sorrow,
Ye that glance 'mid ruins old,
That know not a past, nor expect a morrow,
On many a moonlight Grecian wold!

3.

By sculptured cave and speaking river,
Thee, Dædalus, oft the Nymphs recall;
The leaves with a sound of winter quiver,
Murmur thy name, and withering fall.

4.

Yet are thy visions in soul the grandest
Of all that crowd on the tear-dimmed eye,
Though, Dædalus, thou no more commandest
New stars to that ever-widening sky.

5.

Ever thy phantoms arise before us,
Our loftier brothers, but one in blood;
By bed and table they lord it o'er us,
With looks of beauty and words of Good.

6.

Calmly they show us mankind victorious
O'er all that's aimless, blind, and base;
Their presence has made our nature glorious,
Unveiling our night's illumined face.

7.

Thy toil has won them a godlike quiet,
Thou hast wrought their path to a lovely sphere;
Their eyes to peace rebuke our riot,
And shape us a home of refuge here.

8.

For Dædalus breathed in them his spirit;
  In them their sire his beauty sees;
We too, a younger brood, inherit
  The gifts and blessing bestowed on these.

9.

But ah! their wise and graceful seeming
  Recalls the more that the sage is gone;
Weeping we wake from deceitful dreaming,
  And find our voiceless chamber lone.

10.

Dædalus, thou from the twilight fleest,
  Which thou with visions hast made so bright;
And when no more those shapes thou seest,
  Wanting thine eye they lose their light.

11.

E'en in the noblest of Man's creations,
  Those fresh worlds round this old of ours,
When the seer is gone, the orphaned nations
  See but the tombs of perished powers.

12.

Wail for Dædalus, Earth and Ocean!
  Stars and Sun, lament for him!
Ages, quake in strange commotion!
  All ye realms of life be dim!

13.

Wail for Dædalus, awful voices,
  From earth's deep centre Mankind appall!
Seldom ye sound, and then Death rejoices,
  For he knows that then the mightiest fall.

Also the following, whose measure seems borrowed from Goethe, and is worthy of its source. We insert a part it.

THE WOODED MOUNTAINS.

Woodland mountains in your leafy walks,
  Shadows of the Past and Future blend;
'Mid your verdant windings flits or stalks
  Many a loved and disembodied friend.

With your oaks and pine-trees, ancient brood,
Spirits rise above the wizard soil,
And with these I rove amid the wood;
Man may dream on earth no less than toil.

Shapes that seem my kindred meet the ken;
Gods and heroes glimmer through the shade;
Ages long gone by from haunts of men
Meet me here in rocky dell and glade.

There the Muses, touched with gleams of light,
Warble yet from yonder hill of trees,
And upon the huge and mist-clad height
Fancy sage a clear Olympus sees.

'Mid yon utmost peaks the elder powers
Still unshaken hold their fixed abode,
Fates primeval throned in airy towers,
That with morning sunshine never glowed.

Deep below, amid a hell of rocks,
Lies the Cyclops, and the Dragon coils,
Heaving with the torrent's weary shocks,
That round the untrodden region boils.

But more near to where our thought may climb,
In a mossy, leaf-clad, Druid ring,
Three gray shapes, prophetic Lords of Time,
Homer, Dante, Shakspeare, sit and sing.

Each in his turn his descant frames aloud,
Mingling new and old in ceaseless birth,
While the Destinies hear amid their cloud,
And accordant mould the flux of earth.

Oh! ye trees that wave and glisten round,
Oh! ye waters gurgling down the dell,
Pulses throb in every sight and sound,
Living Nature's more than magic spell.

Soon amid the vista still and dim,
Knights, whom youth's high heart forgetteth not,
Each with scars and shadowy helmet grim,
Amadis, Orlando, Launcelot.

Stern they pass along the twilight green,
  While within the tangled wood's recess
Some lorn damsel sits, lamenting keen,
  With a voice of tuneful amorousness.

Clad in purple weed, with pearly crown,
  And with golden hairs that waving play,
Fairest earthly sight for King and Clown,
  Oriana or Angelica.

But in sadder nooks of deeper shade,
  Forms more subtle lurk from human eye,
Each cold Nymph, the rock or fountain's maid,
  Crowned with leaves that sunbeams never dry.

And while on and on I wander, still
  Passed the plashing streamlet's glance and foam,
Hearing oft the wild-bird pipe at will,
  Still new openings lure me still to roam.

In this hollow smooth by May-tree walled,
  White and breathing now with fragrant flower,
Lo! the fairy tribes to revel called,
  Start in view as fades the evening hour.

Decked in rainbow roof of gossamer,
  And with many a sparkling jewel bright,
Rose-leaf faces, dew-drop eyes are there,
  Each with gesture fine of gentle sprite.

Gay they woo, and dance, and feast, and sing,
  Elfin chants and laughter fill the dell,
As if every leaf around should ring
  With its own aerial emerald bell.

But for man 'tis ever sad to see
  Joys like his that he must not partake,
'Mid a separate world, a people's glee,
  In whose hearts his heart no joy could wake.

Fare ye well, ye tiny race of elves;
  May the moonbeam ne'er behold your tomb;
Ye are happiest childhood's other selves,
  Bright to you be always evening's gloom.

And thou, mountain-realm of ancient wood,
  Where my feet and thoughts have strayed so long,
Now thy old gigantic brotherhood
  With a ghostlier vastness round me throng.

Mound, and cliff, and crag, that none may scale
  With your serried trunks and wrestling boughs,
Like one living presence ye prevail,
  And o'erhang me with Titanian brows.

In your Being's mighty depth of Power,
  Mine is lost and melted all away.
In your forms involved I seem to tower,
  And with you am spread in twilight grey.

In this knotted stem whereon I lean,
  And the dome above of countless leaves,
Twists and swells, and frowns a life unseen,
  That my life with it resistless weaves.

Yet, O nature, less is all of thine
  Than thy borrowings from our human breast;
Thou, O God, hast made thy child divine,
  And for him this world thou hallowest.

The Rose and the Gauntlet we much admire as a ballad, and the tale is told in fewest words, and by a single picture; but we have not room for it here. In Lady Jane Grey, though this again is too garrulous, the picture of the princess at the beginning is fine, as she sits in the antique casement of the rich old room.

The lights through the painted glass

Fall with fondest brightness o'er the form
  Of her who sits, the chamber's lovely dame,
And her pale forehead in the light looks warm,
  And all these colors round her whiteness flame.

Young is she, scarcely passed from childhood's years,
  With grave, soft face, where thoughts and smiles may play,
And unalarmed by guilty aims or fears,
  Serene as meadow flowers may meet the day.

> No guilty pang she knows, though many a dread
> Hangs threatening o'er her in the conscious air,
> And 'mid the beams from that bright casement shut,
> A twinkling crown foreshows a near despair.

The quaint conciseness of this last line pleases me.

He always speaks in marble words of Greece. But I must make no more quotations.

Some part of his poem on Shakspeare is no unfit prelude to a few remarks on his own late work. With such a sense of greatness none could wholly fail.

> With meaning won from him for ever glows
> Each air that England feels, and star it knows;
> And gleams from spheres he first conjoined to earth
> Are blent with rays of each new morning's birth,
> Amid the sights and tales of common things,
> Leaf, flower, and bird, and wars, and deaths of kings,
> Of shore, and sea, and nature's daily round
> Of life that tills, and tombs that load the ground,
> His visions mingle, swell, command, pass by,
> And haunt with living presence heart and eye,
> And tones from him, by other bosoms caught,
> Awaken flush and stir of mounting thought,
> And the long sigh, and deep, impassioned thrill,
> Rouse custom's trance, and spur the faltering will.
> Above the goodly land, more his than ours,
> He sits supreme enthroned in skyey towers.
> And sees the heroic blood of his creation
> Teach larger life to his ennobled nation.
> O! shaping brain! O! flashing fancy's hues!
> O! boundless heart kept fresh by pity's dews!
> O! wit humane and blythe! O! sense sublime
> For each dim oracle of mantled Time!
> Transcendant form of man! in whom we read,
> Mankind's whole tale of Impulse, Thought, and Deed.

Such is his ideal of the great dramatic poet. It would not be fair to measure him, or any man, by his own ideal; that affords a standard of spiritual and intellectual progress, with which the executive powers may not correspond. A clear eye may be associated with a feeble hand, or the reverse. The mode of measurement proposed by the great thinker of our time is not inapplicable. First, show me what aim a man proposes to himself; next, with what degree of earnestness he strives to attain it. In both regards we can look at Mr. Sterling's work with pleasure and admiration. He exhibits to us a great crisis, with noble figures to represent its moving springs. His work is not merely the plea for a principle, or the exposition of a thought, but an exhibition of both at work in life. He opens the instrument and lets us see the machinery without stopping the music. The progress of interest in the piece is imperative, the principal character well brought out, the style clear and energetic, the tone throughout is of a manly dignity, worthy great times. Yet its merit is of a dramatic sketch, rather than a drama. The forms want the roundness, the fulness of life, the thousand charms of spontaneous expression. In this last particular Sterling is as far inferior to Taylor, as Taylor to Shakspeare. His characters, like Miss Baillie's or Talfourd's, narrate rather than express their life. Not elaborately, not pedantically, but yet the effect is that, while they speak we look on them as past, and Sterling's view of them interests us more than themselves. In his view of relations again we must note his inferiority to Taylor, who in this respect is the only contemporary dramatist on whom we can look with complacency. Taylor's characters really meet, really bear upon one another. In contempt and hatred, or esteem, reverence, and melting tenderness, they challenge, bend, and transfuse one another.

Strafford never alters, never is kindled by or kindles the life of any other being, never breathes the breath of the moment. Before us, throughout the play, is the view of his greatness taken by the mind of the author; we are not really made to feel it by those around him; it is echoed from their lips, not from their lives. Lady Carlisle is the only personage, except Strafford, that is brought out into much relief. Everard is only an accessory, and the king, queen, and parliamentary leaders, drawn with a few strokes to give them their historical position. Scarcely more can be said of Hollis; some individual action is assigned him, but not so as to individualize his character. The idea of the relation at this ominous period between Strafford and Lady Carlisle is noble. In these stern times he has put behind him the flowers of tenderness, and the toys of passion.

Lady, believe me, that I loved you truly,
Still think of you with wonder and delight,
Own you the liveliest, noblest heart of woman
This age, or any, knows; but for love ditties
And amorous toys, and kisses ocean-deep,
Strafford and this old Earth are all too sad.

But when the lady had a soul to understand the declaration, and show herself worthy of his friendship, there is a hardness in his action towards her, a want of softness and grace, how different from Van Artevelde's:

My Adriana, victim that thou art.

The nice point indeed, of giving the hero manly firmness, and an even stern self-sufficiency, without robbing him of the beauty of gentle love, was touched with rare success in Van Artevelde. Common men may not be able to show firmness and persistency, without a certain hardness and glassiness of expression; but we expect of the hero, that he should combine the softness with the constancy of Hector.

This failure is the greater here, that we need a private tie to Strafford to give his fall the deepest tragic interest.

Lady Carlisle is painted with some skill and spirit. The name given her by St. John of "the handsome vixen," and the willingness shown by her little page to die, rather than see her after failing to deliver her letter, joined with her own appearance, mark her very well. The following is a prose sketch of her as seen in common life.

Sir Toby Matthew's Portrait of Lucy Percy, Countess of Carlisle.

"She is of too high a mind and dignity, not only to seek, but almost to wish the friendship of any creature: they, whom she is pleased to choose, are such as are of the most eminent condition, both for power and employment; not with any design towards her own particular, either of advantage or curiosity, but her nature values fortunate persons as virtuous. She prefers the conversation of men to that of women; not but she can talk on the fashions with her female friends, but she is too soon sensible that she can set them as she wills; that pre-eminence shortens all equality. She converses with those who are most distinguished for their conversational powers.

"Of love freely will she discourse, listen to all its faults, and mark all its power. She cannot herself love in earnest, but she will play with love, and will take a deep interest for persons of condition and celebrity."—*See Life of Pym; in Lardner Cabinet Cyclopædia,* Vol. xci., p. 213.

The noblest trait, given her in the play, is the justice she is able to do Charles, after his treachery has consigned Strafford to the Tower.

LADY CARLISLE.

And he betrayed you.

STRAFFORD.

He! it cannot be,
There's not a minion in his court so vile,
Holland nor Jermyn, would deceive a trust
Like that I placed in him, nor would belie
So seeming heart felt words as those he spake.

LADY CARLISLE.

He's not entirely vile, and yet he did it.

This, seen in unison with her outpouring of contempt upon the king when present, makes out a character. As a whole, that given her by the poet is not only nobler than the one assigned her in history, but opposed to it in a vital point.

The play closes after Strafford has set forth for the scaffold with the ejaculation from her left in the Tower, where she has waited on his last moments,

"Alone, henceforth forever!"

While history makes her transfer her attachment to Pym, who must have been, in her eyes, Strafford's murderer, on the score of her love of intellectual power, in which all other considerations were merged. This is a character so odious, and in a woman, so unnatural, that we are tempted rather to suppose it was hatred of the king for his base and treacherous conduct towards Strafford, that induced her to betray to Pym the counsels of the court, as the best means of revenge. Such a version of her motives would not be inconsistent with the character assigned her in the play. It would be making her the agent to execute her own curse, so eloquently spoken after she finds the king willing to save himself by the sacrifice of Strafford's life.

KING CHARLES.

The woman's mad; her passion braves the skies!

LADY CARLISLE.

I brave them not; I but invoke their justice
To rain hot curses on a tyrant's head;
Henceforth I set myself apart for mischief,
To find and prompt men capable of hate,
Until some dagger, steeled in Strafford's blood,
Knocks at the heart of Strafford's murderer.

KING CHARLES.

His murderer! O God!—no, no,—not that!
(*Sinks back into a seat.*)

LADY CARLISLE.

And here I call on all the powers above us
To aid the deep damnation of my curse,
And make this treason to the noblest man,
That moves alive within our English seas,
Fatal to him and all his race, whose baseness
Destroys a worth it ne'er could understand.
Stars in your glory, vital air and sun,

And thou, dark earth, our cradle, nurse, and grave,
And more than all, free truth and penal justice,
Conspire with all your dreadful influence
Against his blood, whose crime ye now behold!
Make him a byeword, and a name of woe,
A conquered warrior, and a throneless outcast,
To teach all kings the law of evil power,
Till by an end more friendless and abhorred
Than his great victim's, and with heavier pain,
Let him slink off to a detested grave!
And now I give your majesty leave to go,
And may you carry from my house away,
That fixed incurable ulcer of the heart,
Which I have helped your thoughts to fasten there.

If these burning words had as much power to kindle her own heart, as they must that of the hearer, we only realize our anticipations, when we find her sending to the five members the news of the intention of Charles to arrest them, thus placing him in a position equally ridiculous and miserable, having incurred all the odium of this violent transaction to no purpose. That might well be a proud moment of gratified vengeance to her, when he stood amid the sullen and outraged parliament, baffled like a schoolboy, loathed as a thief, exclaiming, "The birds are flown," and all owing to "the advices of the honorable Lady Carlisle."

The play opens with Strafford's return to London. He is made to return in rather a different temper from what he really did, not only trusting the king, but in his own greatness fearless of the popular hatred. The opening scenes are very good, compact, well wrought, and showing at the very beginning the probable fortunes of the scene, by making the characters the agents of their own destinies. A weight of tragedy is laid upon the heart, and at the same time we are inspired with deep interest as to *how* it shall be acted out.

Strafford appears before us as he does in history, a grand and melancholy figure, whose dignity lay in his energy of will, and large scope of action, not in his perception of principles, or virtue in carrying them out. For his faith in the need of absolute sway to control the herd, does not merit the name of a principle.

> In my thought, the promise of success
> Grows to the self-same stature as the need,
> Which is gigantic. There's a king to guide,
> Three realms to save, a nation to control,
> And by subduing to make blest beyond
> Their sottish dreams of lawless liberty.
> This to fulfil Strafford has pledged his soul
> In the unfaltering hands of destiny.

Nor can we fail to believe, that the man of the world might sincerely take this view of his opponents.

> No wonder they whose life is all deception,
> A piety that, like a sheep-skin drum,
> Is loud because 'tis hollow,—thus can move
> Belief in others by their swollen pretences.
> Why, man, it is their trade; they do not stick
> To cozen themselves, and will they stop at you?

The court and council scenes are good. The materials are taken from history, with Shakspearean adherence to the record, but they are uttered in masculine cadences, sinewy English, worthy this great era in the life of England.

The king and queen and sycophants of the court are too care-essly drawn. Such unmitigated baseness and folly, are unbearable in poetry. The master invests his worst characters with redeeming traits, or at least, touches them with a human interest, that prevents their being objects of disgust rather than contempt or aversion. This is the poetic gift, to penetrate to the truth below the fact. We need to hear the excuses men make to themselves for their worthlessness.

The council of the parliamentary leaders is far better. Here the author speaks his natural language from the lips of grave enthusiastic men. Pym's advice to his daughter is finely worded and contains truths, which, although they have been so often expressed, are not like to find so large reception, as to dispense with new and manifold utterance.

The Lord has power
To guard his own: pray, Mary, pray to Him,
Nor fear what man can do. A rule there is
Above all circumstance, a current deep
Beneath all fluctuations. This who knows,
Though seeming weakest, firmly as the sun
Walks in blind paths where earthly strongest fall,
Reason is God's own voice to man, ordains
All holy duties, and all truth inspires:
And he who fails, errs not by trusting it,
But deafening to the sound his ear, from dread
Of the stern roar it speaks with. O, my child,
Pray still for guidance, and be sure 'twill come.
Lift up your heart upon the knees of God;
Losing yourself, your smallness, and your darkness,
In his great light, who fills and moves the world,
Who hath alone the quiet of perfect motion—
Sole quiet, not mere death.

The speech of Vane is nobly rendered.

The conversations of the populace are tolerably well done. Only the greatest succeed in these; nobody except Goethe in modern times. Here they give, not the character of the people, but the spirit of the time, playing in relation to the main action the part of chorus.

SECOND WOMAN.

There's Master St. John has a tongue
That threshes like a flail.

THIRD WOMAN.

And Master Fiennes
That's a true lamb! He'd roast alive the Bishop.

CITIZEN.

I was close by the coach, and with my nose

Upon the door, I called out, Down with Strafford!
And then just so he fixed his eyes on mine,
And something seemed to choke me in the throat;
In truth, I think it must have been the devil!

THIRD CITIZEN.

I saw him as he stept out of the House,
And then his face was dark, but very quiet;
It seemed like looking down the dusky mouth
Of a great cannon.

Everard says with expressive bitterness as they shout "Down with Strafford,"

I've heard this noise so often, that it seems
As natural as the howling of the wind.

And again—

For forty years I've studied books and men,
But ne'er till these last days have known a jot
Of the true secret madness in mankind.
This morn the whispers leapt from each to each,
Like a petard alight, which every man
Feared might explode in his own hands, and therefore
Would haste to pass it onward to his friend.

Even in our piping times of peace, nullification and the Rhode Island difficulties have given us specimens of the process of fermentation, the more than Virgilian growth of Rumor.

The description of the fanatic preacher by Everard is very good. The poor secretary, not placed in the prominent rank to suffer, yet feeling all that passes, through his master, finds vent to his grief, not in mourning, but a strong causticity:

The sad fanatic preacher,
In whom one saw, by glancing through the eyes,
The last grey curdling dregs of human joy,
Dropped sudden sparks that kindled where they fell.

Strafford draws the line between his own religion and that of the puritans, as it seemed to him, with noble phrase in his last advices to his son.

Say it has ever been his father's mind,
That perfect reason, justice, government,
Are the chief attributes of Him who made,
And who sustains the world, in whose full being,
Wisdom and power are one; and I, his creature,
Would fain have gained authority and rule,
To make the imagined order in my soul
Supreme o'er all, the proper good of man.
But Him to love who shaped us, and whose breast
Is the one home of all things, with a passion
Electing Him amid all other beings,
As if he were beside them, not their all,
This is the snug and dozing deliration
Of men, who filch from woman what is worst,
And cannot see the good. Of such beware.

This is the nobler tone of Strafford's spirit.* That more habitual to him is heard in his presumptuous joy before entering the parliament, into which he went as a conqueror, and came out a prisoner. His confidence is not noble to us, it is not that of Brutus or Van Artevelde, who, knowing what is prescribed by the law of right within the breast, can take no other course but that, whatever the consequences; neither like the faith of Julius Cæsar or Wallenstein in their star, which, though less pure, is not without religion; but it is the presumption of a strong character

* His late biographer says well in regard to the magnanimity of his later days, of so much nobler a tone than his general character would lead us to expect. "It is a mean as well as a hasty judgment, which would attribute this to any unworthy compromise with his real nature. It is probably a juster and more profound view of it, to say that, into a few of the later weeks of his life, new knowledge had penetrated from the midst of the breaking of his fortunes. It was well and beautifully said by a then living poet,

'The soul's dark cottage, battered and decayed,
Lets in new light through chinks that time has made.'"

Forster's Life of Strafford, Lardner's Cabinet Cyclopædia.

which, though its head towers above those of its companions when they are on the same level, yet has not taken a sufficiently high platform, to see what passes around or above it. Strafford's strength cannot redeem his infatuation, while he struggles; vanquished, not overwhelmed, he is a majestic figure, whose features* are well marked in various passages.

> Compared with him, whom I for eighteen years
> Have seen familiar as my friend, all men
> Seem but as chance-born flies, and only he
> Great Nature's chosen and all-gifted son.

†Van Artevelde also bears testimony to the belief of the author, that familiarity breeds no contempt, but the reverse in the service of genuine nobility. A familiarity of eighteen years will not make any but a stage hero, other than a hero to his *valet de chambre*.

King Charles says,

> To pass the bill,—
> Under his eye, with that fixed quiet look
> Of imperturbable and thoughtful greatness,
> I cannot do it.

Strafford himself says, on the final certainty of the king's desertion,

> Dear Everard, peace! for there is nothing here
> I have not weighed before, and made my own.

---

* "A poet, who was present, exclaimed,

> On thy brow
> Sate terror mixed with wisdom, and at once
> Saturn and Hermes in thy countenance."

Life of Strafford, p. 338.

Certainly there could not be a more pointed and pregnant account given of the man than is suggested by this last line.

> † That with familiarity respect
> Doth slacken, is a word of common use;
> I never found it so.

Philip Van Artevelde, 2d Part, p. 29.

And this, no doubt, was true, in a sense. Historians, finding that Strafford expressed surprise, and even indignation, that the king had complied with Strafford's own letter releasing him from all obligation to save his life, have intimated that the letter was written out of policy. But this is a superficial view; it produces very different results from giving up all to another to see him take it; and, though Strafford must have known Charles's weakness too well to expect any thing good from him, yet the consummation must have produced fresh emotion, for a strong character cannot be prepared for the conduct of a weak one; there is always in dishonour somewhat unexpected and incredible to one incapable of it.

The speeches in parliament are well translated from the page of history. The poet, we think, has improved upon it in Strafford's mention of his children; it has not the theatrical tone of the common narrative, and is, probably, nearer truth, as it is more consistent with the rest of his deportment.

He has made good use of the fine anecdote of the effect produced on Pym by meeting Strafford's eye at the close of one of his most soaring passages.

PYM.

The King is King, but as he props the State,
The State a legal and compacted bond,
Tying us all in sweet fraternity,
And that loosed off by fraudful creeping hand,
Or cut and torn by lawless violence,
There is no King because the State is gone;
And in the cannibal chaos that remains
Each man is sovereign of himself alone.
Shall then a drunken regicidal blow
Be paid by forfeit of the driveller's head,
And he go free, who, slaying Law itself,
Murders all royalty and all subjection?
He who, with all the radiant attributes
That most, save goodness, can adorn a man,

Would turn his kind to planless brutishness.
His knavery soars, indeed, and strikes the stars,
Yet is worse knavery than the meanest felon's.
(*Strafford fixes his eyes on Pym, who hesitates.*)
Oh! no, my Lords, Oh! no,
(*Aside to Hampden.*) His eye confounds me; he* was once my friend.
(*Aloud.*) Oh! no, my Lords, the very self-same rule, &c.

The eloquence of this period could not be improved upon; but it is much to select from and use its ebullitions with the fine effect we admire in this play. Whatever view be taken of Strafford, whether as condemnatory as the majority of writers popular among us, the descendants of the puritans, would promote, or that more lenient and discriminating, brought out in this play, for which abundant grounds may be discovered by those who will seek, we cannot view him at this period but with the interest of tragedy as of one suffering unjustly. For however noble the eloquence of the parliamentary leaders in appealing to a law above *the* law, to an eternal justice in the breast, which afforded sufficient sanction to the desired measure, it cannot but be seen, at this distance of time, that this reigned not purely in their own breasts, that his doom, though sought by them from patriotic, not interested, motives, was, in itself, a measure of expediency. He was *the* victim, because the most dreaded foe, because they could not go on with confidence, while the only man lived, who could and would sustain Charles in his absurd and wicked policy. Thus, though

* Through the whole of the speech Strafford is described to have been closely and earnestly watching Pym, when the latter suddenly turning, met the fixed and faded eyes and haggard features of his early associate, and a rush of feelings from other days, so fearfully contrasting the youth and friendship of the past with the love-poisoned hate of the present, and the mortal agony impending in the future, for a moment deprived the patriot of self-possession. "His papers he looked on," says Baillie, "but they could not help him, so he behooved to pass them." For a moment only; suddenly recovering his dignity and self-command, he told the court, &c.—*Life of Pym, Cabinet Cyclopædia.*

he might deserve that the people on whom he trampled should rise up to crush him, that the laws he had broken down should rear new and higher walls to imprison him, though the shade of Eliot called for vengeance on the counsellor who alone had so long saved the tyrant from a speedier fall, and the victims of his own oppressions echoed with sullen murmur to the "silver trumpet" call,* *yet* the greater the peculiar offences of this man, the more need that his punishment should have been awarded in an absolutely pure spirit. And this it was not; it may be respected as an act of just retribution, but not of pure justice.

Men who had such a cause to maintain, as his accusers had, should deserve the praise awarded by Wordsworth to him who,

> In a state where men are tempted still
> To evil for a guard against worse ill,
> And what in quality or act is best
> Doth seldom on a right foundation rest,
> Yet fixes good on good alone, and owes
> To virtue every triumph that he knows.

The heart swells against Strafford as we read the details of his policy. Even allowing that his native temper, prejudices of birth, and disbelief in mankind, really inclined him to a despotic government, as the bad best practicable, that his early espousal of the popular side was only a stratagem to terrify the court, and that he was thus, though a deceiver, no apostate, yet, he *had* been led, from whatever motives, to look on that side; his great intellect was clear of sight, the front presented by better principles in that time commanding. We feel that he was wilful in the course he took, and self-aggrandizement his principal, if not his only motive. We share the hatred of his time, as we see him so triumphant in his forceful, wrongful measures. But we would not have had him hunted down with such a hue and cry,

* "I will not repeat, Sirs, what you have heard from that silver trumpet." One of the parliament speaking of Rudyard.

that the tones of defence had really no chance to be heard. We would not have had papers stolen, and by a son from a father who had entrusted him with a key, to condemn him. And what a man was this thief, one whose high enthusiastic hope never paused at good, but ever rushed onward to the best.

Who would outbid the market of the world,
And seek a holier than a common prize,
And by the unworthy lever of to-day
Ope the strange portals of a better morn.
* * * * *
Begin to-day, nor end till evil sink
In its due grave; and if at once we may not
Declare the greatness of the work we plan,
Be sure, at least, that ever in our eyes
It stand complete before us, as a dome
Of light beyond this gloom; a house of stars,
Encompassing these dusky tents; a thing
Absolute, close to all, though seldom seen,
Near as our hearts, and perfect as the heavens.
Be this our aim and model, and our hands
Shall not wax faint until the work is done.

He is not the first, who, by looking too much at the stars has lost the eye for severe fidelity to a private trust. He thought himself "obliged in conscience to impart the paper to Master Pym." Who that looks at the case by the code of common rectitude can think it was ever his to impart?

What monstrous measures appear the arbitrary construction put on the one word in the minutes which decided the fate of Strafford, the freeing the lords of council from the oath of secrecy under whose protection he had spoken there, the conduct of the House towards Lord Digby, when he declared himself not satisfied that the prisoner could with justice be declared guilty of treason; the burning his speech by the common hangman when he dared print it, to make known the reasons of his course to the world, when placarded as Straffordian, held up as a mark for popular rage for speaking it.* Lord Digby was not a man of honour, but they did not know that, or if they did, it had nothing to do with his right of private judgment. What could Strafford, what could Charles do more high-handed? If they had violated the privileges of parliament, the more reason parliament should respect their privileges, above all the privilege of the prisoner, to be supposed innocent until proved guilty. The accusers, obliged to set aside rule, and appeal to the very foundations of equity, could only have sanctioned such a course by the religion and pure justice of their proceedings. Here the interest of the accusers made them not only demand, but insist upon, the condemnation; the cause was prejudged by the sentiment of the people, and the resentments of the jury, and the proceedings conducted, beside, with the most scandalous disregard to the sickness and other disadvantageous circumstances of Strafford. He was called on to answer "if he will come," just at the time of a most dangerous attack from his cruel distemper; if he *will not come*, the cause is still to be pushed forward. He was denied the time and means he needed to collect his evidence. The aid to be given him by counsel, after being deprived of his chief witness "by a master stroke of policy," was restricted within narrow limits. While he prepared his answers, in full court, for he was never allowed to retire, to the points of accusation, vital in their import, requiring the closest examination, those present talked, laughed, ate, lounged about. None of this disturbed his magnanimous patience; his conduct indeed is so noble, through the whole period, that he and his opponents change places in our minds; at the time, he seems the princely deer, and they the savage hounds.†

* See Parliamentary History, volume ix.

† Who can avoid a profound feeling, not only of compassion, but sympathy, when he reads of Strafford obliged to kneel in Westminster Hall. True, he would, if possible, have brought others as low; but there is a deep pathos in the contrast of his then, and his former state, best shown by the symbol of such an

Well, it is all the better for the tragedy, but as we read the sublime appeals of Pym to a higher state of being, we cannot but wish that all had been done in accordance with them. The art and zeal, with which the condemnation of Strafford was obtained, have had high praise as statesmanlike; we would have wished for them one so high as to preclude this.

No doubt great temporary good was effected for England by the death of Strafford, but the permanence of good is ever in proportion with the purity of the means used to obtain it. This act would have been great for Strafford, for it was altogether in accordance with his views. He met the parliament ready to do battle to the death, and might would have been right, had *he* made rules for the lists; but *they* proposed a different rule for their government, and by that we must judge them. Admit the story of Vane's pilfering the papers not to be true, that the minutes were obtained some other way. This measure, on the supposition of its existence, is defended by those who defend the rest.

Strafford would certainly have come off with imprisonment and degradation from office, had the parliament deemed it safe to leave him alive. When we consider this, when we remember the threat of Pym, at the time of his deserting the popular party, "You have left us, but I will never leave you while your head is on your shoulders," we see not, setting aside the great results of the act, and looking at it by its merits alone, that it differs from the administration of Lynch law in some regions of our own country.

act. Just so we read of Bonaparte's green coat being turned at St. Helena, after it had faded on the right side. He who had overturned the world, to end with having his old coat turned! There is something affecting, Belisarius-like, in the picture. When Warren Hastings knelt in Westminster Hall, the chattering but pleasant Miss Burney tells us, Wyndham, for a moment struck, half shrunk from the business of prosecuting him. At such a sight, whispers in every breast the monition, Had I been similarly tempted, had I not fallen as low, or lower?

Lynch law, with us, has often punished the gamester and the robber, whom it was impossible to convict by the usual legal process; the evil in it is, that it cannot be depended upon, but, while with one hand it punishes a villain, administers with the other as summary judgment on the philanthropist, according as the moral sentiment or prejudice may be roused in the popular breast.

We have spoken disparagingly of the capacities of the drama for representing what is peculiar in our own day, but, for such a work as this, presenting a great crisis with so much clearness, force, and varied beauty, we can only be grateful, and ask for more acquaintance with the same mind, whether through the drama or in any other mode.

Copious extracts have been given, in the belief that thus, better than by any interpretation or praise of ours, attention would be attracted, and a wider perusal ensured to Mr. Sterling's works.

In his mind there is a combination of reverence for the Ideal, with a patient appreciation of its slow workings in the actual world, that is rare in our time. He looks religiously, he speaks philosophically, nor these alone, but with that other faculty which he himself so well describes.

> You bear a brain
> Discursive, open, generally wise,
> But missing ever that excepted point
> That gives each thing and hour a special oneness.
> The little key-hole of the infrangible door,
> The instant on which hangs eternity,
> And not in the dim past and empty future,
> Waste fields for abstract notions.

Such is the demonology of the man of the world. It may rule in accordance with the law of right, but where it does not, the strongest man may lose the battle, and so it was with Strafford.

DIALOGUE

CONTAINING SUNDRY GLOSSES ON POETIC TEXTS

Scene is in a chamber, in the upper story of a city boarding house. The room is small, but neat and furnished with some taste. There are books, a few flowers, even a chamber organ. On the wall hangs a fine engraving from one of Dominichino's pictures. The curtain is drawn up, and shows the moonlight falling on the roofs and chimnies of the city and the distant water, on whose bridges threads of light burn dully.

To Aglauron enter Laurie. A kindly greeting having been interchanged,

Laurie. It is a late hour, I confess, for a visit, but coming home I happened to see the light from your window, and the remembrance of our pleasant evenings here in other days came so strongly over me, that I could not help trying the door.

Aglauron. I do not now see you here so often, that I could afford to reject your visits at any hour.

L. (Seating himself, looks round for a moment with an expression of some sadness.) All here looks the same, your fire burns bright, the moonlight I see you like to have come in as formerly, and we,—we are not changed, Aglauron?

A. I am not.

L. Not towards me?

A. You have elected other associates, as better pleasing or more useful to you than I. Our intercourse no longer ministers to my thoughts, to my hopes. To think of you with that habitual affection, with that lively interest I once did, would be as if the mutilated soldier should fix his eyes constantly on the empty sleeve of his coat. My right hand being taken from me, I use my left.

L. You speak coldly, Aglauron; you cannot doubt that my friendship for you is the same as ever.

A. You should not reproach me for speaking coldly. You have driven me to subdue my feelings by reason, and the tone of reason seems cold because it is calm.

You say your friendship is the same. Your thoughts of your friend are the same, your feelings towards him are not. Your feelings flow now in other channels.

L. Am I to blame for that?

A. Surely not. No one is to blame; if either were so, it would be I, for not possessing more varied powers to satisfy the variations and expansions of your nature.

L. But have I not seemed heartless to you at times?

A. In the moment, perhaps, but quiet thought always showed me the difference between heartlessness and the want of a deep heart.

Nor do I think this will eventually be denied you. You are generous, you love truth. Time will make you less restless, because less bent upon yourself, will give depth and steadfastness to that glowing heart. Tenderness will then come of itself. You will take upon you the bonds of friendship less easily and knit them firmer.

L. And you will then receive me?

A. I or some other; it matters not.

L. Ah! you have become indifferent to me.

A. What would you have? That gentle trust, which seems to itself immortal, cannot be given twice. What is sweet and flower-like in the mind is very timid, and can only be tempted out by the wooing breeze and infinite promise of spring. Those flowers, once touched by a cold wind, will not revive again.

L. But their germs lie in the earth.

A. Yes, to await a new spring! But this conversation is profitless. Words can neither conceal nor make up for the want of flowing love. I do not blame you, Laurie, but I cannot afford to love you as I have done any more, nor would it avail either of us, if I could. Seek elsewhere what you can no longer duly prize from me. Let us not seek to raise the dead from their tombs, but cherish rather the innocent children of to-day.

L. But I cannot be happy unless there is a perfectly good understanding between us.

A. That, indeed, we ought to have. I feel the power of understanding your course, whether it bend my way or not. I need not communication from you, or personal relation to do that,

> "Have I the human kernel first examined,
> Then I know, too, the future will and action."

I have known you too deeply to misjudge you, in the long run.

L. Yet you have been tempted to think me heartless.

A. For the moment only; have I not said it? Thought always convinced me that I could not have been so shallow as to barter heart for anything but heart. I only, by the bold play natural to me, led you to stake too high for your present income. I do not demand the forfeit on the friendly game. Do you understand me?

L. No, I do not understand being both friendly and cold.

A. Thou wilt, when thou shalt have lent as well as borrowed.

I can bring forward on this subject gospel independent of our own experience. The poets, as usual, have thought out the subject for their age. And it is an age where the complex and subtle workings of its spirit make it not easy for the immortal band, the sacred band of equal friends, to be formed into phalanx, or march with equal step in any form.

Soon after I had begun to read some lines of our horoscope, I found this poem in Wordsworth, which seemed to link into meaning many sounds that were vibrating round me.

A COMPLAINT.

There *is* a change, and I am poor;
Your Love hath been, nor long ago,
A Fountain at my fond Heart's door,
Whose only business was to flow;
And flow it did; not taking heed
Of its own bounty, or my need.

What happy moments did I count,
Blest was I then all bliss above;
Now, for this consecrated Fount
Of murmuring, sparkling, living love,
What have I? shall I dare to tell?
A comfortless and hidden WELL.

A Well of love, it may be deep,
I trust it is, and never dry;
What matter? if the Waters sleep
In silence and obscurity,
Such change, and at the very door
Of my fond heart, hath made me poor.

This, at the time, seemed unanswerable; yet, afterwards I found among the writings of Coleridge what may serve as a sufficient answer.

A SOLILOQUY.

Unchanged within to see all changed without
Is a blank lot and hard to bear, no doubt.
Yet why at other's wanings shouldst thou fret?
Then only might'st thou feel a just regret,
Hadst thou withheld thy love, or hid thy light
In selfish forethought of neglect and slight,
O wiselier, then, from feeble yearnings freed,
While, and *on whom*, thou mayst, shine on! nor heed
Whether the object by reflected light
Return thy radiance or absorb it quite;

And though thou notest from thy safe recess
Old Friends burn dim, like lamps in noisome air,
Love them for what they *are;* nor love them less,
Because to *thee* they are not what they *were.*

L. Do you expect to be able permanently to abide by such solace?

A. I do not expect so Olympian a calmness, that at first, when the chain of intercourse is broken, when confidence is dismayed, and thought driven back upon its source, I shall not feel a transient pang, even a shame, as when

"The sacred secret hath flown out of us,
And the heart been broken open by deep care."

The wave receding, leaves the strand for the moment forlorn, and weed-bestrown.

L. And is there no help for this? Is there not a pride, a prudence, identical with self-respect, that could preserve us from such mistakes?

A. If you can show me one that is not selfish forethought of neglect or slight, I would wear it and recommend it as the desired amulet. As yet, I know no pride, no prudence except love of truth.

Would a prudence be desirable that should have hindered our intimacy?

L. Ah, no! it was happy, it was rich.

A. Very well then, let us drink the bitter with as good a grace as the sweet, and for to-night talk no more of ourselves.

L. To talk then of those other, better selves, the poets. I can well understand that Coleridge should have drunk so deeply as he did of this bitter-sweet. His nature was ardent, intense, variable in its workings, one of tides, crises, fermentations. He was the flint from which the spark must be struck by violent collision. His life was a mass in the midst of which fire glowed, but needed time to transfuse it, as his heavenly eyes glowed amid such heavy features. The habit of taking opium was but an outward expression of the transports and depressions to which he was inly prone. In him glided up in the silence, equally vivid, the Christabel, the Geraldine. Through his various mind

"Alph, the sacred river, ran
Through caverns measureless to man,
Down to a sunless sea."

He was one of those with whom

"The meteor offspring of the brain
Unnourished wane,
Faith asks her daily bread,
And fancy must be fed."

And when this was denied,

"Came a restless state, 'twixt yea and nay,
His faith was fixed, his heart all ebb and flow;
Or like a bark, in some half-sheltered bay,
Above its anchor driving to and fro."

Thus we .cannot wonder that he, with all his vast mental resources and noble aims, should have been the bard elect to sing of Dejection, and that the pages of his prose works should be blistered by more painful records of personal and social experiences, than we find in almost any from a mind able to invoke the aid of divine philosophy, a mind touched by humble piety. But Wordsworth, who so early knew, and sought, and found the life and the work he wanted, whose wide and equable thought flows on like a river through the plain, whose verse seemed to come daily like the dew to rest upon the flowers of home affections, we should think he might always have been with his friend, as he describes two who had grown up together,

"Each other's advocate, each other's stay,
And strangers to content, if long apart,
Or more divided than a sportive pair

Of sea-fowl, conscious both that they are hovering
Within the eddy of a common blast,
Or hidden only by the concave depth
Of neighbouring billows from each other's sight."

And that we should not find in him traces of the sort of wound, nor the tone of deep human melancholy that we find in this Complaint, and in the sonnet, " Why art thou silent."

A. I do not remember that.

L. It is in the last published volume of his poems, though probably written many years before.

"Why art thou silent? Is thy love a plant
Of such weak fibre that the treacherous air
Of absence withers what was once so fair?
Is there no debt to pay, no boon to grant?
Yet have my thoughts for thee been vigilant,
(As would my deeds have been) with hourly care,
The mind's least generous wish a mendicant
For naught but what thy happiness could spare.
Speak, though this soft warm heart, once free to hold
A thousand tender pleasures, thine and mine,
Be left more desolate, more dreary cold,
Than a forsaken bird's nest filled with snow,
Mid its own bush of leafless eglantine;
Speak, that my torturing doubts their end may know."

A. That is indeed the most pathetic description of the speechless palsy that precedes the death of love.

"Is there no debt to pay, no boon to grant?"

But Laurie, how could you ever fancy a mind of poetic sensibility would be a stranger to this sort of sadness?

What signifies the security of a man's own position and choice? The peace and brightness of his own lot? If he has this intelligent sensibility can he fail to perceive the throb that agitates the bosom of all nature, or can his own fail to respond to it?

In the eye of man, or in the sunset clouds, from the sobs of literature, or those of the half-spent tempest, can he fail to read the secrets of fate and time, of an over-credulous hope, a too much bewailed disappointment? Will not a very slight hint convey to the mind in which the nobler faculties are at all developed, a sense of the earthquakes which may in a moment upheave his vineyard and whelm his cottage beneath rivers of fire. Can the poet at any time, like the stupid rich man, say to his soul, "Eat, drink, and be merry." No, he must ever say to his fellow man, as Menelaus to his kingly brother,

> "Shall my affairs
> Go pleasantly, while thine are full of woe?"

Oh, never could Wordsworth fail, beside his peaceful lake, to know the tempests of the ocean. And to an equable temperament sorrow seems sadder than it really is, for such know less of the pleasures of resistance.

It needs not that one of deeply thoughtful mind be passionate, to divine all the secrets of passion. Thought is a bee that cannot miss those flowers.

Think you that if Hamlet had held exactly the position best fitted to his nature, had his thoughts become acts, without any violent willing of his own, had a great people paid life-long homage to his design, had he never detected the baseness of his mother, nor found cause to suspect the untimely fate of his father, had that "rose of May, the sweet Ophelia," bloomed safely at his side, and Horatio always been near, with his understanding mind and spotless hands, do you think all this could have preserved Hamlet from the astounding discovery that

> "A man may smile, and smile, and be a villain?"

That line, once written on his tables, would have required the commentary of many years for its explanation.

L. He was one by nature adapted to "consider too curiously," for his own peace.

A. All thoughtful minds are so.

L. All geniuses have not been sad.

A. So far as they are artistic, merely, they differ not from instinctive, practical characters, they find relief in work. But so far as they tend to evolve thought, rather than to recreate the forms of things, they suffer again and again the pain of death, because they open the gate to the next, the higher realm of being. Shakspeare knew both, the joy of creation, the deep pang of knowledge, and this last he has expressed in Hamlet with a force that vibrates almost to the centre of things.

L. It is marvellous, indeed, to hear the beautiful young prince catalogue—

> "The heartache, and the thousand natural shocks
> That flesh is heir to, * * * *
> * * The whips and scorns of time,
> The oppressor's wrong, the proud man's contumely,
> The pangs of despised love, * * *
> * * * * The spurns
> That patient merit of the unworthy takes."

To thee, Hamlet, so complete a nature,

> "The expectancy and rose of the fair state,
> The noble and most sovereign reason,
> The unmatched form and feature of blown youth,"

could such things come so near? Who then shall hope a refuge, except through inborn stupidity or perfected faith?

A. Ay, well might he call his head a globe! It was fitted to comprehend all that makes up that "quintessence of dust, how noble in reason; how infinite in faculties; in form, and moving, how express and admirable; in action how like an angel, in apprehension how like a god; the beauty of the world, the paragon of animals!" yet to him, only a quintessence of dust!

L. And this world only "a sterile promontory."

A. Strange, that when from it one can look abroad into the ocean, its barrenness should be so depressing. But man seems to need some shelter, both from wind and rain.

L. Could he not have found this in the love of Ophelia ?

A. Probably not, since that love had so little power to disenchant the gloom of this period. She was to him a flower to wear in his bosom, a child to play the lute at his feet. We see the charm of her innocence, her soft credulity, as she answers her brother,

"No more, but so ?"

The exquisite grace of her whole being in the two lines

"And I of ladies most deject and wretched
That sucked the honey of his music vows."

She cannot be made to misunderstand him ; his rude wildness crushes, but cannot deceive her heart. She has no answer to his outbreaks but

"O help him, you sweet Heavens !"

But, lovely as she was, and loved by him, this love could have been only the ornament, not, in any wise, the food of his life. The moment he is left alone, his thoughts revert to universal topics ; it was the constitution of his mind, no personal relation could have availed it, except in the way of suggestion. He could not have been absorbed in the present moment. Still it would have been

"Heaven and earth!
Must I remember ?"

L. Have you been reading the play of late ?

A. Yes ; hearing Macready, one or two points struck me that have not before, and I was inclined to try for my thousandth harvest from a new study of it.

Macready gave its just emphasis to the climax—

"I'll call thee Hamlet,
King, father, royal Dane,"

so unlike in its order to what would have been in any other mind, as also to the two expressions in the speech so delicately charac teristic,

"The glimpses of the moon."

and

"With thoughts beyond the reaches of our souls."

I think I have in myself improved, that I feel more than ever what Macready does not, the deep calmness, always apparent beneath the delicate variations of this soul's atmosphere.

"The readiness is all."

This religion from the very first harmonizes all these thrilling notes, and the sweet bells, even when most jangled out of tune, suggest all their silenced melody.

From Hamlet I turned to Timon and Lear; the transition was natural yet surprising, from the indifference and sadness of the heaven-craving soul to the misanthropy of the disappointed affections and wounded trust. Hamlet would well have understood them both, yet what a firmament of spheres lies between his "pangs of despised love," and the anguish of Lear.

"O Regan, Goneril!
Your old kind father, whose frank heart gave you all—
O that way madness lies, let me shun that,
No more of that,

* * * * *

"I tax you not, you elements, with unkindness;
I never gave you kingdom, called you children."

* * * * *

It rends the heart only; no grief would be possible from a Hamlet, which would not, at the same time, exalt the soul.

The outraged heart of Timon takes refuge at once in action, in curses, and bitter deeds. It needs to be relieved by the native baseness of Apemantus's misanthropy, baseness of a soul that never knew how to trust, to make it dignified in our eyes. Timon, estranged from men, could only die; yet the least shade of wrong in this heaven-ruled world would have occasioned Hamlet a deeper pain than Timon was capable of divining. Yet Hamlet could not for a moment have been so deceived as to fancy man worthless, because many men were; he knew *himself* too well, to feel the surprise of Timon when his steward proved true.

"Let me behold
Thy face.—Surely this man was born of woman.—
Forgive my general and exceptless rashness,
You perpetual-sober gods! I do proclaim
One honest man."

He does not deserve a friend that could draw higher inferences from his story than the steward does.

"Poor honest lord, brought low by his own heart,
Undone by goodness! Strange, unusual blood,
When man's worst sin is, he does too much good!
Who then dares to be half so kind again?
For bounty that makes gods, doth still mar men."

Timon tastes the dregs of the cup. He persuades himself that he does not believe even in himself.

"His semblable, even himself, Timon disdains."
* * * * *
"Who dares, who dares
In purity of manhood to stand up
And say *this man's a flatterer*, if one be
So are they all."

L. You seem to have fixed your mind, of late, on the subject of misanthropy!

A. I own that my thoughts *have* turned of late on that low form which despair assumes sometimes even with the well disposed. Yet see how inexcusable would it be in any of these beings. Hamlet is no misanthrope, but he has those excelling gifts, least likely to find due response from those around him. Yet he is felt, almost in his due sense, by two or three.

Lear has not only one faithful daughter, whom he knew not how to value, but a friend beside.

Timon is prized by the only persons to whom he was good, purely from kindliness of nature, rather than the joy he expected from their gratitude and sympathy, his servants.

Tragedy is always a mistake, and the loneliness of the deepest thinker, the widest lover, ceases to be pathetic to us, so soon as the sun is high enough above the mountains.

Were I, despite the bright points so numerous in their history and the admonitions of my own conscience, inclined to despise my fellow men, I should have found abundant argument against it during this late study of Hamlet. In the streets, saloons, and lecture rooms, we continually hear comments so stupid, insolent, and shallow on great and beautiful works, that we are tempted to think that there is no Public for anything that is good; that a work of genius can appeal only to the fewest minds in any one age, and that the reputation now awarded to those of former times is never felt, but only traditional. Of Shakspeare, so vaunted a name, little wise or worthy has been written, perhaps nothing so adequate as Coleridge's comparison of him to the Pine-apple; yet on reading Hamlet, his greatest work, we find there is not a pregnant sentence, scarce a word that men have not appreciated, have not used in myriad ways. Had we never read the play, we should find the whole of it from quotation and illustration familiar to us as air. That exquisite phraseology, so heavy with meaning, wrought out with such admirable minuteness, has become a part of literary diction, the stock of the literary bank; and what set criticism can tell like this fact how great was the work, and that men were worthy it should be addressed to them?

L. The moon looks in to tell her assent. See, she has just got above that chimney. Just as this happy certainty has with you risen above the disgusts of the day.

A. She looks surprised as well as complacent.

L. She looks surprised to find me still here. I must say good night. My friend, good night.

A. Good night, and farewell.

L. You look as if it were for some time.

A. That rests with you. You will generally find me here, and always I think like-minded, if not of the same mind.

An ancient sage had all things deeply tried,
And, as result, thus to his friends he cried,
"O friends, there are no friends." And to this day
Thus twofold moves the strange magnetic sway,
Giving us love which love must take away.
Let not the soul for this distrust its right,
Knowing when changeful moons withdraw their light,
Then myriad stars, with promise not less pure,
New loves, new lives to patient hopes assure,
So long as laws that rule the spheres endure.

LITERATURE AND ART.

PART II.

PAPERS ON LITERATURE AND ART.

POETS OF THE PEOPLE.

RHYMES AND RECOLLECTIONS OF A HAND-LOOM WEAVER.
By William Thom, of Iverury.

> "An' syne whan nichts grew cauld an' lang,
> Ae while he sicht—ae while he sang."

Second Edition, with Additions. London, 1845.

We cannot give a notion of the plan and contents of this little volume better than by copying some passages from the Preface :

"The narrative portion of these pages," says Thom, "is a record of scenes and circumstances interwoven with my experience—with my destiny. * * The feelings and fancies, the pleasure and the pain that hovered about my aimless existence were all my own—my property. These aerial investments I held and fashioned into measured verse. * * The self-portraiture herein attempted is not altogether Egotism neither, inasmuch as the main lineaments of the sketch are to be found in the separate histories of a thousand families in Scotland within these last ten years. That fact, however, being contemplated in mass, and in reference to its bulk only, acts more on the *wonder* than on the *pity* of mankind, as if human sympathies, like the human eye, could not compass an object exceedingly large, and, at the same time, exceedingly near. It is no small share in the end and aim of the present little work, to impart to one portion of the community a glimpse of what is sometimes going on in another; and even if only *that* is accomplished, some good service will be done. I have long had a notion that many of the heart-burnings that run through the Social Whole spring not so much from the distinctiveness of classes as their mutual ignorance of each other. The miserably rich look upon the miserably poor with distrust and dread, scarcely giving them credit for sensibility sufficient to feel their own sorrows. That is ignorance with its gilded side. The poor, in turn foster a hatred of the wealthy as a sole inheritance—look on grandeur as their natural enemy, and bend to the rich man's rule in gall and bleeding scorn. Shallows on the one side and Demagogues on the other, are the portions that come oftenest into contact. These are the luckless things that skirt the great divisions, exchanging all that is offensive therein. 'MAN KNOW THYSELF,' should be written on the right hand; on the left, '*Men, know* EACH OTHER.'"

In this book, the recollections are introduced for the sake of the "Rhymes," and in the same relationship as parent and child, one the offspring of the other; and in that association alone can they be interesting. "I write no more in either than what I knew—and not all of that—so Feeling has left Fancy little to do in the matter."

There are two ways of considering Poems, or the products of literature in general. We may tolerate only what is excellent, and demand that whatever is consigned to print for the benefit of the human race should exhibit fruits perfect in shape, colour, and flavour, enclosing kernels of permanent value.

Those who demand this will be content only with the Iliads and Odysseys of the mind's endeavour.—They can feed no where but at rich men's tables; in the wildest recess of nature roots and berries will not content them. They say, "If you can thus satiate your appetite it is degrading; we, the highly refined in taste and the tissue of the mind, can nowhere be appeased, unless by golden apples, served up on silver dishes."

But, on the other hand, literature may be regarded as the great mutual system of interpretation between all kinds and classes of men. It is an epistolary correspondence between brethren of one family, subject to many and wide separations, and anxious to remain in spiritual presence one of another. These letters may be written by the prisoner in soot and water, illustrated by rude sketches in charcoal;—by nature's nobleman, free to use his inheritance, in letters of gold, with the fair margin filled with exquisite miniatures;—to the true man each will have value, *first*, in proportion to the degree of its revelation as to the life of the human soul, *second,* in proportion to the perfection of form in which that revelation is expressed.

In like manner are there two modes of criticism. One which tries, by the highest standard of literary perfection the critic is capable of conceiving, each work which comes in his way; rejecting all that it is possible to reject, and reserving for toleration only what is capable of standing the severest test. It crushes to earth without mercy all the humble buds of Phantasy, all the plants that, though green and fruitful, are also a prey to insects, or have suffered by drouth. It weeds well the garden, and cannot believe, that the weed in its native soil, may be a pretty, graceful plant.

There is another mode which enters into the natural history of every thing that breathes and lives, which believes no impulse to be entirely in vain, which scrutinizes circumstances, motive and object before it condemns, and believes there is a beauty in each natural form, if its law and purpose be understood. It does not consider a literature merely as the garden of the nation, but as the growth of the entire region, with all its variety of mountain, forest, pasture, and tillage lands. Those who observe in this spirit will often experience, from some humble offering to the Muses, the delight felt by the naturalist in the grasses and lichens of some otherwise barren spot. These are the earliest and humblest efforts of nature, but to a discerning eye they indicate the entire range of her energies.

These two schools have each their dangers. The first tends to hypercriticism and pedantry, to a cold restriction on the unstudied action of a large and flowing life. In demanding that the stream should always flow transparent over golden sands, it tends to repress its careless majesty, its vigour, and its fertilizing power.

The other shares the usual perils of the genial and affectionate;

it tends to indiscriminate indulgence and a leveling of the beautiful with what is merely tolerable. For indeed the vines need judicious pruning if they are to bring us the ruby wine.

In the golden age to which we are ever looking forward, these two tendencies will be harmonized. The highest sense of fulfilled excellence will be found to consist with the largest appreciation of every sign of life. The eye of man is fitted to range all around no less than to be lifted on high.

Meanwhile the spirit of the time, which is certainly seeking, though by many and strange ways, the greatest happiness for the greatest number, by discoveries which facilitate mental no less than bodily communication, till soon it will be almost as easy to get your thought printed or engraved on a thousand leaves as to drop it from the pen on one, and by the simultaneous bubbling up of rills of thought in a thousand hitherto obscure and silent places, declares that the genial and generous tendency shall have the lead, at least for the present.

We are not ourselves at all concerned, lest excellent expression should cease because the power of speech to some extent becomes more general. The larger the wave and the more fish it sweeps along, the likelier that some fine ones should enrich the net. It has always been so. The great efforts of art belong to artistic regions, where the boys in the street draw sketches on the wall and torment melodies on rude flutes; shoals of sonneteers follow in the wake of the great poet. The electricity which flashes with the thunderbolts of Jove must first pervade the whole atmosphere.

How glad then are we to see that such men as Prince and Thom, if they are forced by 'poortith cauld' to sigh much in the long winter night, which brings them neither work nor pleasure, can also sing between.

Thom passed his boyhood in a factory, where, beside the disadvantage of ceaseless toil and din, he describes himself as being under the worst moral influences. These, however, had no power to corrupt his native goodness and sweetness. One of the most remarkable things about him is his disposition to look on the bright side, and the light and gentle playfulness with which he enlivened, when possible, the darkest pages of his life.

The only teachers that found access to the Factory were some works of contemporary poets. These were great contemporaries for him. Scott, Byron, Moore, breathed full enough to fan a good blaze.—But still more important to the Scotsman and the craftsman were the teachings of those commemorated in the following passage which describes the first introduction of them to the literary world, and gives no unfair specimen both of his prose and his poetry :

"Nearer and dearer to hearts like ours was the Ettrick Shepherd, then in his full tide of song and story; but nearer and dearer still than he, or any living songster—to us dearer—was our ill-fated fellow-craftsman, Tannahill, who had just then taken himself from a neglecting world, while yet that world waxed mellow in his lay. Poor weaver chiel! What we owe to thee! Your "Braes o' Balquidder," and "Yon Burnside," and "Gloomy Winter," and the "Minstrel's" wailing ditty, and the noble "Gleneifer." Oh! how they did ring above the rattling of a hundred shuttles! Let me again proclaim the debt we owe those Song Spirits, as they walked in melody from loom to loom, ministering to the low-hearted; and when the breast was filled with everything but hope and happiness, and all but scared, let only break forth the healthy and vigorous chorus "A man's a man for a' that," the fagged weaver brightens up. His very shuttle skytes boldly along, and clatters through in faithful time to the tune of his merrier shopmates!

"Who dare measure in doubt the restraining influences of these very Songs? To us they were all instead of sermons. Had one of us been bold enough to enter a church he must have been ejected for the sake of decency. His forlorn and curiously patched habiliments would have contested the point of attraction with the ordinary eloquence of that period. So for all parties it was better that he kept to his garret, or wandered far "in the deep green wood." Church bells rang not for us. Poets were indeed our Priests. But for those, the last relic of our moral existence would have surely passed away!

"Song was the dew-drops that gathered during the long dark night of despondency, and were sure to glitter in the very first blink of the sun. * * * * To us Virtue, in whatever shape, came only in shadow, but even by that we saw her sweet proportions, and sometimes fain would have sought a kind acquaintance with her.—Thinking that the better features of humanity could not be utterly defaced where song and melody were permitted to exist, and that where they were not all crushed, Hope and Mercy might yet bless the spot, some waxed bold, and for a time took leave of those who were called to "sing ayont the moon," groping amidst the material around and stringing it up, ventured on a home-made lilt.—Short was the search to find a newly kindled love, or some old heart abreaking. Such was aye amongst us and not always unnoticed, nor as ye shall see, unsung.

"It was not enough that we merely chaunted, and listened; but some more ambitious, or idle if ye will, they in time would try a self-conceived song. Just as if some funny little boy, bolder than the rest, would creep into the room where laid Neil Gow's fiddle, and touch a note or two he could not name. How proud he is! how blest! for he had made a sound, and more, his playmates heard it, faith! Here I will introduce one of these early touches, not for any merit of its own, but it will show that we could sometimes bear and even seek for our minds a short residence, though not elegant at least sinless,—a fleeting visit of healthy things, though small they were in size and few in number. Spray from a gushing "linn," if it slackened not the thirst, it cooled the brow.

"The following ditty had its foundation in one of those luckless doings which ever and aye follow misguided attachments; and in our abode of freedom these were almost the only kind of attachments known; so they were all on the wrong side of durability or happiness.

AIR—"*Lass, gin you lo'e me, tell me noo.*"

We'll meet in yon wood, 'neath a starless sky,
When wrestling leaves forsake ilk tree;
We mauna speak mair o' the days gane by,
Nor o' friends that again we *never* maun see:
Nae weak word o' mine shall remembrance gie
O' vows that were made and were broken to me:
I'll seem in my silence to reckon them dead,
A' wither'd and lost as the leaves that we tread.

Alane ye maun meet me, when midnight is near,
By yon blighted auld bush that we fatally ken;
The voice that allured me, O! let me nae hear,
For my heart maun i beat to its music again.

In darkness we'll meet, and in silence remain,'
Ilk word now and look now, were mockful or vain;
Ae mute moment morne the dream that misled,
Syne sinder as cauld as the leaves that we tread.

"This ditty was sung in the weaving shops, and when in the warbling of one who could lend a good voice to the occasion, and could coax the words and air into a sort of social understanding, then was it a song."

Thom had no furtherance for many years after this first appearance. It was hard work at all times to win bread; when work failed he was obliged to wander on foot elsewhere to procure it, losing his youngest child in a barn from the hardships endured one cold night of this untimely "flitting;" his admirable wife too died prematurely from the same cause. At one time he was obliged to go with his little daughter and his flute, (on which he is an excellent performer,) into the streets as a mendicant, to procure bread for his family. This last seems to have been far more cruel than any hardship to the honest pride native to the Scotchman. But there is another side. Like Prince, he was happy, as men in a rank more favoured by fortune seldom are, in his choice of a wife. He had an equal friend, a refined love, a brave, gentle, and uncomplaining companion in every sorrow, and wrote from his own experience the following lines:

THEY SPEAK O' WYLES.

AIR—"*Gin a bodie meet a bodie.*"

They speak o' wyles in woman's smiles,
  An' ruin in her e'e—
I ken they bring a pang at whiles
  That's unco sair to dree;
But mind ye this, the half-ta'en kiss,
  The first fond fa'in' tear,
Is, Heaven kens, fu' sweet amends
  An' tints o' heaven here.

> When twa leal hearts in fondness meet,
>   Life's tempests howl in vain—
> The very tears o' love are sweet
>   When paid with tears again.
> Shall sapless prudence shake its pow,
>   Shall cauldrife caution fear ?
> Oh, dinna, dinna droun the lowe
>   That lichts a heaven here!

He was equally happy in his children, though the motherless bairns had to be sent, the little girl to tend cows, the darling boy to a hospital (where his being subjected, when alone, to a surgical operation, is the occasion of one of the poor Poet's most touching strains.) They were indeed his children in love and sympathy, the source of thought and joy, such as is never known to the rich man who gives up for banks and ships all the immortal riches domestic joys might bring him, leaving his children first to the nursery-maid, then to hired masters, and last to the embrace of a corrupt world. He was also most happy in his "aërial investments," and like Prince, so fortunate, midway in life before his power of resistance was exhausted, and those bitterest of all bitter words Too Late, stamped upon his brow, as to secure the enlightened assistance of one generous journal, the timely assistance of one generous friend, which, though little in money, was large in results. So Thom is far from an unfortunate man, though the portrait which we find in his book is marked with wrinkles of such premature depth. Indeed he declares that while work was plenty and his wife with him, he was blest for "nine years with such happiness as rarely falls to the lot of a human being."

Thom has a poetical mind, rather than is a poet. He has a delicate perception of relations, and is more a poet in discerning good occasions for poems than in using them. Accordingly his prefaces to, or notes upon, his verses, are often, as was the case with Sir Walter Scott, far more poetical than the verses themselves. This is the case as to those which followed this little sketch:

"For a period of seventeen years, I was employed in a great weaving factory in Aberdeen. It contained upwards of three hundred looms, worked by as many male and female weavers. 'Twas a sad place, indeed, and many a curiosity sort of man and woman entered that blue gate. Amongst the rest, that little sly fellow Cupid would steal past 'Willie, the porter' (who never dreamed of such a being)—steal in amongst us, and make a very harvest of it. Upon the remembrance of one of his rather grave doings, the song of 'Mary' is composed. One of our shopmates, a virtuous young woman, fairly though unconsciously, carried away the whole bulk and value of a poor weaver's heart. He became restless and miserable, but could never muster spirit to speak his flame. "*He* never told his love"—yes, he told it to me. At his request, I told it to Mary, and she laughed. Five weeks passed away, and I saw him to the churchyard. For many days ere he died, Mary watched by his bedside, a sorrowful woman, indeed. Never did widow's tears fall more burningly. It is twenty years since then. She is now a wife and a mother; but the remembrance of that, their last meeting, still haunts her sensitive nature, as if she had done a deed of blood."

The charming little description of one of the rural academies known by the name of a "Wifie's Squeel," we reserve to reprint in another connexion.—As we are overstepping all limits, we shall give, in place of farther comments, three specimens of how the Muse sings while she throws a shuttle. They are all interesting in different ways. "One of the Heart's Struggles" is a faithful transcript of the refined feelings of the craftsman, how opposite to the vulgar selfishness which so often profanes the name of Love! "A Chieftain Unknown to the Queen," expresses many thoughts that arose in our own mind as we used to read the bulletins of the Royal Progress through Scotland so carefully transferred to the columns of American journals. "Whisper Low" is perhaps the best specimen of song as song, to be found in this volume.

PRINCE'S POEMS.

By signs too numerous to be counted, yet some of them made fruitful by specification, the Spirit of the Age announces that she is slowly, toilsomely, but surely, working that revolution, whose mighty deluge rolling back, shall leave a new aspect smiling on earth to greet the 'most ancient heavens.' The wave rolls forward slowly, and may be as long in retreating, but when it has retired into the eternal deep, it will leave behind it a refreshed world, in which there may still be many low and mean men, but *no lower classes ;* for it will be understood that it is the glory of a man to labour, and that all kinds of labour have their poetry, and that there is really no more a lower and higher among the world of men with their various spheres, than in the world of stars. All kinds of labour are equally honorable, if the mind of the labourer be only open so to understand them. But as

> "The glory 'tis of Man's estate,—
> For this his dower did he receive,
> That he in mind should contemplate
> What with his hands he doth achieve."
>
> * * * * *
>
> "Observe we sharply, then, what vantage,
> From conflux of weak efforts springs;
> He turns his craft to small advantage
> Who knows not what to light it brings."

It is this that *has* made the difference of high and low, that certain occupations were supposed to have a better influence in liberalizing and refining the higher faculties than others. Now, the tables are turning. The inferences and impressions to be gained from the pursuits that have ranked highest are, for the present, exhausted. They have been written about, prated about, till they have had their day, and need to lie in the shadow and recruit their energies through silence. The mind of the time has detected the truth that as there is nothing, the least, effected in this universe, which does not somehow represent the whole, which it is again the whole scope and effort of human Intelligence to do, no deed, no pursuit can fail, if the mind be 'divinely intended' upon it, to communicate divine knowledge. Thus it is seen that all a man needs for his education is to take whatsoever lies in his way to do, and do it with his might, and think about it with his might, too ; for

> "He turns his craft to small advantage,
> Who knows not what to light it brings."

And, as a mark of this diffusion of the true, the poetic, the philosophic education, we greet the emergence more and more of poets from the working classes—men who not only have poet hearts and eyes, but use them to write and print verses.

Beranger, the man of the people, is the greatest poet, and, in fact, the greatest literary genius of modern France. In other nations if "the lower classes" have not such an one to boast, they at least have many buds and shoots of new talent. Not to speak of the patronized ploughboys and detected merits, they have now an order, constantly increasing, able to live by the day labor of that good right hand which wields the pen at night ; with aims, thoughts, feelings of their own, neither borrowing from nor aspiring to the region of the Rich and Great. Elliott, Nicol, Prince, and Thom find enough in the hedge-rows that border their every-day path ;—they need not steal an entrance to padlocked flower-gardens, nor orchards guarded by man-traps and spring-guns.

Of three of these it may be said, they

> "Were cradled into Poesy by Wrong,
> And learnt in Suffering what they taught in Song."

But of the fourth—Prince, we mean—though he indeed suffered enough of the severest hardships of work-day life, the extreme hardships of life when work could not be got, yet he was no flint that needed such hard blows to strike out the fire, but an easily bubbling naphtha-spring that would have burned much the same, through whatever soil it had reached the open air.

He was born of the poorest laboring people, taught to read and write imperfectly only by means of the Sunday Schools, discouraged in any taste for books by his father lest his time, if any portion were that way bestowed, should not suffice to win his bread,—with no friends of the mind, in youthful years, except a volume of Byron, and an old German who loved to tell stories of his native land ;—married at nineteen, in the hope of mingling some solace with his cup ; plunged by the birth of children into deeper want, going forth to foreign lands a beggar in search of employment, returning to his own country to be received as a pauper, having won nothing but mental treasure which no man wished to buy ; he found his wife and children in the workhouse, and took them thence *home* to lie with him on straw in an unfurnished garret. Thus passed the first half of the span allotted on earth to one made in God's image. And during those years Prince constantly wrote into verse how such things struck him. But we cannot say that his human experiences were deep ; for all these things, that would have tortured other men, only pained him superficially. Into the soul of Elliott, the iron has entered ; the lightest song of Beranger echoes to a melancholy sense of the defects of this world with its Tantalus destinies, a melancholy which touches it at times with celestial pathos. But life has made but little impression on Prince. Endowed by Nature with great purity of instincts, a healthy vigor of feeling more than of thought, he sees, and expresses in all his works, the happiness natural to Man. He sees him growing, gently, gradually, with no more of struggle and labour than is wanted to develope his manly strength, learning his best self from the precious teachings of domestic affections, fully and intelligently the son, the lover, the husband, the father. He sees him walking amid the infinite fair shows of Nature, kingly, yet companionable, too. He sees him offering to his God no sacrifice of blood and tears, whether others' or his own, but the incense of a grateful and obedient heart, ever ready for love and good works.

It is this childishness, rather this virginity of soul, that makes Prince's poems remarkable. He has no high poetic power, not even a marked individuality of expression. There are no lines, verses, or images that strike by themselves; neither human nor external nature are described so as to make the mind of the poet foster-father to its subject. The poems are only easy expression of the common mood of a healthy mind and tender heart, which needs to vent itself in words and metres. Every body should be able to write as good verse,—every body has the same simple, substantial things to put into it. On such a general basis the high constructive faculty, the imagination, might rear her palaces, unafraid of ruin from war or time.

This being the case with Prince, we shall not make detailed remarks upon his poems, but merely substantiate what we have said by some extracts.

1st. We give the description of his Journey and Return. This, to us, presents a delightful picture; the man is so sufficient to himself and his own improvement; so unconquerably sweet and happy.

2d. The poem 'Land and Sea,' as giving a true presentment of the riches of this poor man.

3d. A poem to his Child, showing how a pure and refined sense of the beauty and value of these relations, often unknown in palaces, may make a temple of an unfurnished garret.

4th. In an extract from 'A Vision of the Future,' a presentation of the life fit for man, as seen by a 'reed-maker for weavers;' such as we doubt Mrs. Norton's Child of the Islands would not have vigor and purity of mental sense even to sympathize with, when conceived, far less to conceive.

These extracts speak for themselves; they show the stream of the poet's mind to be as clear as if it had flowed over the sands of Pactolus. But most waters show the color of the soil through which they had to *force* their passage ; this is the case with Elliott, and with Thom, of whose writings we shall soon give some notice.

Prince is an unique, as we sometimes find a noble Bayard, born of a worldly statesman—a sweet shepherdess or nun, of a heartless woman of fashion. Such characters are the direct gift of Heaven, and symbolize nothing in what is now called Society.

THE CHILD OF THE ISLANDS: By the Hon. Mrs. NORTON. London: Chapman and Hull. 1845.

HOURS WITH THE MUSES: By JOHN CRITCHLEY PRINCE. Second Edition. London. Simpkin, Marshall & Co. 1841.

THE *Hon.* Mrs. Norton and Prince, " a reed-maker for weavers," meet upon a common theme—the existing miseries and possible relief of that most wretched body, England's poor: most wretched of the world's sufferers in being worse mocked by pretensions of freedom and glory, most wretched in having minds more awakened to feel their wretchedness.

Mrs. Norton and Prince meet on the same ground, but in strongly contrasted garb and expression, as might be expected from the opposite quarters from which they come. Prince takes this truly noble motto :

" Knowledge and Truth and Virtue were his theme,
And lofty hopes of Liberty divine."—*Shelley.*

Mrs. Norton prefaces a poem on a subject of such sorrowful earnestness, and in which she calls the future sovereign of a groaning land to thought upon his duties, with this weak wish couched in the verse of Moore :

"As, half in shade and half in sun,
This world along its course advances,
May that side the sun's upon
Be all that shall ever meet thy glances."

Thus unconsciously showing her state of mind. It is a very different wish that a good friend, 'let alone' a good angel, would proffer to the Prince of Wales at this moment. Shame indeed will it be for him if he *does* wish to stand in the sun, while the millions that he ought to spend all his blood to benefit are shivering in the cold and dark. The position of the heirs of fortune in that country, under present circumstances, is one of dread, which to a noble soul would bring almost the anguish of crucifixion. How can they enjoy one moment in peace the benefit of their possessions? And how can they give them up, and be sure it will be any benefit to others? The causes of ill seem so deeply rooted in the public economy of England, that, if all her rich men were to sell all they have and give to the poor, it would yield but a temporary relief. Yea! all those heaped-up gems, the Court array of England's beauty; the immense treasures of art, enough to arouse old Greece from her grave; the stately parks, full of dewy glades and bosky dells, haunted by the stately deer and still more thickly by exquisite memories; the enormous wealth of episcopal palaces, might all be given up for the good of the people at large, and not relieve their sufferings ten years. It is not merely that sense of right usually dignified by the name of generosity that is wanted, but wisdom—a deeper wisdom by far as to the conduct of national affairs than the world has ever yet known. It is not enough now for prince or noble to be awakened to good dispositions. Let him not hope at once to be able to do good with the best dispositions; things have got too far from health and simplicity for that; the return must be tedious, and whoever sets out on that path must resign himself to be a patient student, with a painfully studying world for his companion. In work he can for a long time hope no shining results; the miners dig in the dark as yet for the ransom of the suffering million.

Hard is the problem for the whole civilized world at present, hard for bankrupt Europe, hard for endangered America. We say bankrupt Europe, for surely nations are so who have not known how to secure peace, education, or even bodily sustenance for the people at large. The lightest lore of fairy tale is wise enough to show that such nations must be considered bankrupt, notwithstanding the accumulation of wealth, the development of resources, the prodigies of genius and science they have to boast. Some successes have been achieved, but at what a price of blood and tears, of error and of crime!

And, in this hard school-time, hardest must be the lot of him who has outward advantages above the rest, and yet is at all awakened to the wants of all. Has he mind? how shall he learn? time—how employ it? means—where apply them? The poor little "trapper," kept in the dark at his automaton task twelve hours a day, has an easy and happy life before him, compared with the prince on the throne, if that prince possesses a conscience that can be roused, a mind that can be developed.

The position of such a prince is indicated in the following extract which we take from the Schnellpost. Laube says in his late work, called "Three royal cities of the North," "King Oscar still lives in the second story of the castle at Stockholm, where he lived when he was crowned prince. He was out, and his dressing gown thrown upon an elbow chair before the writing table: all was open, showing how he was occupied. I found among the books, that seemed in present use, many in German, among them the "Staats Lexicon," "Julius upon Prisons," "Rotteck's History of the World." It is well known that King Oscar is especially interested in studies for the advantage of the most unhappy classes of citizens, the poor and the prisoners, and has, himself, written upon the subject. His apartment shows domestic habits like those of a writer. No fine library full of books left to accumulate dust, but what he wants, chosen with judgment, ready for use around him. A hundred little things showed what should be the modern kingly character, at home in the intellectual life of our time, earnest for a general culture. Every thing in his simple arrangements showed the manly democratic prince. He is up, early and late, attending with zealous conscientiousness to the duties of his office."

Such a life should England's prince live, and then he would be only one of the many virtuous seekers, with a better chance to try experiments. The genius of the time is working through myriad organs, speaking through myriad mouths, but condescends chiefly to men of low estate. She is spelling a new and sublime spell; its first word we know is *brotherhood*, but that must be well pronounced and learnt *by heart* before we shall hear another so clearly. One thing is obvious, we must cease to worship princes even in genius. The greatest geniuses will in this day rank themselves as the chief servants only. It is not even the most exquisite, the highest, but rather the largest and deepest experience that can serve us. The Prince of Wales, like his poetess, will not be so able a servant on account of the privileges she so gracefully enumerates and cannot persuade herself are not blessings. But they will keep him, as they have kept her, farther from the truth and knowledge wanted than he would have been in a less sheltered position.

Yet we sympathize with Mrs. Norton in her appeal. *Every* boy *should* be a young prince; since it is not so, in the present distorted state of society, it is natural to select some one cherished object as the heir to our hopes. Children become the angels of a better future to all who attain middle age without losing from the breast that chief jewel, the idea of what man and life should be. They must do what we hoped to do, but find time, strength, perhaps even spirit, failing. They show not yet their limitations; in their eyes shines an infinite hope; we can imagine it realized in their lives, and this consoles us for the deficiencies in our own, for the soul, though demanding the beautiful and good every where, can yet be consoled if it is found some where. 'Tis an illusion to look for it in these children more than in ourselves, but it is one we seem to need, being the second strain of the music that cheers our fatiguing march through this part of the scene of life.

There was a good deal of *prestige* about Queen Victoria's coming to the throne. She was young, "and had what in a princess might be styled beauty." She wept lest she should not reign wisely, and that seemed as if she might. Many hoped she might prove another Elizabeth, with more heart, using the privileges of the woman, her high feeling, sympathy, tact and quick penetration in unison with, and as corrective of, the advice of experienced statesmen. We hoped she would be a mother to the country. But she has given no signs of distinguished character; her walk seems a private one. She is a fashionable lady and the mother of a family. We hope she may prove the mother of a good prince, but it will not do to wait for him; the present generation must do all it can. If he does no harm, it is more than is reasonable to expect from a prince--does no harm and is the keystone to keep the social arch from falling into ruins till the time be ripe to construct a better in its stead.

Mrs. Norton, addressing herself to the Child of the Islands, goes through the circling seasons of the year and finds plenty of topics in their changes to subserve her main aim. This is to awaken the rich to their duty. And, though the traces of her education are visible, and weak prejudices linger among newly awakened thoughts, yet, on the whole, she shows a just sense of the relationship betwixt man and man, and musically doth she proclaim her creed in the lines beginning

The stamps of imperfection rests on all
Our human intellect has power to plan.

After an eloquent enumeration of the difficulties that beset our path and our faith, she concludes—

Lo! out of chaos was the world first called,
And Order out of blank Disorder came,
The feebly-toiling heart that shrinks appalled,
In dangers weak, in difficulties tame,
Hath lost the spark of that creative flame
Dimly permitted still on earth to burn,
Working out slowly Order's perfect frame;
Distributed to those whose souls can learn,
As labourers under God, His task-work to discern.

"To discern," ay! that is what is needed. Only these "labourers under God" have that clearness of mind that is needed, and though in the present time they walk as men in a subterranean passage where the lamp sheds its light only a little way onward, yet that light suffices to keep their feet from stumbling while they seek an outlet to the blessed day.

The above presents a fair specimen of the poem. As poetry it is inferior to her earlier verses, where, without pretension to much thought, or commanding view, Mrs. Norton expressed simply the feelings of the girl and the woman. Willis has described them well in one of the most touching of his poems, as being a tale

—"of feelings which in me are cold,
But ah! with what a passionate sweetness told!"

The best passages in the present poem are personal, as where a mother's feelings are expressed in speaking of infants and young children, recollections of a Scotch Autumn, and the description of the imprisoned gipsey.*

* This extract was inserted in the original notice, but must be omitted here for want of room.

In the same soft and flowing style, and with the same unstudied fidelity to nature, is the grief of the gipsey husband painted when he comes and finds her dead. After the first fury of rage and despair is spent, he "weepeth like a child"—

> And many a day by many a sunny bank,
> Or forest pond, close fringed with rushes dank,
> He wails, his clench'd hands on his eyelids prest;
> Or by lone hedges, where the grass grows rank,
> Stretched prone, as travelers deem, in idle rest,
> Mourns for that murdered girl, the dove of his wild nest.

To such passages the woman's heart lends the rhetoric.

Generally the poem is written with considerable strength, in a good style, sustained, and sufficiently adorned, by the flowers of feeling. It shows an expansion of mind highly honourable to a lady placed as Mrs. Norton has been, and for which she, no doubt, is much indebted to her experience of sorrow. She has felt the need of faith and hope, of an enlargement of sympathy. The poem may be read through at once and without fatigue; this is much to say for an ethical poem, filling a large volume. It is, however, chiefly indebted for its celebrity to the circumstances of its authorship. A beautiful lady, celebrated in aristocratic circles, joins the democratic movement, now so widely spreading in light literature, and men hail the fact as a sign of the times. The poem is addressed to the "upper classes," and, even from its defects, calculated to win access to their minds. Its outward garb, too, is suited to attract their notice. The book is simply but beautifully got up, the two stanzas looking as if written for the page they fill, and in a pre-existent harmony with the frame-work and margin. There is only one ugly thing, and that frightfully ugly, the design for the frontispiece by Maclise. The Child of the Islands, represented by an infant form to whose frigid awkwardness there is no correspondence in the most degraded models that can be found in Nature for that age, with the tamest of angels kneeling at his head and feet, angels that have not spirit and sweetness enough to pray away a fly, forms the centre. Around him are other figures of whom it is impossible to say whether they are goblins or fairies, come to curse or bless. The accessories are as bad as the main group, mean in conception, tame in execution. And the subject admitted of so beautiful and noble an illustration by Art! We marvel that a person of so refined taste as Mrs. Norton, and so warmly engaged in the subject, should have admitted this to its companionship.

We intended to have given some account of Prince and his poems, in this connection, but must now wait till another number, for we have spread our words over too much space already.

MISS BARRETT'S POEMS.

A DRAMA OF EXILE: AND OTHER POEMS. By ELIZABETH B. BARRETT, author of THE SERAPHIM AND OTHER POEMS. New-York: Henry G. Langley, No. 8 Astor House, 1845

WHAT happiness for the critic when, as in the present instance, his task is, mainly, how to express a cordial admiration; to indicate an intelligence of beauties, rather than regret for defects!

We have read these volumes with feelings of delight far warmer than the writer, in her sincerely modest preface, would seem to expect from any reader, and cannot hesitate to rank her, in vigour and nobleness of conception, depth of spiritual experience, and command of classic allusion, above any female writer the world has yet known.

In the first quality, especially, most female writers are deficient. They do not grasp a subject with simple energy, nor treat it with decision of touch. They are, in general, most remarkable for delicacy of feeling, and brilliancy or grace in manner.

In delicacy of perception, Miss Barrett may vie with any of her sex. She has what is called a true woman's heart, although we must believe that men of a fine conscience and good organization will have such a heart no less. Signal instances occur to us in the cases of Spenser, Wordsworth and Tennyson. The woman who reads them will not find hardness or blindness as to the subtler workings of thoughts and affections.

If men are often deficient on this score; women, on the other hand, are apt to pay excessive attention to the slight tokens, the little things of life. Thus, in conduct or writing, they tend to weary us by a morbid sentimentalism. From this fault Miss Barrett is wholly free. Personal feeling is in its place; enlightened by Reason, ennobled by Imagination. The earth is no despised resting place for the feet, the heaven bends wide above, rich in starry hopes, and the air flows around exhilarating and free.

The mournful, albeit we must own them tuneful, sisters of the lyre might hush many of their strains at this clear note from one who has felt and conquered the same difficulties.

PERPLEXED MUSIC.

" Experience, like a pale musician, holds
A dulcimer of patience in his hand:
Whence harmonies we cannot understand
Of God's will in his worlds the strain unfolds,
In sad perplexed minors. Deathly colds
Fall on us while we hear and countermand
Our sanguine heart back from the fancy land,
With nightingales in visionary wolds.
We murmur—'Where is any certain tune,
Or measured music in such notes as these?'
But angels leaning from the golden seat,
Are not so minded; their fine ear hath won
The issue of completed cadences;
And smiling down the stars, they whisper—SWEET."

We are accustomed now to much verse on moral subjects, such as follows the lead of Wordsworth and seeks to arrange moral convictions as melodies on the harp. But these tones are never deep, unless the experience of the poet, in the realms of intellect and emotion, be commensurate with his apprehension of truth. Wordsworth moves us when he writes an "Ode to Duty," or "Dion," because he could also write "Ruth," and the exquisitely tender poems on Matthew, in whom nature

"—for a favorite child
Had tempered so the clay,

> That every hour the heart ran wild,
> Yet never went astray."

The trumpet call of Luther's 'Judgment Hymn' sounds from the depths of a nature capable of all human emotions, or it could not make the human ear vibrate as it does. The calm convictions expressed by Miss Barrett in the sonnets come with poetic force, because she was also capable of writing 'The Lost Bower,' 'The Romaunt of the Page,' 'Loved Once,' 'Bertha in the Lane,' and 'A Lay of the Early Rose.' These we select as the finest of the tender poems.

In the 'Drama of Exile' and the 'Vision of Poets,' where she aims at a Miltonic flight or Dantesque grasp—not in any spirit of rivalry or imitation, but because she is really possessed of a similar mental scope—her success is far below what we find in the poems of feeling and experience; for she has the vision of a great poet, but little in proportion of his plastic power. She is at home in the Universe; she sees its laws; she sympathises with its motions. She has the imagination all compact—the healthy archetypal plant from which all forms may be divined, and, so far as now existent, understood. Like Milton, she sees the angelic hosts in real presence; like Dante, she hears the spheral concords and shares the planetary motions. But she cannot, like Milton, marshal the angels so near the earth as to impart the presence other than by sympathy. He who is near her level of mind may, through the magnetic sympathy, see the angels with her. Others will feel only the grandeur and sweetness she expresses in these forms. Still less can she, like Dante, give, by a touch, the key which enables ourselves to play on the same instrument. She is singularly deficient in the power of compression. There are always far more words and verses than are needed to convey the meaning, and it is a great proof of her strength, that the thought still seems strong, when arrayed in a form so Briarean clumsy and many-handed.

We compare her with those great poets, though we have read her preface and see how sincerely she deprecates any such comparison, not merely because her theme is the same as theirs, but because, as we must again repeat, her field of vision and nobleness of conception are such, that we cannot forbear trying her by the same high standard to see what she lacks.

Of the "Drama of Exile" and other poems of the same character, we may say that we shall never read them again, but we are very glad to have read them once, to see how the grand mysteries look to her, to share with her the conception and outline of what would, in the hands of a more powerful artist, have come forth a great poem. Our favorite, above anything we have read of hers, is the "Rhyme of the Duchess May," equally admirable in thought and execution, in poetic meaning and romantic grace.

Were there room here, it should be inserted, as a sufficient evidence of the writer's high claims; but it is too long, and does not well bear being broken. The touches throughout are fine and forcible, but they need the unison of the whole to give them their due effect.

Most of these poems have great originality in the thought and the motive powers. It is these, we suppose, that have made "The Brown Rosarie" so popular. It has long been handed about in manuscript, and hours have been spent in copying it, which would have been spared if the publication of these volumes in America had been expected so soon. It does not please us so well as many of the others. The following, for instance, is just as original, full of grace, and, *almost*, perfectly simple:

THE ROMANCE OF THE SWAN'S NEST.*

How sweetly natural! and how distinct is the picture of the

* Several poems mentioned in these articles, and published in the first instance, are omitted now on account of their length.

little girl, as she sits by the brook. The poem cannot fail to charm all who have treasured the precious memories of their own childhood, and remember how romance was there interwoven with reality.

Miss Barrett makes many most fair and distinct pictures, such as this of the Duchess May at the fatal moment when her lord's fortress was giving way :

Low she dropt her head and lower, till her hair coiled on the floor.
Toll slowly!
And tear after tear you heard, fall distinct as any word
Which you might be listening for.
" Get thee in, thou soft ladie!—here is never a place for thee."
Toll slowly!
" Braid thy hair and clasp thy gown, that thy beauty in its moan
May find grace with Leigh of Leigh."
She stood up in bitter case, with a pale yet steady face,
Toll slowly!
Like a statue thunderstruck, which, though quivering, seems to look
Right against the thunder-place,
And her feet trod in, with pride, her own tears i' the stone beside.
Toll slowly!
Go to, faithful friends, go to!—Judge no more what ladies do,
No, nor how their lords may ride.

and so on. There are passages in that poem beyond praise.

Here are descriptions as fine of another sort of person from

LADY GERALDINE'S COURTSHIP.

Her foot upon the new-mown grass—bareheaded—with the flowing
Of the virginal white vesture, gathered closely to her throat;
With the golden ringlets in her neck, just quickened by her going,
And appearing to breathe sun for air, and doubting if to float,—

With a branch of dewy maple, which her right hand held above her,
And which trembled a green shadow in betwixt her and the skies,—
As she turned her face in going, thus she drew me on to love her,
And to study the deep meaning of the smile hid in her eyes.

For her eyes alone smiled constantly · her lips had serious sweetness,
And her front was calm—the dimple rarely rippled on her cheek:
But her deep blue eyes smiled constantly,—as if they had by fitness
Won the secret of a happy dream, she did not care to speak.

How fine are both the descriptive and critical touches in the following passage:

Ay, and sometimes on the hill-side, while we sat down in the gowans,
With the forest green behind us, and its shadow cast before;
And the river running under; and across it, from the rowens,
A brown partridge whirring near us, till we felt the air it bore—

There, obedient to her praying, did I read aloud the poems
Made by Tuscan flutes, or instruments, more various, of our own;
Read the pastoral parts of Spenser—or the subtle interflowings
Found in Petrarch's sonnets—here's the book—the leaf is folded down!

Or at times a modern volume—Wordsworth's solemn-thoughted idyl,
Howitt's ballad-dew, or Tennyson's god-vocal reverie,—
Or from Browning some "Pomegranate," which, if cut deep down the middle,
Shows a heart within, blood-tinctured, of a veined humanity.

Or I read there, sometimes, hoarsely, some new poem of my making—
Oh, your poets never read their own best verses to their worth,
For the echo, in you, breaks upon the words which you are speaking,
And the chariot-wheels jar in the gate through which you drive them forth.

After, when we were grown tired of books, the silence round us flinging
A slow arm of sweet compression, felt with beatings at the breast,—
She would break out, on a sudden, in a gush of woodland singing,
Like a child's emotion in a god—a naiad tired of rest.

Oh, to see or hear her singing! scarce I know which is divinest—
For her looks sing too—she modulates her gestures on the tune;
And her mouth stirs with the song, like song; and when the notes are finest,
'Tis the eyes that shoot out vocal light, and seem to swell them on.

Then we talked—oh, how we talked! her voice so cadenced in the talking,
Made another singing—of the soul! a music without bars—
While the leafy sounds of woodlands, humming round where we were walking,
Brought interposition worthy-sweet,—as skies about the stars.

And she spake such good thoughts natural, as if she always thought them—
And had sympathies so ready, open-free like bird on branch,
Just as ready to fly east as west, which ever way besought them,
In the birchen wood a chirrup, or a cock-crow in the grange.

In her utmost lightness there is truth—and often she speaks lightly;
And she has a grace in being gay, which mourners even approve;
For the root of some grave earnest thought is understruck so rightly,
As to justify the foliage and the waving flowers above."

We must copy yet one other poem to give some idea of the range of Miss Barrett's power.

THE CRY OF THE CHILDREN.

If it be said that the poetry, the tragedy here is in the facts, yet how rare is it to find a mind that can both feel and upbear such facts.

We have already said, that, as a poet, Miss Barrett is deficient in plastic energy, and that she is diffuse. We must add many blemishes of overstrained and constrained thought and expression. The ways in which words are coined or forced from their habitual meanings does not carry its excuse with it. We find no gain that compensates the loss of elegance and simplicity. One practice which has already had its censors of using the adjective for the noun, as in the cases of "The cry of the Human," "Leaning from the Golden," we, also, find offensive, not only to the habitual tastes, but to the sympathies of the very mood awakened by the writer.

We hear that she has long been an invalid, and, while the knowledge of this increases admiration for her achievements and delight at the extent of the influence,—so much light flowing from the darkness of the sick room,—we seem to trace injurious results, too. There is often a want of pliant and glowing life. The sun does not always warm the marble. We have spoken of the great book culture of this mind. We must now say that this culture is too great in proportion to that it has received from actual life. The lore is not always assimilated to the new form; the illustrations sometimes impede the attention rather than help its course; and we are too much and too often reminded of other minds and other lives.

Great variety of metres are used, and with force and facility. But they have not that deep music which belongs to metres which are the native growth of the poet's mind. In that case, others may have used them, but we feel that, if they had not, he must have invented them; that they are original with him. Miss Barrett is more favoured by the grand and thoughtful, than by the lyric muse.

We have thus pointed out all the faults we could find in Miss Barrett, feeling that her strength and nobleness deserves this act of high respect. She has no need of leniency, or caution. The best comment upon such critiques may be made by subjoining this paragraph from her Preface:

"If it were not presumptuous language on the lips of one to whom life is more than usually uncertain, my favourite wish for this work would be, that it be received by the public as a deposite, ambitious of approaching to the nature of a security for a future offering of more value and acceptability. I would fain do better, and I feel as if I might do better: I aspire to do better. In any case, my poems, while full of faults, as I go forward to my critics and confess, have my life and heart in them. They are not empty shells. If it must be said of me that I have contributed unworthy verses, I also to the many rejected by the age, it cannot, at least be said that I have done so in a light or irresponsible spirit. Poetry has been as serious a thing to me as life itself; and life has been a very serious thing; there has been no playing at skittles for me in either. I never mistook pleasure for the final cause of poetry; nor leisure, for the hour of the poet. I have done my work, so far, as work; not as mere hand and head work apart from the personal being, but as the completest expression of that being to which I could attain; and, as work, I offer it to the public, feeling its faultiness more deeply than any of my readers, because measured from the height of my aspiration, but feeling also that the reverence and sincerity with which the work was done should protect it in the thoughts of the reverent and sincere."

Of the greatest of Grecian sages it was said that he acquired such power over the lower orders of nature, through his purity and intelligence, that wild beasts were abashed and reformed by his admonitions, and that, once, when walking abroad with his disciples, he called down the white eagle, soaring above him, and drew from her willing wing a quill for his use.

We have seen women use with skill and grace, the practical goose-quill, the sentimental crow-quill, and even the lyrical, the consecrated feathers of the swan. But we have never seen one to whom the white eagle would have descended ; and, for a while, were inclined to think that the hour had now, for the first time, arrived. But, upon full deliberation, we will award to Miss Barrett one from the wing of the sea-gull. That is also a white bird, rapid, soaring, majestic, and which can alight with ease, and poise itself upon the stormiest wave.

BROWNING'S POEMS.

Robert Browning is scarcely known in this country, as, indeed, in his own, his fame can spread but slowly, from the nature of his works. On this very account,—of the peculiarity of his genius,—we are desirous to diffuse the knowledge that there is such a person, thinking and writing, so that those who, here and there, need just him, and not another, may know where to turn.

Our first acquaintance with this subtle and radiant mind was through his "Paracelsus," of which we cannot now obtian a copy, and must write from a distant memory.

It is one of those attempts, that illustrate the self-consciousness of this age, to represent the fever of the soul pining to embrace the secret of the universe in a single trance. Men who are once seized with this fever, carry thought upon the heart as a cross, instead of finding themselves daily warmed and enlightened to more life and joy by the sacred fire to which their lives daily bring fresh fuel.

Sometimes their martyrdoms greatly avail, as to positive achievements of knowledge for their own good and that of all men; but, oftener, they only enrich us by experience of the temporary limitations of the mind, and the inutility of seeking to transcend, instead of working within them.

Of this desire, to seize at once as a booty what it was intended we should legitimately win by gradual growth, alchemy and the *elixir vitæ* were, in the middle ages, apt symbols. In seeking how to prolong life, men wasted its exquisite spring-time and splendid summer, lost the clues they might have gained by initiation to the mysteries of the present existence. They sought to make gold in crucibles, through study of the laws which govern the material world, while within them was a crucible and a fire beneath it, which only needed watching, in faith and purity, and they would have turned all substances to treasure, which neither moth nor rust could corrupt.

Paracelsus had one of those soaring ambitions that sought the stars and built no nest amid the loves or lures of life. Incapable of sustaining himself in angelic force and purity, he tainted, after a while, his benefits, by administering them with the arts of a charlatan, seeking too ambitiously the mastery of life, he missed its best instructions.

Yet he who means nobleness, though he misses his chosen aim, cannot fail to bring down a precious quarry from the clouds. Paracelsus won deep knowledge of himself and his God. Love followed, if it could not bless him, and the ecstacies of genius wove music into his painful dreams.

The holy and domestic love of Michal, that *Ave Maria Stella* of his stormy life, the devotion of a friend, who living, for himself, in the humility of a genuine priest, yet is moved by the pangs of sympathy, to take part against and "wrestle with" Heaven in his behalf, the birth and bud of the creative spirit which blesses through the fulness of forms, as expressed in Aprile, all are told with a beauty and, still more, a pregnancy, unsurpassed amid the works of contemporary minds.

"Sordello" we have never seen, and have been much disappointed at not being able to obtain the loan of a copy now existent in New England. It is spoken of as a work more thickly enveloped in refined obscurities than ever any other that really had a meaning; and no one acquainted with Browning's mind can doubt his always having a valuable meaning, though sometimes we may not be willing to take the degree of trouble necessary to ferret it out. His writings have, till lately, been clouded by obscurities, his riches having seemed to accumulate beyond his mastery of them. So beautiful are the picture gleams, so full of meaning the little thoughts that are always twisting their parasites over his main purpose, that we hardly can bear to wish them away, even when we know their excess to be a defect. They seem, each and all, too good to be lopped away, and we cannot wonder the mind from which they grew was at a loss which to reject. Yet, a higher mastery in the poetic art must give him skill and resolution to reject them. Then, all true life being condensed into the main growth, instead of being so much scattered in tendrils, off-shoots and flower-bunches, the effect would be more grand and simple; nor should we be any loser as to the spirit; it would all be there, only more concentrated as to the form, more full, if less subtle, in its emanations. The tendency to variety and delicacy, rather than to a grasp of the subject and concentration of interest, are not so obvious in Browning's minor works as in Paracelsus, and in his tragedy of 'Strafford.' This very difficult subject for tragedy engaged, at about the same time, the attention of Sterling. Both he and Browning seem to have had it brought before their attention by Foster's spirited biography of Strafford. We say it is difficult—though we see how it tempted the poets to dramatic enterprise. The main character is one of tragic force and majesty; the cotemporary agents all splendid figures, and of marked individuality; the march of action necessarily rapid and imposing; the events induced of universal interest. But the difficulty is, that the materials are even too rich and too familiar to every one. We cannot bear any violation of reality, any straining of the common version of this story. Then the character and position of Strafford want that moral interest which is needed to give full pathos to the catastrophe. We admire his greatness of mind and character, we loathe the weakness and treachery of the King; we dislike the stern hunters, notwithstanding their patriotic motives, for pursuing to the death the noble stag; and yet we feel he ought to die. We wish that he had been killed, not by the hands of men, with their spotted and doubtful feelings, but smitten direct by pure fire from heaven. Still we feel he ought to die, and our grief wants the true tragic element which hallows it in the Antigone, the Lear, and even Schiller's "Mary Stuart," or "Wallenstein."

But of the two, Sterling's conception of the character and conduct of the drama is far superior to that of Browning. Both dramas are less interesting and effective than the simple outline history gives, but Browning weakens the truth in his representation of it, while Sterling at least did not falsify the character of Strafford, bitter, ruthlessly ambitious, but strong and majestic throughout. Browning loses, too, his accustomed originality and grace in the details of this work, through a misplaced ambition.

But believing that our poet has not reached that epoch of mastery, when he can do himself full justice in a great work, we would turn rather to the consideration of a series of sketches, dramatic and lyric, which he has been publishing for several years, under the title of "Bells and Pomegranates." We do not know whether this seemingly affected title is assumed in conformity with the catch-penny temper of the present day, or whether these be really in the mind of Robert Browning no more than the glittering fringe of his priestly garment. If so, we shall cherish high hopes, indeed, as to the splendors that will wait upon the unfolding of the main vesture.

The plan of these sketches is original, the execution in many respects, admirable, and the range of talent and perception they display, wider than that of any contemporary poet in England.

"Pippa Passes" is the title of the first of these little two shilling volumes, which seem to contain just about as much as a man who lives wisely, might, after a good summer of mingled work, business and pleasure, have to offer to the world, as the honey he could spare from his hive.

Pippa is a little Italian girl who works in a silk mill. Once a year the workpeople in these mills have an entire day given them for their pleasure. She is introduced at sunrise of such a day, singing her morning thoughts. She then goes forth to wander through the town, singing her little songs of childish gayety and purity. She passes, not through, but by, different scenes of life, passes by a scene of guilty pleasure, by the conspiracies of the malicious, by the cruel undeception of the young sculptor who had dared trust his own heart more fully than is the wont of the corrupt and cautious world. Every where the notes of her song pierce their walls and windows, awakening them to memories of innocence and checking the course of misdeed. The plan of this work is, it will be seen, at once rich and simple. It admits of an enchanting variety, and an unobtrusive unity. Browning has made the best use of its advantages. The slides in the magic lantern succeed one another with perfect distinctness, but, through them all shines the light of this one beautiful Italian day, and the little silk winder, its angel, discloses to us as fine gleams of garden, stream and sky, as we have time to notice while passing such various and interesting groups of human beings.

The finest sketch of these is that of Jules, the sculptor, and his young bride. Jules, like many persons of a lofty mould, in the uncompromising fervour of youth, makes all those among his companions whom he thinks weak, base and vicious, his enviers and bitter enemies. A set of such among his fellow-students have devised this most wicked plan to break his heart and pride at once. They write letters as from a maiden who has distinguished him from the multitude, and knows how to sympathize with all his tastes and aims. They buy of her mother a beautiful young girl, who is to represent the character. The letters assume that she is of a family of rank who will not favour the alliance, and when Jules, enchanted by the union of the beauty of intellect in the letters and the beauty of person of which he has gained glimpses, presses his suit as a lover, marriage is con sented to on condition that he shall not seek to converse with her till after the ceremony. This is the first talk of Jules after he has brought his silent bride to his studio:

Thou by me
And I by thee—this is thy hand in mine—
And side by side we sit—all's true. Thank God!
I have spoken—speak thou!
—O, my life to come!
My Tydeus must be carved that's there in clay,
And how be carved with you about the chamber?
Where must I place you? When I think that once
This room full of rough block-work seemed my heaven
Without you! Shall I ever work again—
Get fairly into my old ways again—
Bid each conception stand while trait by trait
My hand transfers its lineaments to stone?
Will they, my fancies, live near you, my truth—
The live truth—passing and repassing me—
Sitting beside me?
—Now speak!
Only, first,
Your letters to me—was't not well contrived?
A hiding place in Psyche's robe—there lie
Next to her skin your letters; which comes foremost?
Good—this that swam down like a first moonbeam
Into my world.
Those? Books I told you of.
Let your first word to me rejoice them, too,—
This minion of Coluthus, writ in red
Bistre and azure by Bessarion's scribe—
Read this line—no, shame—Homer's be the Greek!
My Odyssey in coarse black vivid type
With faded yellow blossoms 'twixt page and page;
"He said, and on Antinous directed
A bitter shaft"—then blots a flower the rest!

—Ah, do not mind that—better that will look
When cast in bronze—an Almaign Kaiser that,
Swart-green and gold with truncheon based on hip-
This rather, turn to—but a check already—
Or you had recognized that here you sit
As I imagined you, Hippolyta
Naked upon her bright Numidian horse!
—Forgot you this then? "carve in bold relief,"—
So you command me—"carve against I come
A Greek, bay filleted and thunder free,
Rising beneath the lifted myrtle-branch,
Whose turn arrives to praise Harmodius."—Praise him!
Quite round, a cluster of mere hands and arms
Thrust in all senses, all ways, from all sides,
Only consenting at the branches' end
They strain towards, serves for frame to a sole face—
(Place your own face)—the Praiser's, who with eyes
Sightless, so bend they back to light inside
His brain where visionary forms throng up,
(Gaze—I am your Harmodius dead and gone,)
Sings, minding not the palpitating arch
Of hands and arms, nor the quick drip of wine
From the drenched leaves o'erhead, nor who cast off
Their violet crowns for him to trample on—
Sings, pausing as the patron-ghosts approve,
Devoutly their unconquerable hymn—
But you must say a "well" to that—say "well"
Because you gaze--am I fantastic, sweet?
Gaze like my very life's stuff, marble—marbly
Even to the silence—and before I found
The real flesh Phene, I inured myself
To see throughout all nature varied stuff
For better nature's birth by means of art:
With me, each substance tended to one form
Of beauty—to the human Archetype—
And every side occurred suggestive germs
Of that—the tree, the flower—why, take the fruit,
Some rosy shape, continuing the peach,
Curved beewise o'er its bough, as rosy limbs

Depending nestled in the leaves—and just
From a cleft rose-peach the whole Dryad sprung!
But of the stuffs one can be master of,
How I divined their capabilities
From the soft-rinded smoothening facile chalk
That yields your outline to the air's embrace,
Down to the crisp imperious steel, so sure
To cut its one confided thought clean out
Of all the world: but marble!—'neath my tools
More pliable than jelly—as it were
Some clear primordial creature dug from deep
In the Earth's heart where itself breeds itself
And whence all baser substance may be worked;
Refine it off to air you may—condense it
Down to the diamond;—is not metal there
When o'er the sudden specks my chisel trips?
—Not flesh—as flake off flake I scale, approach,
Lay bare these bluish veins of blood asleep?
Lurks flame in no strange windings where surprised
By the swift implements sent home at once,
Flushes and glowings radiate and hover
About its track?—

The girl, thus addressed, feels the wings budding within her, that shall upbear her from the birth-place of pollution in whose mud her young feet have been imprisoned. Still, her first words reveal to the proud, passionate, confiding genius the horrible deception that has been practised on him. After his first anguish, one of Pippa's songs steals in to awaken consoling thoughts. He feels that only because his heart was capable of noble trust could it be so deceived; feels too that the beauty which had enchanted him could not be a mere mask, but yet might be vivified by a soul worthy of it, and finds the way to soar above his own pride and the opinions of an often purblind world.

Another song, with which Pippa passes, contains, in its first stanza, this grand picture:

A king lived long ago,
In the morning of the world,
When Earth was nigher Heaven than now:
And the King's locks curled
Disparting o'er a forehead full
As the milk-white space 'twixt horn and horn
Of some sacrificial bull.
Only calm as a babe new-born;
For he has got to a sleepy mood,
So safe from all decrepitude.
Age with its bane so sure gone by,
(The gods so loved him while he dreamed)
That, having lived thus long there seemed
No need the King should ever die.

Luigi—No need that sort of King should ever die.

Among the rocks his city was;
Before his palace, in the sun,
He sat to see his people pass,
And judge them every one,
From its threshold of smooth stone.

This picture is as good as the Greeks.

Next came a set of Dramatic Lyrics, all more or less good, from which we select

ITALY.

That's my last Duchess painted on the wall,
Looking as if she were alive; I call
That piece a wonder, now; Frà Pandolf's hands
Worked busily a day, and there she stands.
Will't please you sit and look at her? I said
"Frà Pandolf" by design, for never read
Strangers like you that pictured countenance,
The depth and passion of that earnest glance,
But to myself they turned (since none puts by
The curtain I have drawn for you, but I)
And seemed as they would ask me, if they durst,
How such a glance came there; so not the first

Are you to turn and ask thus. Sir, 'twas not
Her husband's presence only, called that spot
Of joy into the Duchess' cheek; perhaps
Frà Pandolf chanced to say "Her mantle laps
"Over my Lady's wrist too much," or "Paint
"Must never hope to reproduce the faint
Half-flush that dies along her throat;" such stuff
Was courtesy, she thought, and cause enough
For calling up that spot of joy. She had
A heart—how shall I say—too soon made glad,
Too easily impressed; she liked whate'er
She looked on, and her looks went every where.
Sir, 'twas all one! My favour at her breast,
The dropping of the daylight in the West,
The bough of cherries some officious fool
Broke in the orchard for her, the white mule
She rode with round the terrace—all and each
Would draw from her alike the forward speech,
Or blush, at least. She thanked men—good; but thanked
Some how—I know not how—as if she ranked
My gift of a nine hundred years' old name
With any body's gift. Who'd stoop to blame
This sort of trifling? Even had you skill
In speech—(which I have not)—could make your will
Quite clear to such an one, and say, "Just this
"Or that in you disgusts me; here you miss,
Or there exceed the mark"—and if she let
Herself be lessoned so, nor plainly set
Her wits to yours, forsooth, and made excuse,
—E'en then would be some stooping, and I chuse
Never to stoop. Oh, Sir, she smiled, no doubt,
Whene'er I passed her; but who passed without
Much the same smile? This grew; I gave commands,
Then all smiles stopped together. There she stands
As if alive. Will't please you rise? We'll meet
The company below then. I repeat,
The Count your master's known munificence
Is ample warrant that no just pretence
Of mine for dowry will be disallowed;
Though his fair daughter's self, as I avowed

At starting, is my object. Nay, we'll go
Together down, Sir! Notice Neptune, though,
Taming a sea-horse, thought a rarity,
Which Claus of Innsbruck cast in bronze for me.

CRISTINA.

To this volume succeeded "King Victor and King Charles," "The Return of the Druses," "A Blot in the 'Scutcheon," and "Colombe's Birthday."

The first we do not so much admire, but the other three have all the same originality of conception, delicate penetration into the mysteries of human feeling, atmospheric individuality, and skill in picturesque detail. All four exhibit very high and pure ideas of Woman, and a knowledge very rare in man of the ways in which what is peculiar in her office and nature works. Her loftiest elevation does not, in his eyes, lift her out of nature. She becomes not a mere saint, but the goddess-queen of nature. Her purity is not cold like marble, but the healthy, gentle energy of the flower, instinctively rejecting what is not fit for it, with no need of disdain to dig a gulf between it and the lower forms of creation. Her office to man is that of the Muse, inspiring him to all good thoughts and deeds. The passions that sometimes agitate these maidens of his verse, are the surprises of noble hearts, unprepared for evil, and even their mistakes cannot cost bitter tears to their attendant angels.

The girl in the "Return of the Druses" is the sort of nature Byron tried to paint in Myrrha. But Byron could only paint women as they were to him. Browning can show what they are in themselves.

In "A Blot in the 'Scutcheon" we see a lily, storm-struck, half broken, but still a lily. In "Colombe's Birthday" a queenly rosebud, which expands into the full glowing rose before our eyes. This is marvelous in this drama, how the characters are unfolded before us by the crisis, which not only exhibits, but calls to life, the higher passions and thoughts which were latent within them.

We bless the poet for these pictures of women, which, however the common tone of society, by the grossness and levity of the remarks bandied from tongue to tongue, would seem to say the contrary, declare there is still in the breasts of men a capacity for pure and exalting passion,—for immortal tenderness.

But we must hasten to conclude with some extracts from another number of "Dramatic Lyrics" lately received. These seem to show that Browning is attaining a more masterly clearness in expression, without seeking to popularize, or omitting to heed the faintest whisper of his genius. He gains without losing as he advances—a rare happiness.

In the former number was a poem called "The Cloister," and in this are two, "The Confessional" and the "Tomb at St. Praxed's," which are the keenest yet a wisely true satire on the forms that hypocrisy puts on in the Romish church. This hateful weed grows rank in all cultivated gardens, but it seems to hide itself, with great care and adroitness, beneath the unnumbered forms and purple gauds of that elaborate system. Accordingly, the hypocrites do not seem so bad, individually, as in other churches, and the satire is continually softening into humour in the "Tomb of St. Praxed's," with its terrible naturalness as to a life-long deception. Tennyson has described the higher kind with a force that will not be surpassed in his Simeon Stylites, but in this piece of Browning's, we find the Flemish school of the same vice.

The "Flight of the Duchess," in its entrancing revelations of the human heart, is a boon to think of. We were, however, obliged to forbear further extracts, with the exception of two from the "Garden Fancies." We regret that these poems, with several others which have been circulated in "The Tribune," could not find room in the present volume.

BELLS AND POMEGRANATES: By ROBERT BROWNING. No. VIII and last. Luria and a Soul's Tragedy. London: Moxon, Dover-st. 1846.

IN closing this series of dramatic and lyrical sketches, Browning explains his plan and title thus:

"Here ends my first series of 'Bells and Pomegranates,' and I take the opportunity of explaining, in reply to inquiries, that I only meant by that title to indicate an endeavour toward something like an alternation or mixture of music with discoursing, sound with sense, poetry with thought, which looks too ambitious, thus expressed, so the symbol was preferred. It is little to the purpose that such is actually one of the most familiar of the Rabbinical (and Patristic) acceptations of the phrase; because I confess that letting authority alone, I supposed the bare words in such juxtaposition would sufficiently convey the desired meaning. 'Faith and good works' is another fancy for instance, and perhaps no easier to arrive at; yet Giotto placed a pomegranate fruit in the hand of Dante, and Raffaelle crowned his Theology with blossoms of the same."

That the poet should have supposed the symbol would be understood at once, marks the nature of his mind, a mind which soars in the creative element, and can only be understood by those who are in a state of congenial activity.

The two pieces before us display, or rather betray, a deep and growing acquaintance with the mysteries of the breast. If one tithe of what informs this little pamphlet were brought out into clear relief by the plastic power of a Shakspeare, the world would stand transfixed before the sad revelation.

In the first piece, Luria, a Moor, is put in command of the Florentine army against Pisa; but spies are set around him, and the base mistress sits in trial on the hero she has won by smiles to fight her battles. His great, simple, fiery nature is captivated by the grace, deep sagacity and self-possession of the Florentines. He glows with delight at feeling in himself the birth of a more intellectual life beneath their influence. But when he finds the treachery hid beneath all this beautiful sculptured outside, he stands amazed, not lost, not overwhelmed, but unable to meet or brave what is so opposite to his own soul. He is, indeed, too noble to resent or revenge, or look on the case other than as God may

Luria—In my own East—if you would stoop to help
My barbarous illustration—it sounds ill,
Yet there's no wrong at bottom—rather praise.
Dom.—Well!
Luria.— We have creatures there which if you saw
The first time, you would doubtless marvel at,
For their surpassing beauty, craft and strength,
And tho' it were a lively moment's shock
Wherein you found the purpose of their tongues—
That seemed innocuous in their lambent play,
Yet, once made known, such grace required a guard,
Your reason soon would acquiesce, I think,
In th' Wisdom which made all things for the best,
So take them, good with ill, contentedly—
The prominent beauty with the secret sting.
I am glad to have seen you, wondrous Florentines.

And having seen them, and staked his heart entirely on the venture, he went through with them—*and lost.* He cannot survive the shock of their treachery. He arranges all things nobly in their behalf, and dies, for he was of that mould, the "precious porcelain of human clay" which

"Breaks with the first fall,"

but not without first exercising a redeeming power upon all the foes and traitors round him. His chivalric antagonist, Tiburzio, needed no conversion, for he is one of the noble race who

"joy to feel
A foeman worthy of their steel,"

and are the best friends of such a foeman. But the shrewd, worldly spy, the supplanted rival, the woman who was guilty of that lowest baseness of wishing to make of a lover the tool of her purposes, all grow better by seeing the action of this noble creature under the crucifixion they have prepared for him; especially the feelings of the rival, who learns from his remorse to understand genius and magnanimity, are admirably depicted. Such repentance always comes too late for the one injured; men kill him first, then grow wiser and mourn; this dreadful and frequent tragedy is shown in Luria's case with its full weight of dark significance, spanned by the rainbow beauty that springs from the perception of truth and nobleness in the victim.

The second piece, "A Soul's Tragedy," is another of the deepest tragedies—a man fancying himself good because he was harsh, honourable because he was not sweet, truer than the lovely and loving natures, because unskilled to use their winning ways. His self-deception is revealed to him by means the most original and admirably managed. Both these dramas are full of genius; both make the heart ache terribly. A text might well suit the cover—a text we must all of us learn ever more and more deeply to comprehend: "Let him who thinketh he standeth take heed lest he fall."

We hope these eight numbers of "Bells and Pomegranates" will now be reprinted here. They would make one volume of proper size to take into the woods and fields.

LIVES OF THE GREAT COMPOSERS;

HAYDN, MOZART, HANDEL, BACH, BEETHOVEN.

THE lives of the musicians are imperfectly written for this obvious reason. The soul of the great musician can only be expressed in music. This language is so much more ready, flexible, full, and rapid than any other, that we can never expect the minds of those accustomed to its use to be expressed by act or word, with even that degree of adequacy, which we find in those of other men. They are accustomed to a higher stimulus, a more fluent existence. We must read them in their works; this, true of artists in every department, is especially so of the high-priests of sound.

Yet the eye, which has followed with rapture the flight of the bird till it is quite vanished in the blue serene, reverts with pleasure to the nest, which it finds of materials and architecture, that, if wisely examined, correspond entirely with all previously imagined of the songster's history and habits. The biography of the artist is a scanty gloss upon the grand text of his works, but we examine it with a deliberate tenderness, and could not spare those half-effaced pencil marks of daily life.

In vain the healthy reactions of nature have so boldly in our own day challenged the love of greatness, and bid us turn from Boswellism to read the record of the village clerk. These obscure men, you say, have hearts also, busy lives, expanding souls. Study the simple annals of the poor, and you find there, only restricted and stifled by accident, Milton, Calderon, or Michel Angelo. Precisely for that, precisely because we might be such as these, if temperament and position had seconded the soul's behest, must we seek with eagerness this spectacle of the occasional manifestation of that degree of development which we call hero, poet, artist, martyr. A sense of the depths of love and pity in "our obscure and private breasts" bids us demand to see their sources burst up somewhere through the lava of circumstance, and Peter Bell has no sooner felt his first throb of penitence and piety, than he prepares to read the lives of the saints.

Of all those forms of life which in their greater achievement shadow forth what the accomplishment of our life in the ages must be, the artist's life is the fairest in this, that it weaves its web most soft and full, because of the material most at command. Like the hero, the statesman, the martyr, the artist differs from other men only in this, that the voice of the demon within the breast speaks louder, or is more early and steadily obeyed than by men in general. But colors, and marble, and paper scores are more easily found to use, and more under command, than the occasions of life or the wills of other men, so that we see in the poet's work, if not a higher sentiment, or a deeper meaning, a more frequent and more perfect fulfilment than in him who builds his temple from the world day by day, or makes a nation his canvass and his pallette.

It is also easier to us to get the scope of the artist's design and its growth as the area where we see it does not stretch vision beyond its power. The Sybil of Michel Angelo indeed shares the growth of centuries, as much as Luther's Reformation, but the first apparition of the one strikes both the senses and the soul, the other only the latter, so we look most easily and with liveliest impression at the Sybil.

Add the benefits of rehearsal and repetition. The grand Napoleon drama could be acted but once, but Mozart's Don Giovanni presents to us the same thought seven times a week, if we wish to yield to it so many.

The artists too are the young children of our sickly manhood, or wearied out old age. On us life has pressed till the form is marred and bowed down, but their youth is immortal, invincible, to us the inexhaustible prophecy of a second birth. From the naive lispings of their uncalculating lives are heard anew the tones of that mystic song we call Perfectibility, Perfection.

Artist biographies, scanty as they are, are always beautiful. The tedious cavil of the Teuton cannot degrade, nor the surley superlatives of the Italian wither them. If any fidelity be preserved in the record, it always casts new light on their works. The exuberance of Italian praise is the better extreme of the two, for the heart, with all its blunders, tells truth more easily than the head. The records before us of the great composers are by the patient and reverent Germans, the sensible, never to be duped Englishman, or the sprightly Frenchman ; but a Vasari was needed also to cast a broader sunlight on the scene. All artist lives are interesting. And those of the musicians, peculiarly so to-day, when Music is *the* living, growing art. Sculpture, Painting, Architecture are indeed not dead, but the life they exhibit is as the putting forth of young scions from an old root. The manifestation is hopeful rather than commanding. But music, after all the wonderful exploits of the last century, grows and towers yet. Beethoven towering far above our heads, still with colossal gesture points above. Music is pausing now to explain, arrange, or explore the treasures so rapidly accumulated ; but how great the genius thus employed, how vast the promise for the next revelation ! Beethoven seems to have chronicled all the sobs, the heart-heavings, and god-like Promethean thefts of the Earth-spirit. Mozart has called to the sister stars, as Handel and Haydn have told to other spheres what has been actually performed in this ; surely they will answer through the next magician.

The thought of the law that supersedes all thoughts, which pierces us the moment we have gone far in any department of knowledge or creative genius, seizes and lifts us from the ground in music. "Were but this known all would be accomplished," is sung to us ever in the triumphs of harmony. What the other arts indicate and philosophy infers, this all-enfolding language declares, nay publishes, and we lose all care for to-morrow or modern life in the truth averred of old, that all truth is comprised in music and mathematics.

> By one pervading spirit
> Of tones and numbers all things are controlled,
> As sages taught where *faith* was found to merit
> Initiation in that mystery old.
>
> WORDSWORTH. "*Stanzas on the power of sound.*"

A very slight knowledge of music makes it the best means of interpretation. We meet our friend in a melody as in a glance of the eye, far beyond where words have strength to climb; we explain by the corresponding tone in an instrument that trait in our admired picture, for which no sufficiently subtle analogy had yet been found. Botany had never touched our true knowledge of our favourite flower, but a symphony displays the same attitude and hues; the philosophic historian had failed to explain the motive of our favourite hero, but every bugle calls and every trumpet proclaims him. He that hath ears to hear, let him hear!

Of course we claim for music only a greater rapidity, fullness, and, above all, delicacy of utterance. All is in each and each in all, so that the most barbarous stammering of the Hottentot indicates the secret of man, as clearly as the rudest zoophyte the perfection of organized being, or the first stop on the reed the harmonies of heaven. But music, by the ready medium, the stimulus and the upbearing elasticity it offers for the inspirations of thought, alone seems to present a living form rather than a dead monument to the desires of Genius.

The feeling naturally given by an expression so facile of the identity and universality of all thought, every thought, is beautifully expressed in this anecdote of Haydn.

When about to compose a symphony he was in the habit of animating his genius by imagining some little romance. An interesting account of one of these is given in Bombet's life of Haydn, p. 75.

"But when his object was not to express any particular affection, or to paint any particular images, all subjects were alike to him. '*The whole art consists*,' said he, '*in taking up a subject and pursuing it.*' Often when a friend entered as he was about to compose a piece, he would say with a smile, 'Give me a subject,'—'Give a subject to Haydn! who would have the courage to do so?' 'Come, never mind,' he would say, 'give me anything you can think of,' and you were obliged to obey."

"Many of his astonishing quartettes exhibit marks of this (piece of dexterity, the French Chevalier is pleased to call it.) They commence with the most insignificant idea, but, by degrees, this idea assumes a character; it strengthens, increases, extends itself, and the dwarf becomes a giant before our wondering eyes."

This is one of the high delights received from a musical composition more than from any other work of art, except perhaps the purest effusions of lyric poetry, that you feel at once both the result and the process. The musician enjoys the great advantage of being able to excite himself to compose by his instrument. This gives him a great advantage above those who are obliged to execute their designs by implements less responsive and exciting. Bach did not consider his pupils as at all advanced, till they could compose from the pure mental harmony, without the outward excitement of the instrument; but, though in the hours of inspiration the work grows of itself, yet the instrument must be of the greatest use to multiply and prolong these hours. We find that all these great composers were continually at the piano. Haydn seated himself there the first thing in the morning, and Beethoven, when so completely deaf, that he could neither tune his violin and piano, nor hear the horrible discords he made upon them, stimulated himself continually by the manual utterance to evolution of the divine harmonies which were lost forever to his bodily ear.

It is mentioned by Bombet, as another advantage which the musician possesses over other artists, that—

"His productions are finished as soon as imagined. Thus Haydn, who abounded in such beautiful ideas, incessantly enjoyed the pleasure of creation. The poet shares this advantage with the composer; but the musician can work faster. A beautiful ode, a beautiful symphony, need only be imagined, to cause, in the mind of the author, that secret admiration, which is the life and soul of artists. But in the studies of the military man, of the architect, the sculptor, the painter, there is not invention enough for them to be fully satisfied with themselves; further labors are necessary. The best planned enterprise may fail in the execution; the best conceived picture may be ill painted; all this leaves in the mind of the inventor an obscurity, a feeling of uncertainty, which renders the pleasure of creation less complete. Haydn, on the contrary, in imagining a symphony, was perfectly happy; there only remained the physical pleasure of hearing it performed, and the moral pleasure of seeing it applauded."

Plausible as this comparison appears at first; the moment you look at an artist like Michel Angelo, who, by deep studies and intensity of survey, had attained such vigor of conception and surety of hand, that forms sprang forth under his touch as fresh, as original, and as powerful, as on the first days when there was light upon the earth, so that he could not turn his pencil this way or that, but these forms came upon the paper as easily as plants from the soil where the fit seed falls,—at Raphael, who seemed to develop at once in his mind the germ of all possible images, so that shapes flowed from his hand plenteous and facile as drops of water from the open sluice, we see that the presence of the highest genius makes all mediums alike transparent, and that the advantages of one over the other respect only the more or less rapid growth of the artist, and the more or less lively effect on the mind of the beholder. All high art says but one thing; but this is said with more or less pleasure by the artist, felt with more or less pleasure by the beholder, according to the flexibility and fulness of the language.

As Bombet's lives of Haydn and Mozart are accessible here through an American edition, I shall not speak of these masters with as much particularity as of the three other artists. Bombet's book, though superficial, and in its attempts at criticism totally wanting in that precision which can only be given by a philosophical view of the subject, is lively, informed by a true love for beauty, and free from exaggeration as to the traits of life which we most care for. The life of Haydn is the better of the two, for the calm and equable character of this great man made not much demand on insight. It displays throughout the natural decorum and freedom from servile and conventional restraints, the mingling of dignity and tenderness, the singleness of aim, and childlike simplicity in action proper to the artist life. It flowed a gentle, bounteous river, broadening ever beneath the smiles of a "calm pouring sun." A manly uniformity makes his life intelligible alike to the genius and the citizen. Set the picture in its proper frame, and we think of him with great pleasure, sitting down nicely dressed, with the diamond on his finger given him by the King of Prussia, to compose the Creation, or the Seven Words. His life was never little, never vehement, and an early calm hallowed the gush of his thoughts. We have no regret, no cavil, little thought for this life of Haydn. It is simply the fitting vestibule to the temple of his works.

The healthy energy of his nature is well characterized by what is said of his "obstinate joy,"

"The magic of his style seems to me to consist in a predominating character of liberty and joy. This joy of Haydn is a perfectly natural, pure, and continual exaltation; it reigns in the *allegros*, it is perceptible even in the grave parts, and pervades the *andantes* in a sensible degree

"In these compositions, where it is evident from the rhythm, the tone, and the general character, that the author intends to inspire melancholy, this obstinate joy, being unable to show itself openly, is transformed into energy and strength. Observe, this sombre gravity is not pain; it is joy constrained to disguise itself which might be called the concentrated joy of a savage; but never sadness, dejection, or melancholy. Haydn has never been really melancholy more than two or three times; in a verse of his *Stabat Mater*, and in two of the adagios of the *Seven Words*.

"This is the reason why he has never excelled in dramatic music. Without melancholy, there can be no impassioned music."

All the traits of Haydn's course, his voluntary servitude to Porpora, his gratitude shown at so dear a rate to his Mæcenas, the wig-maker, his easy accommodation to the whims of the Esterhazies, and his wise views of the advantage derived to his talent from being forced to compose nightly a fresh piece for the baryton of Prince Nicholas, the economy of his time, and content with limited means, each and all show the man moderate because so rich, modest because so clear-sighted, robust, ample, nobly earnest, rather than fiery and aspiring. It is a great character, one that does not rouse us to ardent admiration, but always commands, never disappoints. Bombet compares him in his works to Ariosto, and the whole structure of his character reminds us of the "Ariosto of the North," Walter Scott. Both are examples of that steady and harmonious action of the faculties all through life, so generally supposed inconsistent with gifts like theirs; both exhibit a soil fertile from the bounties of its native forests, and unaided by volcanic action.

The following passage is (to say nothing of its humor) very significant on the topic so often in controversy, as to whether the descriptive powers of music are of the objective or subjective character.

Of an opera, composed by Haydn to Curtz's order, at the age of nineteen—

"Haydn often says, that he had more trouble in finding out a mode of representing the waves in a tempest in this opera, than he afterwards had in writing fugues with a double subject. Curtz, who had spirit and taste, was difficult to please; but there was also another obstacle. Neither of the two authors had ever seen either sea or storm. How can a man describe what he knows nothing about? If this happy art could be discovered, many of our great politicians would talk better about virtue. Curtz, all agitation, paced up and down the room, where the composer was seated at the piano forte. 'Imagine,' said he, 'a mountain rising, and then a valley sinking; and then another mountain, and then another valley; the mountains and the valleys follow one after another, with rapidity, and at every moment, alps and abysses succeed each other.'

"This fine description was of no avail. In vain did harlequin add the thunder and lightning. 'Come describe for me all these horrors,' he repeated incessantly, 'but particularly represent distinctly these mountains and valleys.'

"Haydn drew his fingers rapidly over the key board, ran through the semitones, tried abundance of *sevenths*, passed from the lowest notes of the bass to the highest of the treble. Curtz was still dissatisfied. At last, the young man, out of all patience, extended his hands to the two ends of the harpsichord, and, bringing them rapidly together, exclaimed 'The devil take the tempest.' 'That's it, that's it,' cried the harlequin, springing upon his neck and nearly stifling him. Haydn added, that when he crossed the Straits of Dover, in bad weather, many years afterwards, he laughed during the whole of the passage in thinking of the storm in *The Devil on two Sticks.*

"'But how,' said I to him, 'is it possible, by sounds, to describe a tempest, and that *distinctly* too? As this great man is indulgence itself, I added, that, by imitating the peculiar tones of a man in terror or despair, *an author of genius may communicate to an auditor the sensations which the sight of a storm would cause;* but,' said I, 'music can no more represent a tempest, than say 'Mr. Hadyn lives near the barrier of Schonbrunn.' 'You may be right,' replied he, 'but recollect, nevertheless, that words and especially scenery guide the imagination of the spectator.'"

Let it be an encouragement to the timidity of youthful genius to see that an eaglet like Haydn has ever groped and flown so sidewise from the aim.

In later days, though he had the usual incapacity of spontaneous genius, as to giving a reason for the faith that was in him, he had also its perfect self-reliance. He, too, would have said, when told that the free expression of a thought was contrary to rule, that he would make it a rule then, and had no reason to give why he put a phrase or note here, and thus, except "It was best so. It had the best effect so." The following anecdote exhibits in a spirited manner the contrast between the free genius and the pedant critic.

"Before Hadyn had lost his interest in conversation, he related with pleasure many anecdotes respecting his residence in London. A nobleman passionately fond of music, according to his own account, came to him one morning, and asked him to give him some lessons in counterpoint, at a guinea a lesson. Haydn, seeing that he had some knowledge of music, accepted his proposal. 'When shall we begin?' 'Immediately, if you please,' replied the nobleman; and he took out of his pocket a quartett of Haydn's. 'For the first lesson,' continued he, 'let us examine this quartett, and tell me the reason of certain modulations, and of the general management of the composition, which I cannot altogether approve, since it is contrary to the rules.'

"Haydn, a little surprised, said, that he was ready to answer his questions. The nobleman began, and, from the very first bar, found something to remark upon every note. Haydn, with whom invention was a habit, and who was the opposite of a pedant, found himself a good deal embarrassed, and replied continually, 'I did so because it has a good effect; I have placed this passage here, because I think it suitable.' The Englishman, in whose opinion these replies were nothing to the purpose, still returned to his proofs, and demonstrated very clearly, that his quartett was good for nothing. 'But, my Lord, arrange this quartett in your own way; hear it played, and you will then see which of the two is best.' 'How can yours, which is contrary to the rules be the best?' 'Because it is the most agreeable.' My Lord still returned to the subject. Haydn replied as well as he was able; but, at last, out of patience, 'I see, my Lord,' said he, 'that it is you who are so good as to give lessons to me, and I am obliged to confess, that I do not merit the honour of having such a master.' The advocate of the rules went away, and cannot to this day understand how an author, who adheres to them, should fail of producing a *Matrimonio Segreto.*"

I must in this connexion, introduce a passage from the life of Handel. "The highest effort of genius here (in music) consists in direct violations of rule. The very first answer of the fugue in the overture to Mucius Scævola affords an instance of this kind. Geminiani, the strictest observer of rule, was so charmed with this direct transgression of it, that, on hearing its effect, he cried out, *Quel semitono* (meaning the f sharp) *vale un mondo.* That semitone is worth a world."

I should exceedingly like to quote the passage on Haydn's quartetts, and the comparison between the effect produced by one of his and one of Beethoven's. But room always fails us in this little magazine. I cannot, however, omit a passage, which gave me singular pleasure, referring to Haydn's opinion of the importance of the air. For the air is the *thought* of the piece, and ought never to be disparaged from a sense of the full flow of concord.

"Who would think it? This great man, under whose authority our miserable pedants of musicians, without genius, would fain shelter themselves, repeated incessantly; 'Let your *air* be good, and your composition, whatever it be, will be so likewise, and will assuredly please.'

"'It is the soul of music,' continued he; 'it is the life, the spirit, the essence of a composition. Without this, Tartini may find out the most singular and learned chords, but nothing is heard but a labored sound; which, though it may not offend the ear, leaves the head empty and the heart cold.'"

The following passage illustrates happily the principle.

"Art is called *Art,* because it is not Nature."

"In music the best physical imitation is, perhaps, that which only just indicates its object; which shows it to us through a veil, and abstains from scrupulously representing nature exactly as she is. This kind of imitation is the perfection of the descriptive department. You are aware, my friend, that all the arts are founded to a certain degree on what is not true; an obscure doctrine, notwithstanding its apparent clearness, but from which the most important principles are derived. It is thus that from a dark grotto springs the river, which is to water vast provinces. You have more pleasure in seeing a beautiful picture of the garden of the Tuilleries, than in beholding the same garden, faithfully reflected from one of the mirrors of the chateau; yet the scene displayed in the mirror has far more variety of colouring than the painting, were it the work of Claude Lorraine; the figures have motion; everything is more true to nature; still you cannot help preferring the picture. A skilful artist never departs from that degree of falsity which is allowed in the art he professes. He is well aware, that it is not by imitating nature to such a degree as to produce deception, that the arts give pleasure; he makes a distinction between those accurate daubs, called eye-traps, and the St. Cecilia of Raphael. Imitation should produce the effect which the object imitated would have upon us, did it strike us in those fortunate moments of sensibility and enjoyment, which awaken the passions."

The fault of this passage consists in the inaccurate use of the words *true* and *false*. Bombet feels distinctly that truth to the ideal is and must be above truth to the actual; it is only because he feels this, that he enjoys the music of Haydn at all; and yet from habits of conformity and complaisance he well nigh mars his thought by use of the phraseology of unthinking men, who apprehend no truth beyond that of facts apparent to the senses.

Let us pass to the life of Handel. We can but glance at these great souls, each rich enough in radiating power to be the centre of a world; and can only hope to indicate, not declare, their different orbits and relations. Haydn and Mozart both looked to Handel with a religious veneration. Haydn was only unfolded to his greatest efforts after hearing, in his latest years, Handel's great compositions in England.

"One day at Prince Schwartzenberg's, when Handel's Messiah was performed, upon expressing my admiration of one of the sublime choruses of that work, Haydn said to me thoughtfully, *This man is the father of us all.*

"I am convinced, that, if he had not studied Handel, he would never have written the *Creation ;* his genius was fired by that of this master. It was remarked by every one here, that, after his return from London, there was more grandeur in his ideas; in short, he approached, as far as is permitted to human genius, the unattainable object of his songs. Handel is simple; his accompaniments are written in three parts only; but, to use a Neapolitan phrase of Gluck's, *There is not a note that does not draw blood.*"—Bombet, p. 180.

"Mozart most esteemed Porpora, Durante, Leo, and Alessandro Scarlatti, but he placed Handel above them all. He knew the principal works of that great master by heart. He was accustomed to say, Handel knows best of all of us what is capable of producing a great effect. When he chooses, he strikes like the thunderbolt."—Ibid. p. 291.

Both these expressions, that of Gluck and that of Mozart, happily characterize Handel in the vigor and grasp of his genius, as Haydn, in the amplitude and sunny majesty of his career, is well compared to the gazing, soaring eagle.

I must insert other beautiful tributes to the genius of Handel.

After the quarrel between Handel and many of the English nobles, which led to their setting up an opera in opposition to his, they sent to engage Hasse and Porpora, as their composers. When Hasse was invited over, the first question he asked was, whether Handel was dead. Being answered in the negative, he long refused to come, thinking it impossible that a nation, which might claim the benefit of Handel's genius, could ask aid from any other.

When Handel was in Italy, Scarlatti saw him first at the carnival, playing on the harpsichord, in his mask. Scarlatti immediately affirmed it could be none but the famous Saxon or the devil.

Scarlatti, pursuing the acquaintance, tried Handel's powers in every way.

"When they came to the organ, not a doubt remained as to which the preference belonged. Scarlatti himself declared the superiority of his antagonist, and owned that until he had heard him upon this instrument, he had no conception of his powers. So greatly was he struck with his peculiar way of playing, that he followed him all over Italy, and was never so happy as when he was with him. And ever afterwards, Scarlatti, as often as he was admired for his own great execution, would mention Handel, and cross himself in token of veneration."—*Life of Handel.*

These noble rivalries, this tender enthusiastic conviction of the superiority of another, this religious

—" joy to feel
A foeman worthy of our steel,"

one instance of which delights us more than all the lonely achievements of intellect, as showing the twofold aspect of the soul, and linking every nature, generous enough for sympathy, in the golden chain, which upholds the earth and the heavens, are found everywhere in the history of high genius. Only the little men of mere talent deserve a place at Le Sage's supper of the authors. Genius cannot be forever on the wing; it craves a home, a holy land; it carries reliquaries in the bosom; it craves cordial draughts from the goblets of other pilgrims. It is always pious, always chivalric; the artist, like the Preux, throws down his shield to embrace the antagonist, who has been able to pierce it; and the greater the genius, the more do we glow with delight at his power of feeling,—need of feeling reverence not only for the creative soul, but for its manifestation through fellow men. What melody of Beethoven's is more melodious, than his letter of regal devotion to Cherubini, or the transports with which he calls out on first hearing the compositions of Schubert; "Wahrlich in dem Schubert wohnt ein göttlicher Funke." Truly in Schubert dwells a divine fire.*

But to return to Handel. The only biography of him I have

* As Schubert's music begins to be known among ourselves, it may be interesting to record the names of those songs, which so affected Beethoven. They are Ossian's Gesange, Die Burgschaft, Die junge Nonne, and Die Grenze der Menschheit.

seen is a little volume from the library of the University at Cambridge, as brief, and, in the opinion of the friend who brought it to me, as dry and scanty as possible. I did not find it so. It is written with the greatest simplicity, in the style of the days of Addison and Steele ; and its limited technology contrasts strongly with the brilliancy of statement and infinite "*nuances*" of the present style of writing on such subjects. But the writer is free from exaggeration, without being timid or cold ; and he brings to his work the requisites of a true feeling of the genius of Handel, and sympathy with his personal character. This lies, indeed, so deep, that it never occurs to him to give it distinct expression ; it is only implied in his selection, as judicious as simple, of anecdotes to illustrate it.

For myself, I like a dry book, such as is written by men who give themselves somewhat tamely to the task in hand. I like to read a book written by one who had no higher object than mere curiosity, or affectionate sympathy, and never draws an inference. Then I am sure of the facts more nakedly true, than when the writer has any theory of his own, and have the excitement all the way of putting them into new relations. The present is the gentle, faithful narrative of a private friend. He does not give his name, nor pretend to anything more than a slight essay towards giving an account of so great a phenomenon as Handel.

The vigour, the ready decision, and independence of Handel's character are displayed in almost every trait of his youthful years. At seven years old he appears as if really inspired by a guardian genius. His father was going to Weissenfels, to visit an elder son, established at court there. He refused to take the little Handel, thinking it would be too much trouble. The boy, finding tears and entreaties of no avail, stole out and followed the carriage on foot. When his father perceived him persist in this, he could resist no longer, but took him into the carriage and carried him to Weissenfels. There the Duke, hearing him play by accident in the chapel, and finding it was but a little child, who had been obliged too to cultivate his talent by stealth, in opposition to the wishes of his father, interfered, and removed all obstruction from the course of his destiny.

Like all the great musicians he was precocious. This necessarily results from the more than usually delicate organization they must possess, though, fortunately for the art, none but Mozart has burnt so early with that resplendence that prematurely exhausted his lamp of life. At nine years of age Handel composed in rule, and played admirably on more than one instrument. At fifteen he insisted on playing the first harpsichord at the Hamburg opera house, and again his guardian genius interfered in a manner equally picturesque and peculiar.

"The elder candidate was not unfit for the office, and insisted on the right of succession. Handel seemed to have no plea, but that of natural superiority, of which he was conscious, and from which he would not recede."

Parties ran high; the one side unwilling that a boy should arrogate a place above a much older man, one who had a prior right to the place, the other maintaining that the opera-house could not afford to lose so great a composer as Handel gave promise of becoming, for a punctilio of this kind. Handel at last obtained the place.

"Determined to make Handel pay dear for his priority, his rival stifled his rage for the present, only to wait an opportunity of giving it full vent. One day, as they were coming out of the orchestra, he made a push at Handel with a sword, which being aimed full at his heart, would forever have removed him from the office he had usurped, but for the friendly score which he accidentally carried in his bosom, and through which to have forced the weapon would have demanded the might of Ajax himself. Had this happened in the early ages, not a mortal but would have been persuaded that Apollo himself had interfered to preserve him, in the shape of a music-book."

The same guardian demon presided always over his outward fortunes. His life, like that of Haydn, was one of prosperity. The only serious check he ever experienced (at a very late day in England) was only so great as to stimulate his genius to manifest itself by a still higher order of efforts, than before (his oratorios.) And these were not only worthy of his highest aspirations, but successful with the public of his own day.

It is by no means the case in the arts, that genius must not expect sympathy from its contemporaries. Its history shows it in many instances, answering as much as prophesying. And Haydn, Handel, and Mozart seemed to culminate to a star-gazing generation.

While yet in his teens, Handel met the Grand Duke of Tuscany, who was very desirous to send him to Italy, at his own expense, that he might study the Italian music in its native land. "But he refused to accept the Duke's offer, though determined to go as soon as he could make up a privy purse for the purpose. And this noble independency he preserved through life," and we may add the twin sister, liberality, for we find scattered through his life numerous instances of a wise and princely beneficence.

When he at last went to Italy, he staid six years, a period of inestimable benefit to his growth. I pause with delight at this rare instance of a mind obtaining the food it craves, just at the time it craves it. The *too early* and *too late*, which prevent so many "trees from growing up into the heavens," withered no hour of Handel's life. True, the compensating principle showed itself in his regard, for he had neither patience nor fortitude, which the usual training might have given. But it seems as if what the man lost, the genius gained, and we cannot be displeased at the exception which proves the rule.

The Italians received him with that affectionate enthusiasm, which they show as much towards foreign as native talent. The magnanimous delight with which they greeted West, and, as it is said, now greet our countryman Powers, which not many years since made their halls resound with the cry, "there is no tenor like Braham," was heard in shouts of "Viva il caro Sassone!" at every new composition given by Handel on their stage. The people followed him with rapture; the nobles had musical festivals prepared in his honour; Scarlatti's beautiful homage has been mentioned above; and the celebrated Corelli displayed the same modest and noble deference to his instructions. He too, addressed him as "*Caro Sassone.*"

A charming anecdote of Corelli is not irrelevant here.

"A little incident relating to Corelli shows his character so strongly, that I shall be excused for reciting it, though foreign to our present purpose. He was requested one evening to play, to a large and polite company, a fine solo which he had lately composed. Just as he was in the midst of his performance, some of the number began to discourse together a little unseasonably; Corelli gently lays down his instrument. Being asked whether anything was the matter with him; nothing, he replied, he was only afraid that he interrupted the conversation, The elegant propriety of this silent censure, joined with his genteel and good-humoured answer, afforded great pleasure, even to the persons who occasioned it. They begged him to resume his instrument, assuring him at the same time, that he might depend on all the attention which the occasion required, and which his merit ought before to have commanded."—*Life of Handel.*

His six years' residence in Italy educated Handel's genius into a certainty, vigour and command of resources that made his after career one track of light. The forty years of after life are one continued triumph, a showering down of life and joy on an expectant world.

Although Germany offered every encouragement both from people and princes, England suited him best, and became the birthplace of his greatest works. For nine years after he began to conduct the opera-house, his success with the public and happiness in his creative life appears to have been perfect. Then he came for brief space amid the breakers. It is, indeed, rather wonderful that he kept peace so long with those most refractory subjects, the singers, than that it should fail at last. Fail at last it did! Handel was peremptory in his requisitions, the singing-birds obstinate in their disobedience; the public divided, and the majority went against Handel. The following little recital of one of his many difficulties, with his prima-donnas, exhibits his character with amusing fidelity.

"Having one day some words with Cuzzoni on her refusing to sing *Cara Immagine* in *Ottone*, 'Oh Madame,' said he, 'je sais bien que vous êtes une veritable Diable, mais je vous ferai sçavoir, moi, que je suis Beelzebub le *Chef* des diables.' With this he took her up by the waist, swearing that, if she made any more words, he would fling her out of the window. It is to be noted, (adds the biographer with Counsellor Pleydel-like facetiousness,) that this was formerly one of the methods of executing criminals in Germany, a process not unlike that of the Tarpeian rock, and probably derived from it."—*Life of Handel.*

Senesino, too, was one of Handel's malcontent aids, the same of whom the famous anecdote is told, thus given in the Life of Haydn.

"Senesino was to perform on a London theatre the character of a tyrant, in I know not what opera; the celebrated Farinelli sustained that of an oppressed prince. Farinelli, who had been giving concerts in the country, arrived only a few hours before the representation, and the unfortunate hero and the cruel tyrant saw one another for the first time on the stage. When Farinelli came to his first air, in which he supplicates for mercy, he sung it with such sweetness and expression, that the poor tyrant, totally forgetting himself, threw himself upon his neck and repeatedly embraced him."

The refined sensibility and power of free abandonment to the life of the moment, displayed in this anecdote, had made Senesino the darling, the spoiled child of the public, so that they were ungrateful to their great father, Handel. But he could not bow to the breeze. He began life anew at the risk of the wealth he had already acquired, and these difficulties only urged him to new efforts. The Oratorio dawned upon his stimulated mind, and we may, perhaps, thank the humours of Senesino and Faustina for the existence of the Messiah.

The oratorios were not brought forward without opposition. That part of the public, which in all ages, walks in clogs on the green-sward, and prefers a candle to the sun, which accused Socrates of impiety, denounced the Tartuffe of Moliere as irreligious, which furnishes largely the Oxford press in England, and rings its little alarm bell among ourselves at every profound and universal statement of religious experience, was exceedingly distressed, that Handel should profane the details of biblical history by wedding them to his God-given harmonies. Religion, they cried, was lost; she must be degraded, familiarized; she would no longer speak with authority after she had been sung. But, happily, owls hoot in vain in the ear of him whose soul is possessed by the muse, and Handel, like all the great, could not even understand the meaning of these petty cavils. Genius is fearless; she never fancies herself wiser than God, as prudence does. She is faithful, for she has been trusted, and feels the presence of God in herself too clearly to doubt his government of the world.

Handel's great exertions at this period brought on an attack of paralysis, which he cured by a course that shows his untamed, powerful nature, and illustrates in a homely way the saying, Fortune favors the brave.

Like Tasso, and other such fervid and sanguine persons, if he could at last be persuaded to use a remedy for any sickness, he always overdid the matter. As for this palsied arm,—

" It was thought best for him to have recourse to the vapor baths at Aix-la-Chapelle, over which he sat three times as long as hath ever been the practice. Whoever knows anything of the nature of these baths, will, from this instance, form some idea of his surprising constitution. His sweats were profuse beyond what can well be imagined. His cure, from the manner as well as the quickness with which it was wrought, passed with the nuns for a miracle. When, but a few hours from the time of his leaving the bath, they heard him at the organ in the principal church, as well as convent, playing in a manner so much beyond what they had ever heard or even imagined, it is not wonderful, that they should suppose the interposition of a higher power."

He remained, however, some weeks longer at the baths to confirm the cure, thus suddenly effected by means that would have destroyed a frame of less strength and energy. The more cruel ill of blindness fell upon his latest years, but he had already run an Olympian course, and could sit still with the palm and oak crowns upon his brows.

Handel is a Greek in the fullness and summer glow of his nature, in his directness of action and unrepentant steadfastness. I think also with a pleasure, in which I can hardly expect sympathy, since even his simple biographer shrinks from it with the air of "a person of quality," on the fact that he was fond of good eating, and also ate a great deal. As he was neither epicure nor gourmand, I not only accept the excuse of the biographer, that a person of his choleric nature, vast industry and energy, needed a great deal of sustenance; but it seems to me perfectly in character for one of his large heroic mould. I am aware that these are total abstinence days, especially in the regions of art and romance; but the Greeks were wiser and more beautiful, if less delicate than we; and I am strongly reminded by all that is said of Handel, of a picture painted in their golden age. The subject was Hercules at the court of Admetus; in the background handmaids are mourning round the corpse of the devoted Alceste, while in the foreground the son of Jove is satisfying what seem to his attendants an interminable hunger. They are heaping baskets, filling cans, toiling up the stairs with huge joints of meat; the hero snaps his fingers, impatient for the new course, though many an empty trencher bears traces of what he has already devoured. For why; a journey to Tartarus and conquest of gloomy Dis would hardly, in the natural state of society, be undertaken on a biscuit and a glass of lemonade. And when England was yet fresh from her grand revolution, and John Bull still cordially enjoyed his yule logs and Christmas feasts, "glorious John Dryden" was not ashamed to write thus of the heroes,—

"And when the *rage of hunger* was appeased."

Then a man was not ashamed of being not only a man in mind, but every inch a man. And Handel surely did not neglect to labour after he had feasted. Beautiful are the upward tending, slender stemmed plants! Not less beautiful and longer lived, those of stronger root, more powerful trunk, more spreading branches! Let each be true to his law; concord, not monotony, is music. We thank thee, Nature, for Handel, we thank thee for Mozart! Yet one story from the Life of Handel ere we pass on. It must interest all who have observed the same phenomenon of a person exquisitely alive to the music of verse, stupified and bewildered by other music.

"Pope often met Handel at the Earl of Burlington's. One day after Handel had played some of the finest things he ever composed, Mr. Pope declared that they gave him no sort of pleasure; that his ears were of that untoward make, and reprobate cast, as to receive his music, which he was persuaded was the best that could be, with as much indifference as the airs of a common ballad. A person of his excellent understanding, it is hard to suspect of affectation. And yet it is as hard to conceive how an ear, so perfectly attentive to all the delicacies of rhythm and poetical numbers, should be totally insensible to the charm of musical sounds. An attentiveness, too, which was as discernible in his manner of reading, as it is in his method of writing."—*Life of Handel.*

The principal facts of that apparition which bore the name of Mozart, are well known. His precocious development was far more precocious than that of any other artist on record. (And here let us observe another correspondence between music and mathematics, that is, the early prodigies in childish form, which seem to say that neither the art nor the science requires the slow care of the gardener, Experience, but are plants indigenous to the soil, which need only air and light to lure them up to majestic stature.) Connected with this is his exquisite delicacy of organization, unparalleled save in the history of the fairy Fine Ear, so that at six years old he perceived a change of half a quarter of a note in the tuning of a violin, and fainted always at sound of the trumpet. The wonderful exploits which this accurate perception of and memory for sounds enabled him to perform, are known to every one, but I could read the story a hundred times yet, so great is its childish beauty. Again, allied with this are his extreme tenderness and loving nature. In this life (Schlichtegroll's, translated by Bombet) it is mentioned, "He would say ten times a day to those about him, 'Do you love me well?' and whenever in jest they said 'No,' the tears would roll down his cheeks." I remember to have read elsewhere an anecdote of the same engaging character. "One day, when Mozart, (then in his seventh year,) was entering the presence chamber of the empress, he fell and hurt himself. The other young princesses laughed, but Marie Antoinette took him up, and consoled him with many caresses. The little Mozart said to her, "You are good; I will marry you." Well for the lovely princess, if common men could have met and understood her lively and genial nature as genius could, in its childlike need of love.

With this great desire for sympathy in the affections was linked, as by nature it should be, an entire self-reliance in action. Mozart knew nothing but music; on that the whole life of his soul was shed, but there he was as unerring and undoubting, as fertile and aspiring.

"At six years of age, sitting down to play in presence of the emperor Francis, he addressed himself to his majesty and asked; 'Is not M. Wagenseil here? We must send for *him; he* understands the thing.'

The emperor sent for Wagenseil, and gave up his place to him by the side of the piano. 'Sir,' said Mozart to the composer, 'I am going to play one of your concertos ; you must turn over the leaves for me.' The emperor said, in jest, to the little Wolfgang ; 'It is not very difficult to play with all one's fingers, but to play with only one, without seeing the keys, would indeed be extraordinary.' Without manifesting the least surprise at this strange proposal, the child immediately began to play with a single finger, and with the greatest possible precision and clearness. He afterwards desired them to cover the keys of the piano, and continued to play in the same manner, as if he had long practiced it.

From his most tender age, Mozart, animated with the true feeling of his art, was never vain of the compliments paid him by the great. He only performed insignificant trifles when he had to do with people unacquainted with music. He played, on the contrary, with all the fire and attention of which he was capable, when in the presence of connoisseurs ; and his father was often obliged to have recourse to artifice, in order to make the great men, before whom he was to exhibit, pass for such with him."

Here, in childlike soft unconsciousness, Mozart acts the same part that Beethoven did, with cold imperial sarcasm, when the Allied Sovereigns were presented to him at Vienna. "I held myself 'vornehm,'" said Beethoven, that is, treated them with dignified affability ; and his smile is one of saturnine hauteur, as he says it ; for the nature, so deeply glowing towards man, was coldly disdainful to those who would be more than men, merely by the aid of money and trappings. Mozart's attitude is the lovelier and more simple ; but Beethoven's lion tread and shake of the mane are grand too.

The following anecdote shows, that Mozart (rare praise is this) was not less dignified and clear-sighted as a man than in his early childhood.

"The Italians at the court of the Emperor, Joseph the Second, spoke of Mozart's first essays (when he was appointed chapel-master) with more jealousy than fairness, and the emperor, who scarcely ever judged for him self, was easily carried away by their decisions. One day after hearing the rehearsal of a comic opera, which he had himself demanded of Mozart, he said to the composer, 'My dear Mozart, that is too fine for my ears; there are too many notes there.' 'I ask your majesty's pardon,' replied Mozart, dryly; 'there are just as many notes as there should be.' The emperor said nothing, and appeared rather embarrassed by the reply; but when the opera was performed, he bestowed on it the greatest encomiums."

This anecdote certainly shows Joseph the Second to be not a mean man, if neither a sage nor a connoisseur.

Read in connexion with the foregoing, the traits recorded of the artist during his wife's illness, (Life of Mozart, p. 309,) and you have a sketch of a most beautiful character.

Combined with this melting sweetness, and extreme delicacy, was a prophetic energy of deep-seated fire in his genius. He inspires while he overwhelms you. The vigour, the tenderness, and far-reaching ken of his conceptions, were seconded by a range, a readiness, and flexibility in his talents for expression, which can only be told by the hackneyed comparison between him and Raphael. A life of such unceasing flow and pathetic earnestness must at any rate have early exhausted the bodily energies. But the high-strung nerves of Mozart made him excessive alike in his fondness for pleasure, and in the melancholy which was its reaction. His life was too eager and keen to last. The gift of presentiment, as much developed in his private history as in his works, offers a most interesting study to the philosophic observer, but one of too wide a scope for any discussion here.

I shall not speak of Mozart as a whole man, for he was not so; but rather the exquisite organ of a divine inspiration. He scarcely took root on the soil; not knowing common purposes, cares, or discretions, his life was all crowded with creative efforts, and vehement pleasures, or tender feelings between. His private character was that of a child, as ever he loved to be stimulated to compose by having fairy tales told to him by the voice of affection. And when we consider how any art tends to usurp the whole of a man's existence, and music most of all to unfit for other modes of life, both from its stimulus to the senses and exaltation of the soul, we have rather reason to wonder that the other four great ones lived severe and manlike lives, than that this remained a voluptuary and a fair child. The virtues of a child he had,—sincerity, tenderness, generosity, and reverence. In the generosity with which he gave away the precious works of his genius, and the princely sweetness with which he conferred these favours, we are again reminded of Raphael. There are equally fine anecdotes of Haydn's value for him, and his for Haydn. Haydn answered the critics of "Don Giovanni," "I am not a judge of the dispute; all that I know is, that Mozart is the greatest composer now existing." Mozart answered the critic on Haydn, "Sir, if you and I were both melted down together, we should not furnish materials for one Haydn."

Richard Cœur de Lion and Saladin!

We never hear the music of Mozart to advantage, yet no one can be a stranger to the character of his melodies. The idea charms me of a symbolical correspondence, not only between the soul of man and the productions of nature, but of a like harmony, pervading every invention of his own. It seems he has not only "builded better than he knew," when following out the impulse of his genius, but in every mechanical invention, so that all the furniture of man's life is necessarily but an aftergrowth of nature. It seems clear that not only every hue, every gem, every flower, every tree, has its correspondent species in the race of man, but the same may be said of instruments, as obviously of the telescope, microscope, compass. It is clearly the case with the musical instruments. As a child I at once thought of Mozart as the Flute, and to this day, cannot think of one without the other. Nothing ever occurred to confirm this fancy, till a year or two since, in the book now before me, I found with delight the following passage.

" The most remarkable circumstance in his music, independently of the genius displayed in it, is the novel way in which he employs the orchestra, especially the wind instruments. He draws surprising effect from *the flute*, an instrument of which Cimarosa hardly ever made any use "

Ere bidding adieu to Mozart, to whom I have only turned your eyes, as the fowler directs those of the by-standers to the bird glancing through the heavens, which he had not skill to bring down, and consoles himself with thinking the fair bird shows truer, if farther, on the wing, I will insert three sonnets, so far interesting as showing the degree of truth with which these objects appear to one, who has enjoyed few opportunities of hearing the great masters, and is only fitted to receive them by a sincere love of music, which caused a rejection of the counterfeits that have been current among us. They date some years back, and want that distinctness of expression, so attainable to-day ; but, if unaided by acquaintance with criticism on these subjects, have therefore the merit of being a pure New England growth, and deserve recording like Sigismund Biederman's comparison of Queen Margaret to his favourite of the Swiss pasture. " The queen is a stately creature. The chief cow of the herd, who carries the bouquets and garlands to the chalet, has not a statelier pace."—*Anne of Geierstein.*

INSTRUMENTAL MUSIC.

The charms of melody, in simple airs,
By human voices sung, are always felt ;
With thoughts responsive, careless hearers melt,
Of secret ills, which our frail nature bears.
We listen, weep, forget. But when the throng
Of a great Master's thoughts, above the reach
Of words or colors, wire and wood can teach

By laws which to the spirit-world belong,—
When several parts, to tell one mood combined,
Flash meaning on us we can ne'er express,
Giving to matter subtlest powers of Mind,
Superior joys attentive souls confess.
The harmony which suns and stars obey,
Blesses our earth-bound state with visions of supernal day.

BEETHOVEN.

Most intellectual master of the art,
Which, best of all, teaches the mind of man
The universe in all its varied plan,—
What strangely mingled thoughts thy strains impart!
Here the faint tenor thrills the inmost heart,
There the rich bass the Reason's balance shows;
Here breathes the softest sigh that Love e'er knows;
There sudden fancies, seeming without chart,
Float into wildest breezy interludes;
The past is all forgot,—hopes sweetly breathe,
And our whole being glows,—when lo! beneath
The flowery brink, Despair's deep sob concludes!
Startled, we strive to free us from the chain,—
Notes of high triumph swell, and we are thine again!

MOZART.

If to the intellect and passions strong
Beethoven speak, with such resistless power,
Making us share the full creative hour,
When his wand fixed wild Fancy's mystic throng,
Oh nature's finest lyre! to thee belong
The deepest, softest tones of tenderness,
Whose purity the listening angels bless,
With silvery clearness of seraphic song.
Sad are those chords, oh, heavenward striving soul!
A love, which never found its home on earth,
Pensively vibrates, even in thy mirth,
And gentle laws thy lightest notes control;
Yet dear that sadness! Spheral concords felt
Purify most those hearts which most they melt.

We have spoken of the widely varying, commanding, yet, bright and equable life of Haydn; of the victorious procession, and regal Alexandrine aspect of Handel; of the tender, beloved, overflowing, all too intense life of Mozart. They are all great and beautiful; look at them from what side you will, the foot stands firm, the mantle falls in wide and noble folds, and the eye flashes divine truths. But now we come to a figure still more Roman, John Sebastian Bach, all whose names we give to distinguish him from a whole family of geniuses, a race through which musical inspiration had been transmitted, without a break, for six generations; nor did it utterly fail, after coming to its full flower in John Sebastian; his sons, though not equal to their father, were not unworthy their hereditary honours.

The life of Bach which I have before me, (translated from the German of J. N. Forkel, author also of the "Complete History of Music,") is by far the best of any of these records. It is exceedingly brief and simple, very bare of facts, but the wise, quiet enthusiasm of its tone, and the delicate discrimination of the remarks on the genius of Bach, bring us quite home to him and his artist-life. Bach certainly shines too lonely in the sky of his critic, who has lived in and by him, till he cannot see other souls in their due places, but would interrupt all hymns to other deities with "Great is Diana of the Ephesians!" But his worship is true to the object, if false to the All, and the pure reverence of his dependence has made him fit to reproduce the genius which has fed his inmost life. All greatness should enfranchise its admirers, first from all other dominions, and then from its own. We cannot but think that Forkel has seen, since writing this book, that he deified Bach too exclusively, but he can never feel the shame of blind or weak obsequiousness. His, if idolatry, was yet in the spirit of true religion.

The following extract from the preface, gives an idea of the spirit in which the whole book is written.

"How do I wish I were able to describe, according to its merit, the sublime genius of this first of all artists, whether German or foreign! After the honour of being so great an artist, so preëminent above all as he was, there is perhaps no greater than that of being able duly to appreciate so entirely perfect an art, and to speak of it with judgment. He who can do the last, must have a mind not wholly uncongenial to that of the artist himself, and has therefore, in some measure, the flattering probability in his favour, that he might perhaps have been capable of the first, if similar external relations had led him into the proper career. But I am not so presumptuous as to believe, that I could ever attain to such an honour. I am, on the contrary, thoroughly convinced, that no language in the world is rich enough to express all that might and should be said of the astonishing extent of such a genius. The more intimately we are acquainted with it, the more does our admiration increase. All our eulogiums, praises, and admiration, will always be, and remain no more than well-meant prattle. Whoever has had an opportunity of comparing together the works of art, of several centuries, will not find this declaration exaggerated ; he will rather have adopted the opinion, that Bach's works cannot be spoken of, by him who is fully acquainted with them, except with rapture, and some of them even with a kind of sacred awe. We may indeed conceive and explain his management of the internal mechanism of the art; but how he contrived at the same time to inspire into this mechanic art, which he alone has attained in such high perfection, the living spirit which so powerfully attaches us even in his smallest works, will probably be always felt and admired only, but never conceived."

Of the materials for this narrative he says,

"I am indebted to the two eldest sons of J. S. Bach. I was not only personally acquainted with both, but kept up a constant correspondence with them for many years, chiefly with C. Ph. Emanuel. The world knows that they were both great artists; but it perhaps does not know that to the last moment of their lives they never spoke of their father's genius without enthusiasm and admiration. As I had from my early youth felt the same veneration for the genius of their father, it was a frequent theme of discussion with us, both in our conversations and correspondence. This made me by degrees so acquainted with everything relative to J. S. Bach's life, genius, and works, that I may now hope to be able to give to the public not only some detailed, but also useful information on the subject.

"I have no other object whatever than to call the attention of the public to an undertaking, the sole aim of which is to raise a worthy monument to German art, to furnish the true artist with a gallery of the most instructive models, and to open to the friends of musical science an inexhaustible source of the sublimest enjoyment."

The deep, tender repose in the contemplation of genius, the fidelity in the details of observation, indicated in this passage, are the chief requisites of the critic. But he should never say of any object, as Forkel does, it is the greatest that ever was or ever will be, for that is limiting the infinite, and making himself a bigot, gentle and patient perhaps, but still a bigot. All are so who limit the divine within the boundaries of their present knowledge.

The founder of the Bach family (in its musical phase) was a Thuringian miller. "In his leisure hours he amused himself with his guitar, which he even took with him into the mill, and played upon it amidst all the noise and clatter." The same love of music, for its own sake, continued in the family for six generations. After enumerating the geniuses who illustrated it before the time of John Sebastian, Forkel says,

"Not only the above-mentioned, but many other able composers of the earlier generations of the family might undoubtedly have obtained much more important musical offices, as well as a more extensive reputation, and a more brilliant fortune, if they had been inclined to leave their native province, and to make themselves known in other countries. But we do not find that any one of them ever felt an inclination for such an emigration. Temperate and frugal by nature and education, they required but little to live; and the intellectual enjoyment, which their art procured them, enabled them not only to be content without the gold chains, which used at that time to be given by great men to esteemed artists, as especial marks of honour, but also without the least envy to see them worn by others, who perhaps without these chains would not have been happy."

Nothing is more pleasing than the account of the jubilee which this family had once a year. As they were a large family, and scattered about in different cities, they met once a year and had this musical festival.

"Their amusements during the time of their meeting were entirely musical. As the company wholly consisted of chanters, organists, and town musicians, who had all to do with the Church, and as it was besides a general custom to begin everything with religion, the first thing they did, when they were assembled, was to sing a hymn in chorus. From this pious commencement they proceeded to drolleries, which often made a very great contrast with it. They sang, for instance, popular songs, the contents of which are partly comic and partly licentious, all together, and extempore, but in such a manner that the several songs thus extemporized made a kind of harmony together, the words, however, in every part being different. They called this kind of extemporary chorus 'a Quodlibet,' and not only laughed heartily at it themselves, but excited an equally hearty and irresistible laughter in every body that heard them. Some persons are inclined to consider these facetiæ as the beginning of comic operettas in Germany; but such quodlibets were usual in Germany at a much earlier period. I possess myself a printed collection of them, which was published at Vienna in 1542."

In perfect harmony with what is intimated of the family, of their wise content, loving art, purely and religiously for its own sake, unallured by ambition or desire for excitement, deep and true, simple and modest in the virtues of domestic life, was the course of the greatest of them, John Sebastian. No man of whom we read has lived more simply the grand, quiet, manly life, "without haste, without rest." Its features are few, its outline large and tranquil. His youth was a steady aspiration to the place nature intended him to fill; as soon as he was in that place, his sphere of full, equable activity, he knew it, and was content. After that he was known by his fruits. As for outward occasions and honours, it was with him as always with the "Happy Warrior," who must

"In himself possess his own desire
Who *comprehends his trust*, and to the same
Keeps faithful with a singleness of aim;
And therefore does not stoop, nor lie in wait
For wealth, or honours, or for worldly state;

Whom they must follow, on whose head must fall,
Like showers of manna, if they come at all."

A pretty story of his childhood shows that he was as earnest in the attainment of excellence, as indifferent to notoriety..

" J. S. Bach was left an orphan at ten years of age, and was obliged to have recourse to an elder brother, John Christopher, who was organist at Ordruff. From him he received the first instructions in playing on the clavichord. But his inclination and talent for music must have been already very great at that time, since the pieces which his brother gave him to learn were so soon in his power, that he began with much eagerness to look out for some that were more difficult. He had observed that his brother had a book, in which were pieces by the most famous composers of the day, such as he wanted, and earnestly begged him to give it him. But it was constantly denied. His desire to possess the book was increased by the refusal, so that he at length sought means to get possession of it secretly. As it was kept in a cupboard, which had only a lattice door, and his hands were still small enough to pass through, so that he could roll up the book, which was merely stitched in paper, and draw it out, he did not long hesitate to make use of these favorable circumstances. But, for want of a candle, he could only copy it in moonlight nights; and it took six whole months before he could finish his laborious task. At length, when he thought himself safely possessed of the treasure, and intended to make good use of it in secret, his brother found it out, and took from him, without pity, the copy which had cost him so much pains; and he did not recover it till his brother's death, which took place soon after."

Without pity indeed! What a tale is told by these few words of all the child suffered from disappointment of the hopes and plans, which had been growing in his heart all those six months of secret toil; hopes and plans too, so legitimate, on which a true parent or guardian would have smiled such delighted approval! One can scarcely keep down the swelling heart at these instances of tyranny to children, far worse than the knouts and Siberia of the Russian despot, in this, that the domestic tyrant cannot be wholly forgetful of the pain he is inflicting, though he may be too stupid or too selfish to forsee the consequences of these early wrongs, through long years of mental conflict. A nature so strong and kindly as that of Bach could not be crushed in such ways. But with characters of less force the consequences are more cruel. I have known an instance of life-long injury from such an act as this. An elder brother gave a younger a book; then, as soon as the child became deeply interested in reading it, tore out two or three leaves. Years after the blood boiled, and the eyes wept bitter tears of distrust in human sympathy, at remembrance of this little act of wanton wrong. And the conduct of Bach's brother is more coldly cruel.

The facts of his life are simple. Soon his great abilities displayed themselves, so as to win for him all that he asked from life, a moderate competency, a home, and a situation in which he could cultivate his talents with uninterrupted perseverance. A silent happiness lit up his days, deliberately, early he grew to giant stature, deeply honoured wherever known, only not more widely known because indifferent to being so. No false lure glitters on his life from any side. He was never in a hurry, nor did he ever linger on the syren shore, but passed by, like Orpheus, not even hearing their songs, so rapt was he in the hymns he was singing to the gods.

Haydn is the untouched green forest in the fulness of a June day; Handel the illuminated garden, where splendid and worldly crowds pause at times in the dark alleys, soothed and solemnized by the white moonlight; with Mozart the nightingale sings, and the lonely heron waves his wings, beside the starlit, secret lake, on whose bosom gazes the white marble temple. Bach is the towering, snowy mountain, "itself earth's Rosy Star," and the green, sunny, unasking valley, all in one. Earth and heaven are not lonely while such men live to answer to their meaning.

I had marked many passages which give a clear idea of Bach's vast intellectual comprehension, of the happy balance between the intuitive and the reasoning powers in his nature, the depth of his self-reliance, the untiring severity of his self-criticism, and the glad, yet solemn religious fulness of his mental life. But already my due limits are overstepped, and I am still more desirous to speak at some length of Beethoven. I shall content myself with two or three passages, which not only indicate the peculiar scope of this musician, but are of universal application to whatever is good in art or literature.

Bombet mentions this anecdote of Jomelli.

> " On arriving at Bologna, he went to see the celebrated Father Martini, without making himself known, and begged to be received into the number of his pupils. Martini gave him a subject for a *fugue;* and finding that he executed it in a superior manner, 'Who are you?' said he, 'are you making game of me? It is I who need to learn of you.' 'I am Jomelli, the professor, who is to write the opera to be performed here next autumn, and I am come to ask you to teach me the great art of never being embarrassed by my own ideas.' "

There seems to have been no time in Bach's life when he needed to ask this question, the great one which Genius ever asks of Friendship. He did not need to flash out into clearness in another atmosphere than his own. Always he seems the master, possessing, not possessed by, his idea. These creations did not come upon him as on the ancient prophets, dazzling, unexpected, ever flowing from the centre of the universe. He was not possessed by the muse; he had not intervals of the second sight. The thought and the symbol were one with him, and like Shakspeare, he evolved from his own centre, rather than was drawn to *the* centre. He tells the universe by living a self-centred world.

As becomes the greatest, he is not hasty, never presumptuous. We admire it in the child Mozart, that he executed at once the musical *tour de force* prepared by the Emperor Francis. We admire still more Bach's manly caution and sense of the importance of his art, when visiting, at an advanced age, the grea Frederic, who seems to have received him king-like.

"The musicians went with him from room to room, and Bach was in vited everywhere to try and to play unpremeditated compositions. Afte he had gone on for some time, he asked the King to give him a subject for a fugue, in order to execute it immediately, without any preparation. The King admired the learned manner in which his subject was thus executed extempore; and, probably to see how far such art could be carried, expressed a wish to hear a fugue with six obligato parts. But as it is not every subject that is fit for such full harmony, Bach chose one himself, and immediately executed it, to the astonishment of all present, in the same magnificent and learned manner as he had done that of the King."

The following anecdote shows the same deeply intellectual modesty and candour, and when compared with the inspired rapidity of Mozart, marks the distinction made by the French between "une savante originalité" and "une rayonnante originalité."

"He at length acquired such a high degree of facility, and, we may almost say, unlimited power over his instrument in all the modes, that there were hardly any more difficulties for him. As well in his unpremeditated fantasies, as in executing his other compositions, in which it is well known that all the fingers of both hands are constantly employed. and have to make motions which are as strange and uncommon as the melodies themselves; he is said to have possessed such certainty that he never missed a note. He had besides such an admirable facility in reading and executing the compositions of others, (which, indeed, were all easier than his own,) that he once said to an acquaintance, that he really believed he could play everything, without hesitating, at the first sight. He was, however, mistaken; and the friend, to whom he had thus expressed his opinion, convinced him of it before a week was passed. He invited him one morning to breakfast, and laid upon the desk of his instrument, among other pieces, one which at the first glance appeared to be very trifling. Bach came, and, according to his custom, went immediately to the instrument, partly to play, partly to look over the music that lay on the desk. While he was turning over and playing them, his friend went into the next room to prepare breakfast. In a few minutes, Bach got to the piece which was destined to make him change his opinion, and began to play it. But he had not proceeded far when he came to a passage at which he stopped. He looked at it, began anew, and again stopped at the same passage. 'No,' he called out to his friend, who was laughing to himself in the next room, at the same time going away from the instrument, 'one cannot play everything at first sight; it is not possible.'"

A few more extracts which speak for themselves.

"The clavichord and the organ are nearly related, but the style and mode of managing both instruments are as different as their respective destination. What sounds well, or expresses something on the clavichord, expresses nothing on the organ, and vice versa. The best player on the clavichord, if he is not duly acquainted with the difference in the destination and object of the two instruments, and does not know constantly how to keep it in view, will always be a bad performer on the organ, as indeed is usually the case. Hitherto I have met with only two exceptions. The one is John Sebastian himself, and the second his eldest son, William Friedemann. Both were elegant performers on the clavichord; but, when they came to the organ, no trace of the harpsichord player was to be perceived. Melody, harmony, motion, all was different; that is, all was adapted to the nature of the instrument and its destination. When I heard Will Friedemann on the harpsichord, all was delicate, elegant, and agreeable. When I heard him on the organ, I was seized with reverential awe. There, all was pretty, here, all was grand and solemn. The same was the case with John Sebastian, but both in a much higher degree of perfection. W. Friedemann was here but a child to his father, and he most frankly concurred in this opinion. The organ compositions of this extraordinary man are full of the expression of devotion, solemnity, and dignity; but his unpremeditated voluntaries on the organ, where nothing was lost in writing down, are said to have been still more devout, solemn, dignified, and sublime. What is it that is most essential in this art? I will say what I know; much, however, cannot be said, but must be felt."

Then after some excellent observations upon the organ, he says,

"Bach, even in his secular compositions, disdained every thing common; but in his compositions for the organ, he kept himself far more distant from it; so that here he does not appear like a man, but as a true disembodied spirit, who soars above everything mortal."

It does indeed seem, from all that is said of Bach on this score, that, as the organ was his proper instrument, and represents him, as the flute or violin might Mozart, so he that heard him on it enjoyed the sense of the true Miltonic Creation, thought too plenteous to be spoken of as rill, or stream, or fountain, but rolling and surging like a tide, marking its course by the large divisions of seas and continents.

I wish there was room to quote the fine story of the opera house at Berlin, p. 34, which shows how rapid and comprehensive was his intellectual sight in his own department; or the remarks on the nature of his harmony in that it was a multiplied melody, pp. 42, 43, or on the severe truth and dignity of his conduct to his pupils and the public, p. 76. But I must content myself with the following passages, which, beside, lose much by mutilation.

"The ideas of harmony and modulation can scarcely be separated, so nearly are they related to each other. And yet they are different. By harmony we must understand the concord or coincidence of the various parts; by modulation, their progression.

"In most composers you find that their modulation, or if you will, their harmony, advances slowly. In musical pieces to be executed by numerous performers, in large buildings, as, for example, in churches, where a loud sound can die away but slowly, this arrangement indisputably shows the prudence of a composer, who wishes to have his work produce the best possible effect. But in instrumental or chamber music, that slow progress is not a proof of prudence, but, far oftener, a sign that the composer was not sufficiently rich in ideas. Bach has distinguished this very well. In his great vocal compositions, he well knew how to repress his fancy, which, otherwise, overflowed with ideas; but, in his instrumental music this reserve was not necessary. As he, besides, never worked for the crowd, but always had in his mind his ideal of perfection, without any view to approbation or the like, he had no reason whatever for giving less than he had, and could give, and in fact he has never done this. Hence in the modulation of his instrumental works, every advance is a new thought, a constantly progressive life and motion, within the circle of the modes chosen, and those nearly related to them. Of the harmony which he adopts he retains the greatest part, but, at every advance he mingles something related to it; and in this manner he proceeds to the end of a piece, so softly, so gently, and gradually, that no leap, or harsh transition is to be felt; and yet no bar (I may almost say, no part of a bar,) is like another. With him, every transition was required to have a connexion with the preceding idea, and appears to be a necessary consequence of it. He knew not, or rather he disdained those sudden sallies, by which many composers attempt to surprise their hearers. Even in his chromatics, the advances are so soft and tender, that we scarcely perceive their distances, though often very great."

"In other departments he had rivals; but in the fugue, and all the kinds of canon and counterpoint related to it, he stands quite alone, and so alone, that all around him, is, as it were, desert and void. * * * It (his fugue) fulfils all the conditions which we are otherwise accustomed to demand, only of more free species of composition. A highly characteristic theme, an uninterrupted principal melody, wholly derived from it, and equally characteristic from the beginning to the end; not mere accompaniment in the other parts, but in each of them an independent melody, according with the others, also from the beginning to the end; freedom, lightness, and fluency in the progress of the whole, inexhaustible variety of modulation combined with perfect purity; the exclusion of every arbitrary note, not necessarily belonging to the whole; unity and diversity in the style, rhythmus, and measure; and lastly, a life diffused through the whole, so that it sometimes appears to the performer or hearer, as if every single note were animated; these are the properties of Bach's fugue,—properties which excite admiration and astonishment in every judge, who knows what a mass of intellectual energy is required for the production of such works. I must say still more. All Bach's fugues, composed in the years of his maturity, have the above-mentioned properties in common; they are all endowed with equally great excellencies, but each in a different manner. Each has his own precisely defined character; and dependent upon that, its own turns in melody and harmony. When we know and can perform *one*, we really know only *one*, and can perform but *one;* whereas we know and can play whole folios full of fugues by other composers of Bach's time, as soon as we have comprehended and rendered familiar to our hand, the turns of a single one."

He disdained any display of his powers. If they were made obvious otherwise than in the beauty and fullness of what was produced, it was in such a way as this.

"In musical parties, where quartettes or other fuller pieces of instrumental music were performed, he took pleasure in playing the tenor. With this instrument, he was, as it were, in the middle of the harmony, whence he could both hear and enjoy it, on both sides. When an opportunity offered, in such parties, he sometimes accompanied a trio or other pieces on the harpsichord. If he was in a cheerful mood, ***and knew that the composer of the piece, if present, would not take it amiss,*** he used to make extempore out of the figured bass a new trio, or of three single parts a quartette. These, however, are the only cases in which he proved to others how strong he was.

"He was fond of hearing the music of other composers. If he heard in a church a fugue for a full orchestra, and one of his two eldest sons stood near him, he always, as soon as he had heard the introduction to the theme, said beforehand what the composer ought to introduce, and what possibly might be introduced. If the composer had performed his work well, what he had said happened; then he rejoiced, and jogged his son to make him observe it."

He did not publish a work till he was forty years of age. He never laid aside the critical file through all his life, so that an edition of his works, accompanied by his own corrections, would be the finest study for the musician.

This severe ideal standard, and unwearied application in realizing it, made his whole life a progress, and the epithet *old*, which too often brings to our minds associations of indolence or decay, was for him the title of honour. It is noble and imposing when Frederic the Second says to his courtiers, "with a kind of agitation, 'Gentlemen, Old Bach has come.'"

"He laboured for himself, like every true genius; he fulfilled his own wish, satisfied his own taste, chose his subjects according to his own opinion, and lastly, derived the most pleasure from his own approbation. The applause of connoisseurs could not then fail him, and, in fact, never did fail him. How else could a real work of art be produced? The artist, who endeavours to make his works so as to suit some particular class of amateurs, either has no genius, or abuses it. To follow the prevailing taste of the many, needs, at the most, some dexterity in a very partial manner of treating tones. Artists of this description may be compared to the mechanic, who must also make his goods so that his customers can make use of them. Bach never submitted to such conditions. He thought the artist may form the public, but that the public does not form the artist."

But it would please me best, if I could print here the whole of the concluding chapter of this little book. It shows a fulness and depth of feeling, objects are seen from a high platform of culture, which make it invaluable to those of us who are groping in a denser atmosphere after the beautiful. It is a slight scroll, which implies ages of the noblest effort, and so clear a perception of laws, that its expression, if excessive in the particular, is never extravagant on the whole; a true and worthy outpouring of homage, so true that its most technical details suggest the canons by which all the various exhibitions of man's genius are to be viewed, and silences, with silver clarion tone, the barking of partial and exclusive connoisseurship. The person who should republish such a book in this country would be truly a benefactor. Both this and the Life of Handel I have seen only in the London edition. The latter is probably out of print; but the substance of it, or rather the only pregnant traits from it have been given here. This life of Bach should be read, as its great subject should be viewed, as a whole.

The entertaining memoir of Beethoven by Ries and Wegeler has been, in some measure, made known to us through the English periodicals. I have never seen the book myself. That to which I shall refer is the life of Beethoven by Schindler, to whom Beethoven confided the task of writing it, in case of the failure of another friend, whom he somewhat preferred.

Schindler, if inadequate to take an observation of his subject from any very high point of view, has the merit of simplicity, fidelity, strict accuracy according to his power of discerning, and a devout reverence both for the art, and this greatest exemplar of the art. He is one of those devout Germans who can cling for so many years to a single flower, nor feel that they have rifled all its sweets. There are in Rome, Germans who give their lives to copy the great masters in the art of painting, nor ever feel that they can get deep enough into knowledge of the beauty already produced to pass out into reproduction. They would never weary through the still night of tending the lights for the grand Mass. Schindler is of this stamp ; a patient student, most faithful, and, those of more electric natures will perhaps say, a little dull.

He is very indignant at the more sprightly sketches of Ries and Bettina Brentano. Ries, indeed, is probably inaccurate in detail, yet there is a truth in the whole impression received from him. It was in the first fervour of his youth that he knew Beethoven ; he was afterwards long separated from him ; in his book we must expect to see rather Ries, under the influence of Beethoven, than the master's self. Yet there is always deeper truth in this manifestation of life through life, if we can look at it aright, than in any attempt at an exact copy of the original. Let only the reader read poetically, and Germany *by* Madame de Staël, Wallenstein *by* Schiller, Beethoven *by* Ries, are not the less true for being inaccurate. It is the same as with the Madonna *by* Guido, or *by* Murillo.

As for Bettina, it was evident to every discerning reader that the great man never talked so ; the whole narration is overflowed with Bettina rose-colour. Schindler grimly says, the good Bettina makes him appear as a *Word Hero ;* and we cannot but for a moment share his contempt, as we admire the granite laconism of Beethoven's real style, which is beyond any other, the short hand of Genius. Yet "the good Bettina" gives us the soul of the matter. Her description of his manner of seizing a melody and then gathering together from every side all that belonged to it, and the saying, "other men are touched by something good. Artists are fiery ; they do not weep," are Beethoven's, whether he really said them or not. "You say that Shakspeare never meant to express this! What then? his genius meant it!"

The impression Schindler gives of Beethoven differs from that given by Ries or Bettina only in this, that the giant is seen through uncoloured glass; the lineaments are the same in all the three memoirs.

The direction left by Beethoven himself to his biographer is as follows. "Tell the truth with severe fidelity of me and all connected with me, without regard to whom it may hit, whether others or myself."

He was born 17th Dec. 1770. It is pleasing to the fancy to know that his mother's name was Maria Magdalena. She died when he was seventeen, so that a cabalistic number repeats itself the magical three times in the very first statement of his destiny.

The first thirty years of his life were all sunshine. His genius was early acknowledged, and princely friends enabled him to give it free play, by providing for his simple wants in daily life. Notwithstanding his uncompromising democracy, which, from the earliest period, paid no regard to rank and power, but insisted that those he met should show themselves worthy as men and citizens, before he would have anything to do with them, he was received with joy into the highest circles of Vienna. Van Swieten, the emperor's physician, one of those Germans, who, after the labors of the day, find rest in giving the whole night to music, and who was so situated that he could collect round him all that was best in the art, was one of his firmest friends. Prince and Princess Lichnowsky constituted themselves his foster-parents, and were not to be deterred from their wise and tender care by the often perverse and impetuous conduct of their adopted son, who indeed tried them severely, for he was (ein gewaltig natur) "a vehement nature," that broke through all limits and always had to run his head against a barrier, before he could be convinced of its existence. Of the princess, Beethoven says:

"With love like that of a grandmother, she sought to educate and foster me, which she carried so far as often to come near having a glass bell put over me, lest somewhat unworthy should touch or even breathe on me." Their house is described as "eine freihafen der Humanitat und feinem sitte," the home of all that is genial, noble and refined.

In these first years, the displays of his uncompromising nature affect us with delight, for they have not yet that hue of tragedy, which they assumed after he was brought more decidedly into opposition with the world. Here wildly great and free, as afterwards sternly and disdainfully so, he is, waxing or waning, still the same orb; here more fairly, there more pathetically noble.

He early took the resolution, by which he held fast through life, "against criticisms or attacks of any kind, so long as they did not touch his honour, but were aimed solely at his artist-life, never to defend himself. He was not indifferent to the opinion of the good, but ignored as much as possible the assaults of the bad, even when they went so far as to appoint him a place in the mad house." For that vein in human nature, which has flowed unexhausted ever since the days of "I am not mad, most noble Festus," making men class as magic or madness all that surpasses the range of their comprehension and culture, manifested itself in full energy among the contemporaries of Beethoven. When he published one of his greatest works, the critics declared him "*now* (in the very meridian of his genius) ripe for the mad-house." For why? "WE do not understand it; WE never had such thoughts; we cannot even read and execute them." Ah men! almost your ingratitude doth at times convince that you are wholly unworthy the visitations of the Divine!

But Beethoven "was an artist-nature;" he had his work to do, and could not stop to weep, either pitying or indignant tears. "If it amuses those people to say or to write such things of me, do not disturb them," was his maxim, to which he remained true through all the calamities of his "artist-life."

Gentleness and forbearance were virtues of which he was incapable. His spirit was deeply loving, but stern. Incapable himself of vice or meanness, he could not hope anything from men that were not so. He could not try experiments; he could not pardon. If at all dissatisfied with a man, he had done with him forever. This uncompromising temper he carried out even in his friendliest relations. The moment a man ceased to be important to him or he to the man, he left off seeing him, and they did not meet again, perhaps for twenty years. But when they *did* meet, the connexion was full and true as at first. The inconveniences of such proceedings in the conventional world are obvious, but Beethoven knew only the world of souls.

> "In man he saw only the man. Rank and wealth were to him mere accidents, to which he attached no importance. To bow before Mammon and his ministers he considered absolute blasphemy; the deepest degradation to the man who had genius for his dower. The rich man must show himself noble and beneficent, if he would be honoured by the least attention from Beethoven." "He thought that the Spirit, the Divine in man, must always maintain its preëminence over the material and temporary; that, being the immediate gift of the Creator, it obliged its possessor to go before other men as a guiding light."

How far his high feeling of responsibility, and clear sight of his own position in the universe were from arrogance, he showed always by his aversion to servile homage. He left one of his lodging houses because the people would crowd the adjacent bridge to gaze on him as he went out; another because the aristocratic proprietor, abashed before his genius, would never meet him without making so many humble reverences, as if to a domesticated god. He says, in one of the letters to Julietta, "I am persecuted by kindness, which I think I wish to deserve as little as I really do deserve it. Humility of man before man,—it pains me; and when I regard myself in connexion with the universe, what am I? and what is he whom they name Greatest? And yet there *is* the godlike in man."

"Notwithstanding the many temptations to which he was exposed, he, like each other demigod, knew how to preserve his virtue without a stain. Thus his inner sense for virtue remained ever pure, nor could he suffer anything about him of dubious aspect on the moral side. In this respect he was conscious of no error, but made his pilgrimage through life in untouched maidenly purity. The serene muse, who had so highly gifted and elected him to her own service, gave in every wise to his faculties the upward direction, and protected him, even in artistical reference, against the slightest contact with vulgarity, which, in life as in art, was to him a torture."—"Ah, had he but carried the same clearness into the business transactions of his life!"

So sighs the friend, who thinks his genius was much impeded by the transactions, in which his want of skill entangled him with sordid, contemptible persons.

Thus in unbroken purity and proud self-respect, amid princely bounties and free, manly relations, in the rapid and harmonious development of his vast powers, passed the first thirty years of his life. But towards the close of that period, crept upon him the cruel disorder, to him of all men the most cruel, which immured him a prisoner in the heart of his own kingdom, and beggared him for the rest of his life of the delights he never ceased to lavish on others.

After his fate was decided he never complained, but what lay in the secret soul is shown by the following paper.

"During the summer he lived at Heiligenstadt, by the advice of his physician, and in the autumn wrote the following testament:—

"For my brothers Carl and —— Beethoven.

"O ye men, who esteem or declare me unkind, morose, or misanthropic, what injustice you do me; you know not the secret causes of that which so seems. My heart and my mind were from childhood disposed to the tender feelings of good will. Even to perform great actions was I ever disposed. But think only that for six years this ill has been growing upon me, made worse by unwise physicians; that from year to year I have been deceived in the hope of growing better; finally constrained to the survey of this as a permanent evil, whose cure will require years, or is perhaps impossible. Born with a fiery, lively temperament, even susceptible to the distractions of society, must I early sever myself, lonely pass my life. If I attempted, in spite of my ill, intercourse with others, O how cruelly was I then repulsed by the doubly gloomy experience of my bad hearing; and yet it was not possible for me to say to men, speak louder, scream, for I am deaf! Ah, how would it be possible for me to make known the weakness of a sense which ought to be more perfect in me than in others, a sense which I once possessed in the greatest perfection, in a perfection certainly beyond most of my profession. O I cannot do it Therefore pardon, if you see me draw back when I would willingly mingle with you. My misfortune is a double woe, that through it I must be misunderstood. For me the refreshment of companionship, the finer pleasures of conversation, mutual outpourings can have no place. As an exile must I live! If I approach a company, a hot anguish falls upon me, while I fear to be put in danger of exposing my situation. So has it been this half year that I have passed in the country. The advice of my friendly physician, that I should spare my hearing, suited well my present disposition, although many times I have let myself be misled by the desire for society. But what humiliation, when some one stood near me, and from afar heard the flute, and I heard *nothing, or heard the Shepherd sing*,* and I heard nothing. Such occurrences brought me near to despair; little was wanting that I should, myself, put an end to my life. Only she, Art, she held me back! Ah! it seemed to me impossible to leave the world before I had brought to light all which lay in my mind. And so I lengthened out this miserable life, so truly miserable, as that a swift change can throw me from the best state into the worst. *Patience*, it is said, I must now take for my guide. I have so. Constant, I hope, shall my resolution be to endure till the inexorable Fates shall be pleased to break the thread. Perhaps goes it better, perhaps not, I am prepared. Already in my twenty-eighth year constrained to become a philosopher. It is not easy, for the artist harder than any other man. O God, thou lookest down upon my soul, thou knowest that love to man and inclination to well-doing dwell there. O men, when you at some future time read this, then think that you have done me injustice, and the unhappy, let

* See Ries.

him be comforted by finding one of his race, who in defiance of all hindrances of nature has done all possible to him to be received in the rank of worthy artists and men. You, my brothers, Carl and ——*, so soon as I am dead, if Professor Schmidt is yet living, pray him in my name that he will describe my disease, and add this writing to the account of it, that at least as much as possible the world may be reconciled with me after my death. At the same time I declare you two the heirs of my little property, (if I may call it so). Divide it honourably, agree, and help one another. What you have done against me has been, as you know, long since pardoned. Thee, brother Carl, I especially thank for thy lately shown attachment. My wish is that you may have a better life, freer from care than mine. Recommend to your children virtue, that alone can make happy, not gold. I speak from experience. For this it was that raised up myself from misery; this and my art I thank, that I did not end my life by my own hand. Farewell and love one another. All friends I thank, especially Prince Lichnowsky and Professor Schmidt. I wish the instruments given me by Prince L. to be preserved with care by one of you, yet let no strife arise between you on that account. So soon as they are needed for some more useful purpose, sell them. Joyful am I that even in the grave I may be of use to you. Thus with joy may I greet death; yet comes it earlier than I can unfold my artist powers, it will, notwithstanding my hard destiny, come too early, and I would wish it delayed; however I would be satisfied that it freed me from a state of endless suffering. Come when thou wilt, I go courageously to meet thee. Farewell, and forget me not wholly in death; I have deserved that you should not, for in my life I thought often of you, and of making you happy; be so.

"LUDWIG VAN BEETHOVEN.

"Heiligenstadt, 6th October, 1802."

"Postscript. 10th October, 1802.

"So take I then a sad farewell of thee. Yes! the beloved hope, which I brought hither, to be cured at least to a certain point, must now wholly leave me. As the leaves fall in autumn, are withered, so has also this withered for me. Almost as I came hither, so go I forth, even the high courage, which inspired me oft in the fair summer days, is vanished. O Providence, let once again a clear day of joy shine for me, so long already

* He seems to have forgotten at the moment the name of his younger brother.

has the inward echo of true joy been unknown to me. When, when, O God, can I feel it again in the temple of nature and of man?—Never? No! that would be too cruel!"

The deep love shown in these words, love such as only proud and strong natures know, was not only destined to be wounded in its general relations with mankind through this calamity. The woman he loved, the inspiring muse of some of his divinest compositions, to whom he writes, "Is not our love a true heavenly palace, also as firm as the fortress of heaven," was unworthy. In a world where millions of souls are pining and perishing for want of an inexhaustible fountain of love and grandeur, this soul, which was indeed such an one, could love in vain. This eldest son, this rightful heir of nature, in some secret hour, writes at this period, "Only love, that alone could give thee a happier life. O my God, let me only find at last that which may strengthen me in virtue, which to me is lawful. A love which is permitted, (erlaubt)."

The prayer was unheard. He was left lonely, unsustained, unsolaced, to wrestle with, to conquer his fate. Pierced here in the very centre of his life, exposed both by his misfortune and a nature which could neither anticipate nor contend with the designs of base men, to the anguish of meeting ingratitude on every side, abandoned to the guardianship of his wicked brothers, Beethoven walked in night, as regards the world, but within, the heavenly light ever overflowed him more and more.

Shall lesser beings repine that they do not receive their dues in this short life with such an example before them, how large the scope of eternal justice must be? Who can repine that thinks of Beethoven? His was indeed the best consolation of life. "To him a God gave to tell what he suffered," as also the deep joys of knowledge that spring from suffering. As he descends to "the divine deeps of sorrow," and calls up, with spells known only to those so initiated, forms so far more holy, radiant, and commanding than are known in regions of cheerful light, can we wish him a happier life? He has been baptized with fire, others only with water. He has given all his life and won the holy sepulchre and a fragment, at least, of the true cross. The solemn command, the mighty controul of various forces which makes us seem to hear

> "Time flowing in the middle of the night,
> And all things (rushing) to the day of doom,"

the searching through all the caverns of life for the deepest thought, and the winged uprise of feeling when it is attained; were not these wonders much aided by the calamity, which took this great genius from the outward world, and forced him to concentrate just as he had attained command of his forces?

Friendly affection, indeed, was not wanting to the great master; but who could be his equal friend? It was impossible; he might have found a love, but could not a friend in the same century with himself. But men were earnest to serve and women to venerate him. Schindler, as well as others, devoted many of the best years of life to him. A beautiful trait of affection is mentioned of the Countess Marie Erdödy, a friend dear to Beethoven, who, in the park which surrounds her Hungarian palace, erected a temple which she dedicated to him.

Beethoven had two brothers. The one, Johann, seems to have been rather stupid and selfish than actively bad. The character of his mind is best shown by his saying to the great master, "you will never *succeed* as well as I have." We have all, probably, in memory instances where the reproving angel of the family, the one whose thinking mind, grace, and purity, may possibly atone for the worthless lives of all the rest, is spoken of as the unsuccessful member, because he has not laid up treasures there where moth or rust do corrupt, and ever as we hear such remarks, we are tempted to answer by asking, "what is the news from Sodom and Gomorrah?" But the farce of *Beethoven's not succeeding* is somewhat broad, even in a world where many such sayings echo through the streets. At another time Johann, having become proprietor of a little estate, sent into Beethoven's lodging a new year card on which was written Johann van Beethoven *Gutsbesitzer*, (possessor of an estate,) to which the Master returned one inscribed Ludwig van Beethoven *Hirnbesitzer*, (possessor of a brain.) This Gutsbesitzer refused his great brother a trifling aid in his last illness, applied for by the friends who had constituted themselves his attendants, and showed towards him systematic selfishness and vulgarity of feeling. Carl, the other brother, under the mask of affectionate attention, plundered him both of his gains and the splendid presents often made him, and kept away by misrepresentations and falsehood all those who would have sincerely served him. This was the easier, in that the usual unfortunate effect of deafness of producing distrust was increased in Beethoven's case by signal instances of treachery, shown towards him in the first years of incapacity to manage his affairs as he had done before his malady. This sad distrust poisoned the rest of his life; but it was his only unworthiness; let us not dwell upon it. This brother, Carl, was Beethoven's evil genius, and his malignant influence did not cease with his life. He bequeathed to his brother the care of an only son, and Beethoven assumed the guardianship with that high feeling of the duties it involved, to be expected from one of his severe and pure temper. The first step he was obliged to take was to withdraw the boy from the society and care of his mother, an unworthy woman, under whose influence no good could be hoped from anything done for him. The law-suit, instituted for this purpose, which lasted several years, was very injurious to Beethoven's health, and effectually impeded the operations of his poetic power. For he was one "who so abhorred vice and meanness that he could not bear to hear them spoken of, much less suffer them near him; yet now was obliged to think of them, nay, carefully to collect evidence in proof of their existence, and that in the person of a near connexion." This quite poisoned the atmosphere of his ideal world, and destroyed for the time all creative glow. On account of the *van* prefixed to his name, the cause was, at first, brought before the tribunal of nobility. They called on Beethoven to show them his credentials of noble birth. "Here!" he replied, putting his hand to head and heart. But as these nobles mostly derived their titles from the head and heart of some remote ancestor, they would not recognize this new peerage, and Beethoven, with indignant surprise, found himself referred to the tribunal of the common burghers.

The lawsuit was spun out by the obstinate resistance of his sister-in-law for several years, and when Beethoven at last obtained possession of the child, the seeds of vice were already sown in his breast. An inferior man would have been more likely to eradicate them than Beethoven, because a kindred consciousness might have made him patient. But the stern Roman spirit of Beethoven could not demand less than virtue, less than excellence, from the object of his care. For the youth's sake he made innumerable sacrifices, toiled for him as he would not for himself, was lavish of all that could conduce to his true good, but imperiously demanded from him truth, honour, purity and aspiration. No tragedy is deeper than the perusal of his letters to the young man, so brief and so significant, so stern and so tender. The joy and love at every sign of goodness, the profound indignation at failure and falsehood, the power of forgiving but not of excusing, the sentiment of the true value of life, so rocky calm, that with all its height it never seems exalted, make these letters a biblical chapter in the protest of modern days against the backslidings of the multitude. The lover of man, the despiser of men, he who writes, "Recommend to your children virtue; that alone can make happy, not gold; *I speak from experience*," is fully painted in these letters.

In a lately published novel, "Night and Morning," Bulwer has well depicted the way in which a strong character overshoots its mark in the care of a weak one. The belief of Philip that his weaker brother will abide by a conviction or a promise, with the same steadfastness that he himself could; the unfavourable action of his disinterested sacrifices on the character of his charge, and the impossibility that the soft, selfish child should sympathize with the conflicts or decisions of the strong and noble mind; the undue rapidity with which Philip draws inferences, false to the subject because too large for it; all this tragedy of common life is represented with Rembrandt power of shadow in the history of Beethoven and his nephew. The ingratitude of the youth is unsurpassed, and the nature it wronged was one of the deepest capacity for suffering from the discovery of such baseness. Many years toiled on the sad drama; its catastrophe was the death of this great master, caused by the child of his love neglecting to call a physician, because he wanted to play at billiards.

His love was unworthy; his adopted child unworthy; his brothers unworthy. Yet though his misfortunes in these respects seem singular, they sprang from no chance. Here, as elsewhere, "mind and destiny are two names for one idea." His colossal step terrified those around him; they wished him away from the earth, lest he should trample down their mud-hovels; they bound him in confiding sleep, or, Judas-like, betrayed with a base kiss of fealty. His genius excited no respect in narrow minds; his entire want of discretion in the economy of life left him, they thought, their lawful prey. Yet across the dark picture shines a gleam of almost unparalleled lustre, for "she, Art, she held him up."

I will not give various instances of failure in promises from the rich and noble, piracy from publishers, nor even some details of his domestic plagues, in which he displays a breadth of humour, and stately savage sarcasm, refreshing in their place. But

I will not give any of these, nor any of his letters, because the limits forbid to give them all, and they require light from one another. In such an account as the present, a mere sketch is all that can be attempted.

A few passages will speak for themselves. Goethe neglected to lend his aid to the artist for whom he had expressed such admiration, at a time when he might have done so without any inconvenience. Perhaps Beethoven's letter (quoted No. V. of the Dial, Essay on Goethe) may furnish an explanation of this. Cherubini omitted to answer Beethoven's affectionate and magnanimous letter, though he complied with the request it contained. But "the good Bettina" was faithful to her professions, and of essential use to Beethoven, by interesting her family in the conduct of his affairs.

He could not, for any purpose, accommodate himself to courts, or recognize their claims to homage. Two or three orders given him for works, which might have secured him the regard of the imperial family, he could not obey. Whenever he attempted to compose them, he found that the degree of restriction put upon him by the Emperor's taste hampered him too much. The one he did compose for such a purpose, the "Glorreiche Augenblick," Schindler speaks of as one of the least excellent of his works.

He could not bear to give lessons to the Archduke Rudolph, both because he detested giving regular lessons at all, and because he could not accommodate himself to the ceremonies of a court. Indeed it is evident enough from a letter of the Archduke's, quoted by Schindler as showing most condescending regard, how unfit it was for the lion-king to dance in gilded chains amid these mummeries.

Individuals in that princely class he admired, and could be just to, for his democracy was very unlike that fierce vulgar radicalism which assumes that the rich and great *must* be bad. His was only vindication of the rights of man; he could see merit if seated on a throne, as clearly as if at a cobbler's stall. The Archduke Karl, to whom Körner dedicated his heroic muse, was the object of his admiration also. The Empress of Russia, too, he admired.

"Whoever wished to learn of him was obliged to follow his steps everywhere, for to teach, or say anything, at an appointed time was to him impossible. Also he would stop immediately, if he found his companion not sufficiently versed in the matter to keep step with him." He could not harangue; he must always be drawn out.

Amid all the miseries of his housekeeping or other disturbances, (and here, did space permit, I should like to quote his humourous notice of his "four bad days," when he was almost starved,) he had recourse to his art. "He would be fretted a little while; then snatch up the score and write 'noten im nothen,' as he was wont to call them, and forget the plague."

When quite out of health and spirits he restored himself by the composition of a grand mass. This "great, solemn mass," as he calls it in his letter to Cherubini, was offered to the different courts of Europe for fifty ducats. The Prussian ambassador in a diplomatic letter attempted to get it for an order and ribbon. Beethoven merely wrote in reply, "fifty ducats." He indeed was as disdainful of gold chains and orders as Bach was indifferent to them.

Although thus haughty, so much so that he would never receive a visit from Rossini, because, though he admitted that the Italian had genius, he thought he had not cultivated it with that devout severity proper to the artist, and was, consequently, corrupting the public taste, he was not only generous in his joy at any exhibition of the true spirit from others, but tenderly grateful for intelligent sympathy with himself, as is shown in the following beautiful narratives.

"Countess S. brought him on her return from ——, German words by Herr Scholz, written for his first mass. He opened the paper as we were seated together at the table. When he came to the 'Qui tollis,' tears streamed from his eyes, and he was obliged to stop, so deeply was he moved by the inexpressibly beautiful words. He cried, 'Ja! so habe ich gefühlt, als ich dieses schrieb,' 'yes, this was what I felt when I wrote it.' It was the first and last time I ever saw him in tears."

They were such tears as might have been shed on the jubilee of what he loved so much, Schiller's Ode to Joy.

"Be welcome, millions,
This embrace for the whole world."

Happy the man, who gave the bliss to Beethoven of feeling his thought not only recognised, but understood. Years of undiscerning censure, and scarcely less undiscerning homage, are obliterated by the one true vibration from the heart of a fellow-man. *Then* the genius is at home on earth, when another soul knows not only what he writes, but what he felt when he wrote it. "The music is not the lyre nor the hand which plays upon it, but when the two meet, that arises which is neither, but gives each its place."

A pleasure almost as deep was given him on this occasion. Rossini had conquered the German world also; the public had almost forgotten Beethoven. A band of friends, in whose hearts the care for his glory and for the high, severe culture of art was still living, wrote him a noble letter, in which they entreated him to give to the public one of his late works, and, by such a musical festival, eclipse at once these superficial entertainments. The spirit of this letter is thoughtful, tender, and shows so clearly the German feeling as to the worship of the beautiful, that it would have been well to translate it, but that it is too long. It should be a remembrancer of pride and happiness to those who signed their names to it. Schindler knew when it was to be sent, and after Beethoven had time to read it, he went to him.

"I found Beethoven with the memorial in his hand. With an air of unwonted serenity, he reached it to me, placing himself at the window to gaze at the clouds drawing past. His inly deep emotion could not escape my eye. After I had read the paper I laid it aside, and waited in silence for him to begin the conversation. After a long pause, during which his looks constantly followed the clouds, he turned round, and said, in an elevated tone that betrayed his deep emotion, 'Es ist doch recht schön. Es freut mich.' 'It is indeed right fair. It rejoices me.' I assented by a motion of the head. He then said, 'Let us go into the free air.' When we were out he spoke only in monosyllables, but the spark of desire to comply with their requests glimmered visibly in him."

This musical festival at last took place after many difficulties, caused by Beethoven's obstinacy in arranging all the circumstances in his own way. He could never be brought to make allowance anywhere for ignorance or incapacity. So it must be or no how! He could never be induced to alter his music on account of the incapacity of the performers, (the best, too, on that occasion, anywhere to be had,) for going through certain parts. So that they were at last obliged to alter parts in their own fashion, which was always a great injury to the final effect of his works. They were at this time unwearied in their efforts to please him, though Sontag playfully told him he was "a very tyrant to the singing organs."

This festival afforded him a complete triumph. The audience applauded and applauded, till, at one time, when the acclamations rose to their height, Sontag perceiving that Beethoven did not hear, as his face was turned from the house, called his attention. The audience then, as for the first time realizing the extent of his misfortune, melted into tears, then all united in a still more rapturous expression of homage. For once at least the man excited the tenderness, the artist the enthusiasm he deserved.

His country again forgot one who never could nor would call attention to himself; she forgot in the day him for whom she in the age cherishes an immortal reverence, and the London Philharmonic Society had the honour of ministering to the necessities of his last illness. The generous eagerness with which they sent all that his friendly attendants asked, and offered more whenever called for, was most grateful to Beethoven's heart, which had in those last days been frozen by such ingratitude. It roused his sinking life to one last leap of flame; his latest days were passed in revolving a great work which he wished to compose for the society, and which those about him thought would, if finished, have surpassed all he had done before.

No doubt, if his situation had been known in Germany, his country would have claimed a similar feeling from him. For she was not to him a step-dame; and, though in his last days taken up with newer wonders, would not, had his name been spoken, have failed to listen and to answer.

Yet a few more interesting passages. He rose before daybreak both in winter and summer, and worked till two or three o'clock, rarely after. He would never correct, to him the hardest task, as, like all great geniuses, he was indefatigable in the use of the file, in the evening. Often in the midst of his work he would run out into the free air for half an hour or more, and return laden with new thoughts. When he felt this impulse he paid no regard to the weather.

Plato and Shakspeare were his favourite authors; especially he was fond of reading Plato's Republic. He read the Greek and Roman classics much, but in translations, for his education, out of his art, was limited. He also went almost daily to coffee-houses, where he read the newspapers, going in and out by the back door. If he found he excited observation, he changed his haunt.

"He tore without ceremony a composition submitted to him by the great Hummel, which he thought bad. Moscheles, dreading a similar fate for one of his which was to pass under his criticism, wrote at the bottom of the last page, 'Finis. With the help of God.' Beethoven wrote beneath, 'Man, help thyself.'"

Obviously a new edition of Hercules and the Wagoner.

"He was the most open of men, and told unhesitatingly all he thought, unless the subject were art and artists. On these subjects he was often inaccessible, and put off the inquirer with wit or satire." "On two subjects he would never talk, thorough bass and religion. He said they were both things complete within themselves, (in sich abgeschlossene dinge,) about which men should dispute no farther."

"As to the productions of his genius, let not a man or a nation, if yet in an immature stage, seek to know them. They require a certain degree of ripeness in the inner man to be understood.

"From the depth of the mind arisen, she, (Poesie,) is only to the depth of the mind either useful or intelligible."

I cannot conclude more forcibly than by quoting Beethoven's favourite maxim. It expresses what his life was, and what the life must be of those who would become worthy to do him honour.

"The barriers are not yet erected which can say to aspiring talent and industry, thus far and no farther."

Beethoven is the only one of these five artists whose life can be called unfortunate. They all found early the means to unfold their powers, and a theatre on which to display them. But Beethoven was, through a great part of his public career, deprived of the satisfaction of guiding or enjoying the representation of his thoughts. He was like a painter who could never see his pictures after they are finished. Probably, if he could himself have directed the orchestra, he would have been more pliable in making corrections with an eye to effect. Goethe says that no one can write a successful drama without familiarity with the stage, so as to know what can be expressed, what must be merely indicated. But in Beethoven's situation, there was not this reaction, so that he clung more perseveringly to the details of his work than great geniuses do, who live in more immediate contact with the outward world. Such an one will, indeed, always answer like Mozart to an ignorant criticism, "There are just as many notes as there should be." But a habit of intercourse with the minds of men gives an instinctive tact as to meeting them, and Michel Angelo, about to build St. Peter's, takes into consideration, not only his own idea of a cathedral, but means, time, space, and prospects.

But the misfortune, which fettered the outward energies, deepened the thought of Beethoven. He travelled inward, downward, till downward was shown to be the same as upward, for the centre was passed.

Like all princes, he made many ingrates, and his powerful lion nature, was that most capable of suffering from the amazement of witnessing baseness. But the love, the pride, the faith, which survive such pangs are those which make our stair to heaven. Beethoven was not only a poet, but a victorious poet, for having drunk to its dregs the cup of bitterness, the fount of inward nobleness remained undefiled. Unbeloved, he could love; deceived in other men, he yet knew himself too well to despise human nature; dying from ingratitude, he could still be grateful.

Schindler thinks his genius would have been far more productive, if he had had a tolerably happy home, if instead of the cold discomfort that surrounded him, he had been blessed, like Mozart, with a gentle wife, who would have made him a sanctuary in her unwearied love. It is, indeed, inexpressibly affecting to find the "vehement nature," even in his thirty-first year, writing thus; "At my age one sighs for an equality, a harmony of outward existence," and to know that he never attained it. But the lofty ideal of the happiness which his life could not attain, shone forth not the less powerfully from his genius. The love of his choice was not "firm as the fortress of heaven," but his heart remained the gate to that fortress. During all his latter years, he never complained, nor did Schindler ever hear him advert to past sorrows, or the lost objects of affection. Perhaps we are best con-

5*

tented that earth should not have offered him a home; where is the woman who would have corresponded with what we wish from his love? Where is the lot in which he could have reposed with all that grandeur of aspect in which he now appears to us? Where Jupiter, the lustrous, lordeth, there may be a home for thee, Beethoven.

We will not shrink from the dark clouds which became to his overflowing light cinctures of pearl and opal; we will not, even by a wish, seek to amend the destiny through which a divine thought glows so clearly. Were there no Œdipuses there would be no Antigones.

Under no other circumstances could Beethoven have ministered to his fellows in the way he himself indicates.

"The unhappy man, let him be comforted by finding one of his race who in defiance of all hinderances of nature, has done all possible to him to be received in the rank of worthy artists and men."

In three respects these artists, all true artists, resemble one another. Clear decision. The intuitive faculty speaks clear in those devoted to the worship of Beauty. They are not subject to mental conflict, they ask not counsel of experience. They take what they want as simply as the bird goes in search of its proper food, so soon as its wings are grown.

Like nature they love to work for its own sake. The philosopher is ever seeking the thought through the symbol, but the artist is happy at the implication of the thought in his work. He does not reason about "religion or thorough bass." His answer is Haydn's, "I thought it best so." From each achievement grows up a still higher ideal, and when his work is finished, it is nothing to the artist who has made of it the step by which he ascended, but while he was engaged in it, it was all to him, and filled his soul with a parental joy.

They do not criticise, but affirm. They have no need to deny aught, much less one another. All excellence to them was genial; imperfection only left room for new creative power to display itself. An everlasting yes breathes from the life, from the work of the artist. Nature echoes it, and leaves to society the work of saying no, if it will. But it will not, except for the moment. It weans itself for the moment, and turns pettishly away from genius, but soon stumbling, groping, and lonely, cries aloud for its nurse. The age cries *now*, and what an answer is prophesied by such harbinger stars as these at which we have been gazing. We will engrave their names on the breastplate, and wear them as a talisman of hope.

A RECORD OF IMPRESSIONS

PRODUCED BY THE EXHIBITION OF MR. ALLSTON'S PICTURES IN THE SUMMER OF 1839.

THIS is a record of impressions. It does not aspire to the dignity of criticism. The writer is conscious of an eye and taste, not sufficiently exercised by study of the best works of art, to take the measure of one who has a claim to be surveyed from the same platform. But, surprised at finding that an exhibition, intended to promote thought and form the tastes of our public, has called forth no expression* of what it was to so many, who almost daily visited it; and believing that comparison and discussion of the impressions of individuals is the best means to ascertain the sum of the whole, and raise the standard of taste, I venture to offer what, if not true in itself, is at least true to the mind of one observer, and may lead others to reveal more valuable experiences.

Whether the arts can ever be at home among us; whether the desire now manifested to cultivate them be not merely one of our modes of imitating older nations; or whether it springs from a need of balancing the bustle and care of daily life by the unfolding of our calmer and higher nature, it is at present difficult to decide. If the latter, it is not by unthinking repetition of the technics of foreign connoisseurs, or by a servile reliance on the judgment of those, who assume to have been formed by a few

* Since the above was written, we see an article on the Exhibition in the North American Review for April, 1840.

hasty visits to the galleries of Europe, that we shall effect an object so desirable, but by a faithful recognition of the feelings naturally excited by works of art, not indeed flippant, as if our raw, uncultivated nature was at once competent to appreciate those finer manifestations of nature, which slow growths of ages and peculiar aspects of society have occasionally brought out, to testify to us what we may and should be. We know it is not so; we know that if such works are to be assimilated at all by those who are not under the influences that produced them, it must be by gradually educating us to their own level. But it is not blind faith that will educate us, that will open the depths and clear the eye of the mind, but an examination which cannot be too close, if made in the spirit of reverence and love.

It was as an essay in this kind that the following pages were written. They are pages of a journal, and their form has not been altered, lest any attempt at a more fair and full statement should destroy that freshness and truth of feeling, which is the chief merit of such.

July, 1839.

On the closing of the Allston exhibition, where I have spent so many hours, I find myself less a gainer than I had expected, and feel that it is time to look into the matter a little, with such a torch or penny rush candle as I can command.

I have seen most of these pictures often before; the Beatrice and Valentine when only sixteen. The effect they produced upon me was so great, that I suppose it was not possible for me to avoid expecting too large a benefit from the artist.

The calm and meditative cast of these pictures, the ideal beauty that shone *through* rather than *in* them, and the harmony of colouring were as unlike anything else I saw, as the Vicar of Wakefield to Cooper's novels. I seemed to recognise in painting that self-possessed elegance, that transparent depth, which I most admire in literature; I thought with delight that such a man as this had been able to grow up in our bustling, reasonable community, that he had kept his foot upon the ground, yet never lost sight of the rose-clouds of beauty floating above him. I saw, too, that he had not been troubled, but possessed his own soul with the blandest patience; and I hoped, I scarce knew what; probably the *mot d'enigme* for which we are all looking. How the poetical mind can live and work in peace and good faith! how it may unfold to its due perfection in an unpoetical society!

From time to time I have seen other of these pictures, and they have always been to me sweet silvery music, rising by its clear tone to be heard above the din of life; long forest glades glimmering with golden light, longingly eyed from the window of some crowded drawing room.

But now, seeing so many of them together, I can no longer be content merely to feel, but must judge these works. I must try to find the centre, to measure the circumference; and I fare somewhat as I have done, when I have seen in periodicals detached thoughts by some writer, which seemed so full of meaning and suggestion, that I would treasure them up in my memory, and think about them, till I had made a picture of the author's mind, which his works when I found them collected would not justify. Yet the great writer would go beyond my hope and abash my fancy; should not the great painter do the same?

Yet, probably, I am too little aware of the difficulties the artist encounters, before he can produce anything excellent, fully to appreciate the greatness he has shown. Here, as elsewhere. I suppose the first question should be, What ought we to expect under the circumstances?

There is no poetical ground-work ready for the artist in our country and time. Good deeds appeal to the understanding. Our religion is that of the understanding. We have no old established faith, no hereditary romance, no such stuff as Catholicism, Chivalry afforded. What is most dignified in the Puritanic modes of thought is not favourable to beauty. The habits of an industrial community are not propitious to delicacy of sentiment.

He, who would paint human nature, must content himself with selecting fine situations here and there; and he must address himself, not to a public which is not educated to prize him, but to the small circle within the circle of men of taste.

If, like Wilkie or Newton, he paints direct from nature, only selecting and condensing, or choosing lights and draperies, I suppose he is as well situated now as he could ever have been; but if, like Mr. Allston, he aims at the Ideal, it is by no means the same. He is in danger of being sentimental and picturesque, rather than spiritual and noble. Mr. Allston has not fallen into these faults; and if we can complain, it is never of blemish or falsity, but of inadequacy. Always he has a high purpose in what he does, never swerves from his aim, but sometimes fails to reach it.

The Bible, familiar to the artist's youth, has naturally furnished subjects for his most earnest efforts. I will speak of four pictures on biblical subjects, which were in this exhibition.

Restoring the dead man by the touch of the Prophet's Bones. I should say there was a want of artist's judgment in the very choice of the subject.

In all the miracles where Christ and the Apostles act a part, and which have been favourite subjects with the great painters, poetical beauty is at once given to the scene by the moral dignity, the sublime exertion of faith on divine power in the person of the main actor. He is the natural centre of the picture, and the emotions of all present grade from and cluster round him. So in a martyrdom, however revolting or oppressive the circumstances, there is room in the person of the sufferer for a similar expression, a central light which shall illuminate and dignify all round it.

But a miracle effected by means of a relique, or dry bones,

has the disagreeable effect of mummery. In this picture the foreground is occupied by the body of the patient in that state of deadly rigidity and pallor so offensive to the sensual eye. The mind must reason the eye out of an instinctive aversion, and force it to its work,—always an undesirable circumstance.

In such a picture as that of the *Massacre of the Innocents,* painful as the subject is, the beauty of forms in childhood, and the sentiment of maternal love, so beautiful even in anguish, charm so much as to counterpoise the painful emotions. But here, not only is the main figure offensive to the sensual eye, thus violating one principal condition of art; it is incapable of any expression at such a time beyond that of physical anguish during the struggle of life suddenly found to re-demand its dominion. Neither can the assistants exhibit any emotions higher than those of surprise, terror, or, as in the case of the wife, an overwhelming anxiety of suspense.

The grouping and colouring of this picture are very good, and the individual figures managed with grace and discrimination, though without much force.

The subjects of the other three pictures are among the finest possible, grand no less than beautiful, and of the highest poetical interest. They present no impediment to the manifestation of genius. Let us look first at *Jeremiah in prison dictating to Baruch.*

The strength and dignity of the Jew physique, and the appropriateness of the dress, allowed fair play to the painter's desire to portray inspiration manifesting itself by a suitable organ. As far as the accessories and grouping of the figures nothing can be better. The form of the prophet is brought out in such noble relief, is in such fine contrast to the pale and feminine sweetness of the scribe at his feet, that for a time you are satisfied. But by and by you begin to doubt, whether this picture is not rather imposing than majestic. The dignity of the prophet's appearance seems to lie rather in the fine lines of the form and drapery, than in the expression of the face. It was well observed by one who looked on him, that, if the eyes were cast down, he would become an ordinary man. This is true, and the expression of the bard must not depend on a look or gesture, but beam with mild electricity from every feature. Allston's Jeremiah is not the mournfully indignant bard, but the robust and stately Jew, angry that men will not mark his word and go his way. But Baruch is admirable! His overwhelmed yet willing submission, the docile faith which turns him pale, and trembles almost tearful in his eye, are given with infinite force and beauty. The *coup d'œil* of this picture is excellent, and it has great merit, but not the highest.

Miriam. There is hardly a subject which, for the combination of the sublime with the beautiful could present greater advantages than this. Yet this picture also, with all its great merits, fails to satisfy our highest requisitions.

I could wish the picture had been larger, and that the angry clouds and swelling sea did not need to be looked for as they do. For the whole attention remains so long fixed on the figure of Miriam, that you cannot for some time realize who she is. You merely see this bounding figure, and the accessories are so kept under, that it is difficult to have the situation full in your mind, and feel that you see not merely a Jewish girl dancing, but the representative of Jewry rescued and triumphant! What a figure this might be! The character of Jewish beauty is so noble and profound! This maiden had been nurtured in a fair and highly civilized country, in the midst of wrong and scorn indeed, but beneath the shadow of sublime institutions. In a state of abject bondage, in a catacomb as to this life, she had embalmed her soul in the memory of those days, when God walked with her fathers, and did for their sakes such mighty works. Amid all the pains and penances of slavery, the memory of Joseph, the presence of Moses, exalt her soul to the highest pitch of national pride. The chords had of late been strung to their greatest tension, by the series of prodigies wrought in behalf of the nation of which her family is now the head. Of these the last and grandest had just taken place before her eyes.

Imagine the stately and solemn beauty with which such nurture and such a position might invest the Jewish Miriam. Imagine her at the moment when her soul would burst at last the shackles in which it had learned to move freely and proudly, when her lips were unsealed, and she was permitted before her brother, deputy of the Most High, and chief of their assembled nation, to sing the song of deliverance. Realize this situation, and oh, how far will this beautiful picture fall short of your demands!

The most unimaginative observers complain of a want of depth in the eye of Miriam. For myself, I make the same complaint, as much as I admire the whole figure. How truly is she upborne, what swelling joy and pride in every line of her form! And the face, though inadequate, is not false to the ideal. Its beauty is mournful, and only wants the heroic depth, the cavernous flame of eye, which should belong to such a face in such a place.

The Witch of Endor is still more unsatisfactory. What a tragedy was that of the stately Saul, ruined by his perversity of will, despairing, half mad, refusing to give up the sceptre which he feels must in a short time be wrenched from his hands, degrading himself to the use of means he himself had forbid as unlawful and devilish, seeking the friend and teacher of his youth by means he would most of all men disapprove. The mournful significance of the crisis, the stately aspect of Saul as celebrated in the history, and the supernatural events which had filled his days, gave authority for investing him with that sort of beauty and majesty proper to archangels ruined. What have we here? I don't know what is generally thought about the introduction of a ghost on canvass, but it is to me as ludicrous as the introduction on the stage of the ghost in Hamlet (*in his night-gown*) as the old play book direction was. The effect of such a representation seems to me unattainable in a picture. There cannot be due distance and shadowy softness.

Then what does the picture mean to say ? In the chronicle, the witch, surprised and affrighted at the apparition, reproaches the king, "Why hast thou deceived me ? for thou art Saul."

But here the witch (a really fine figure, fierce and *prononcé* as that of a Norna should be) seems threatening the king, who is in an attitude of theatrical as well as degrading dismay. To me this picture has no distinct expression, and is wholly unsatisfactory, maugre all its excellencies of detail.

In fine, the more I have looked at these pictures, the more I have been satisfied that the grand historical style did not afford the scope most proper to Mr. Allston's genius. The Prophets and Sibyls are for the Michael Angelos. The Beautiful is Mr. Allston's dominion. There he rules as a Genius, but in attempts such as I have been considering, can only show his appreciation of the stern and sublime thoughts he wants force to reproduce.

But on his own ground we can meet the painter with almost our first delight.

A certain bland delicacy enfolds all these creations as an atmosphere. Here is no effort, they have floated across the painter's heaven on the golden clouds of phantasy.

These pictures (I speak here only of figures, of the landscapes a few words anon) are almost all in repose. The most beautiful are Beatrice, The Lady reading a Valentine, The Evening Hymn, Rosalie, The Italian Shepherd Boy, Edwin, Lorenzo and Jessica. The excellence of these pictures is subjective and even feminine. They tell us the painter's ideal of character. A graceful repose, with a fitness for moderate action. A capacity of emotion, with a habit of reverie. Not one of these beings is in a state of *epanchement*, not one is, or perhaps could be, thrown off its equipoise. They are, even the softest, characterized by entire though unconscious self-possession.

While looking at them would be always coming up in my mind the line,

"The genius loci, feminine and fair."

Grace, grace always.

Mr. Allston seems to have an exquisite sensibility to colour, and a great love for drapery. The last sometimes leads him to direct our attention too much to it, and sometimes the accessories are made too prominent; we look too much at shawls, curtains, rings, feathers, and carcanets.

I will specify two of these pictures, which seem to me to indicate Mr. Allston's excellences as well as any.

The Italian Shepherd boy is seated in a wood. The form is almost nude, and the green glimmer of the wood gives the flesh the polished whiteness of marble. He is very beautiful, this boy; and the beauty, as Mr. Allston loves it best, has not yet unfolded all its leaves. The heart of the flower is still a perfumed secret. He sits as if he could sit there forever, gracefully lost in reverie, steeped, if we may judge from his mellow brown eye, in the present loveliness of nature, in the dimly anticipated ecstasies of love.

Every part of nature has its peculiar influence. On the hill-top one is roused, in the valley soothed, beside the waterfall absorbed. And in the wood, who has not, like this boy, walked as far as the excitement of exercise would carry him, and then, with "blood listening in his frame," and heart brightly awake, seated himself on such a bank. At first he notices everything, the clouds doubly soft, the sky deeper blue, as seen shimmering through the leaves, the fyttes of golden light seen through the long glades, the skimming of a butterfly ready to light on some starry wood-flower, the nimble squirrel peeping archly at him, the flutter and wild notes of the birds, the whispers and sighs of the trees,—gradually he ceases to mark any of these things, and becomes lapt in the Elysian harmony they combine to form. Who has ever felt this mood understands why the observant Greek placed his departed great ones in groves. While, during this trance, he hears the harmonies of Nature, he seems to become her and she him; it is truly the mother in the child, and the Hamadryads look out with eyes of tender twilight approbation from their beloved and loving trees. Such an hour lives for us again in this picture.

Mr. Allston has been very fortunate in catching the shimmer and glimmer of the woods, and tempering his greens and browns to their peculiar light.

Beatrice. This is spoken of as Dante's Beatrice, but I should think can scarcely have been suggested by the Divine Comedy. The painter merely having in mind how the great Dante loved a certain lady called Beatrice, embodied here his own ideal of a poet's love.

The Beatrice of Dante was, no doubt, as pure, as gentle, as high-bred, but also possessed of much higher attributes than this fair being.

How fair, indeed, and not unmeet for a poet's love. But there lies in her no germ of the celestial destiny of Dante's saint. What she is, what she can be, it needs no Dante to discover.

She is not a lustrous, bewitching beauty, neither is she a high and poetic one. She is not a concentrated perfume, nor a flower, nor a star; yet somewhat has she of every creature's best. She has the golden mean, without any touch of the mediocre. She can venerate the higher and compassionate the lower, and do to all honour due with most grateful courtesy and nice tact. She is velvet-soft, her mild and modest eyes have tempered all things round her, till no rude sound invades her sphere; yet, if need were, she could resist with as graceful composure as she can favour or bestow.

No vehement emotion shall heave that bosom, and the tears shall fall on those cheeks more like dew than rain. Yet are her feelings delicate, profound, her love constant and tender, her resentment calm but firm.

Fair as a maid, fairer as a wife, fairest as a lady mother and ruler of a household, she were better suited to a prince than a poet. Even if no prince could be found worthy of her, I would not wed her to a poet, if he lived in a cottage. For her best graces demand a splendid setting to give them their due lustre, and she should rather enhance than cause her environment.

There are three pictures in the comic kind, which are good. It is genteel comedy, not rich, easily taken in and left, but having the lights and shades well marked. They show a gentlemanlike playfulness. In *Catharine and Petruchio*, the Gremio is particularly good, and the tear-distained Catharine, whose head shoulder, knee, and foot seem to unite to spell the word *Pout*, is next best.

The Sisters—a picture quite unlike those I have named—does not please me much, though I should suppose the execution remarkably good. It is not in repose nor in harmony, nor is it rich in suggestion, like the others. It aims to speak, but says little, and is not beautiful enough to fill the heart with its present moment. To me it makes a break in the chain of thought the other pictures had woven.

Scene from Gil Blas—also unlike the other in being perfectly objective, and telling all its thought at once. It is a fine painting.

Mother and Child. A lovely little picture. But there is to my taste an air of got up naiveté and delicacy in it. It seems selected, arranged by "an intellectual effort." It did not flow into the artist's mind like the others. But persons of better taste than I like it better than I do!

Jews—full of character. Isaac is too dignified and sad; gold never rusted the soul of the man that owned that face.

The Landscapes. At these I look with such unalloyed delight, that I have been at moments tempted to wish that the artist had concentrated his powers on this department of art, in so high a degree does he exhibit the attributes of the master; a power of sympathy, which gives each landscape a perfectly individual character. Here the painter is merged in his theme, and these pictures affect us as parts of nature, so absorbed are we in contemplating them, so difficult is it to remember them as pictures. How the clouds float! how the trees live and breathe out their mysterious souls in the peculiar attitude of every leaf. Dear companions of my life, whom yearly I know better, yet into whose heart I can no more penetrate than see your roots, while you live and grow, I feel what you have said to this painter; I can in some degree appreciate the power he has shown in repeating here the gentle oracle.

The soul of the painter is in these landscapes, but not his character. Is not that the highest art? Nature and the soul combined; the former freed from slight crudities or blemishes, the latter from its merely human aspect.

These landscapes are too truly works of art, their language is too direct, too lyrically perfect, to be translated into this of words, without doing them an injury.

To those, who confound praise with indiscriminate eulogium, and who cannot understand the mind of one, whose highest expression of admiration is a close scrutiny, perhaps the following lines will convey a truer impression, than the foregoing remarks, of the feelings of the writer. They were suggested by a picture painted by Mr. Allston for a gentleman of Boston, which has never yet been publicly exhibited. It is of the same class with his *Rosalie* and *Evening Hymn*, pictures which were not particularized in the above record, because they inspired no thought except of their excelling beauty, which draws the heart into itself.

These two sonnets may be interesting, as showing how similar trains of thought were opened in the minds of two observers.

"To-day I have been to see Mr. Allston's new picture of *The Bride*, and am more convinced than ever of the depth and value of his genius, and of how much food for thought his works contain. The face disappointed me at first by its want of beauty. Then I observed the peculiar expression of the eyes, and that of the lids, which tell such a tale, as well as the strange complexion, all heightened by the colour of the background, till the impression became very strong. It is the story of the lamp of love, lighted, even burning with full force in a being that cannot yet comprehend it. The character is domestic, far more so than that of the ideal and suffering Rosalie, of which, nevertheless, it reminds you.

"TO W. ALLSTON, ON SEEING HIS 'BRIDE.'

"Weary and slow and faint with heavy toil,
The fainting traveller pursues his way,
O'er dry Arabian sands the long, long day,
Where at each step floats up the dusty soil;
And when he finds a green and gladsome isle,
And flowing water in that plain of care,
And in the midst a marble fountain fair,
To tell that others suffered too erewhile,
And then appeased their thirst, and made this fount
To them a sad remembrance, but a joy
To all who follow—his tired spirits mount
At such dim-visioned company—so I
Drink of thy marble source, and do not count
Weary the way in which thou hast gone by."

TO ALLSTON'S PICTURE, 'THE BRIDE.'

Not long enough we gaze upon that face,
Not pure enough the life with which we live,
To be full trancèd by that softest grace,
To win all pearls those lucid depths can give;
Here Phantasy has borrowed wings of Even,
And stolen Twilight's latest, sacred hues,
A Soul has visited the woman's heaven,
Where palest lights a silver sheen diffuse,
To see aright the vision which he saw,
We must ascend as high upon the stair,
Which leads the human thought to heavenly law,
And see the flower bloom in its natal air;
Thus might we read aright the lip and brow,
Where Thought and Love beam too subduing for our senses now.

AMERICAN LITERATURE;

ITS POSITION IN THE PRESENT TIME, AND PROSPECTS FOR THE FUTURE.

Some thinkers may object to this essay, that we are about to write of that which has, as yet, no existence.

For it does not follow because many books are written by persons born in America that there exists an American literature. Books which imitate or represent the thoughts and life of Europe do not constitute an American literature. Before such can exist, an original idea must animate this nation and fresh currents of life must call into life fresh thoughts along its shores.

We have no sympathy with national vanity. We are not anxious to prove that there is as yet much American literatnre. Of those who think and write among us in the methods and of the thoughts of Europe, we are not impatient; if their minds are still best adapted to such food and such action. If their books express life of mind and character in graceful forms, they are good and we like them. We consider them as colonists and useful schoolmasters to our people in a transition state; which lasts rather longer than is occupied in passing, bodily, the ocean which separates the new from the old world.

We have been accused of an undue attachment to foreign continental literature, and, it is true, that in childhood, we had well nigh "forgotten our English," while constantly reading in other languages. Still, what we loved in the literature of continental Europe was the range and force of ideal manifestation in forms of national and individual greatness. A model was before us in the great Latins of simple masculine minds seizing upon life with unbroken power. The stamp both of nationality and individuality was very strong upon them ; their lives and thoughts stood out in clear and bold relief. The English character has the iron force of the Latins, but not the frankness and expansion. Like their fruits, they need a summer sky to give them more sweetness and a richer flavour. This does not apply to Shakspeare, who has all the fine side of English genius, with the rich colouring, and more fluent life, of the Catholic countries. Other poets, of England also, are expansive more or less, and soar freely to seek the blue sky, but take it as a whole, there is in English literature, as in English character, a reminiscence of walls and ceilings, a tendency to the arbitrary and conventional that repels a mind trained in admiration of the antique spirit. It is only in later days that we are learning to prize the peculiar greatness which a thousand times outweighs this fault, and which has enabled English genius to go forth from its insular position and conquer such vast dominion in the realms both of matter and of mind.

Yet there is, often, between child and parent, a reaction from excessive influence having been exerted, and such an one we have experienced, in behalf of our country, against England. We use her language, and receive, in torrents, the influence of her thought, yet it is, in many respects, uncongenial and injurious to our constitution. What suits Great Britain, with her insular position and consequent need to concentrate and intensify her life, her limited monarchy, and spirit of trade, does not suit a mixed race, continually enriched with new blood from other stocks the most unlike that of our first descent, with ample field and verge enough to range in and leave every impulse free, and abundant opportunity to develope a genius, wide and full as our rivers, flowery, luxuriant and impassioned as our vast prairies, rooted in strength as the rocks on which the Puritan fathers landed.

That such a genius is to rise and work in this hemisphere we are confident; equally so that scarce the first faint streaks of that day's dawn are yet visible. It is sad for those that foresee, to know they may not live to share its glories, yet it is sweet, too, to know that every act and word, uttered in the light of that foresight, may tend to hasten or ennoble its fulfilment.

That day will not rise till the fusion of races among us is more complete. It will not rise till this nation shall attain sufficient moral and intellectual dignity to prize moral and intellectual, no less highly than political, freedom, not till, the physical resources of the country being explored, all its regions studded with towns, broken by the plow, netted together by railways and telegraph lines, talent shall be left at leisure to turn its energies upon the higher department of man's existence. Nor then shall it be seen till from the leisurely and yearning soul of that riper time national ideas shall take birth, ideas craving to be clothed in a thousand fresh and original forms.

Without such ideas all attempts to construct a national literature must end in abortions like the monster of Frankenstein, things with forms, and the instincts of forms, but soulless, and therefore revolting. We cannot have expression till there is something to be expressed.

The symptoms of such a birth may be seen in a longing felt here and there for the sustenance of such ideas. At present, it shows itself, where felt, in sympathy with the prevalent tone of society, by attempts at external action, such as are classed under the head of social reform. But it needs to go deeper, before we can have poets, needs to penetrate beneath the springs of action, to stir and remake the soil as by the action of fire.

Another symptom is the need felt by individuals of being even sternly sincere. This is the one great means by which alone progress can be essentially furthered. Truth is the nursing mother of genius. No man can be absolutely true to himself, eschewing cant, compromise, servile imitation, and complaisance, without becoming original, for there is in every creature a fountain of life which, if not choked back by stones and other dead rubbish, will create a fresh atmosphere, and bring to life fresh beauty. And it is the same with the nation as with the individual man.

The best work we do for the future is by such truth. By use of that, in whatever way, we harrow the soil and lay it open to the sun and air. The winds from all quarters of the globe bring seed enough, and there is nothing wanting but preparation of the soil, and freedom in the atmosphere, for ripening of a new and golden harvest.

We are sad that we cannot be present at the gathering in of this harvest. And yet we are joyous, too, when we think that though our name may not be writ on the pillar of our country's fame, we can really do far more towards rearing it, than those who come at a later period and to a seemingly fairer task. *Now*, the humblest effort, made in a noble spirit, and with religious hope, cannot fail to be even infinitely useful. Whether we introduce some noble model from another time and clime, to encourage aspiration in our own, or cheer into blossom the simplest wood-flower that ever rose from the earth, moved by the genuine impulse to grow, independent of the lures of money or celebrity; whether we speak boldly when fear or doubt keep others silent, or refuse to swell the popular cry upon an unworthy occasion, the spirit of truth, purely worshipped, shall turn our acts and forbearances alike to profit, informing them with oracles which the latest time shall bless.

Under present circumstances the amount of talent and labour given to writing ought to surprise us. Literature is in this dim and struggling state, and its pecuniary results exceedingly pitiful. From many well known causes it is impossible for ninety-nine out of the hundred, who wish tc use the pen, to ransom, by its use, the time they need. This state of things will have to be changed in some way. No man of genius writes for money; but it is essential to the free use of his powers, that he should be able to disembarrass his life from care and perplexity. This is very difficult here; and the state of things gets worse and worse, as less and less is offered in pecuniary meed for works demanding great devotion of time and labour (to say nothing of the ether engaged) and the publisher, obliged to regard the transaction as a matter of business, demands of the author to give him only what will find an immediate market, for he cannot afford to take any thing else. This will not do! When an immortal poet was secure only of a few copyists to circulate his works, there were princes and nobles to patronize literature and the arts. Here is only the public, and the public must learn how to cherish the nobler and rarer plants, and to plant the aloe, able to wait a hundred years for its bloom, or its garden will contain, presently, nothing but potatoes and pot-herbs. We shall have, in the course of the next two or three years, a convention of authors to inquire into the causes of this state of things and propose measures for its remedy. Some have already been thought of that look promising, but we shall not announce them till the time be ripe; that date is not distant, for the difficulties increase from day to day, in consequence of the system of cheap publication, on a great scale.

The ranks that led the way in the first half century of this republic were far better situated than we, in this respect. The country was not so deluged with the dingy page, reprinted from Europe, and patriotic vanity was on the alert to answer the question, "Who reads an American book?" And many were the books written, worthy to be read, as any out of the first class in

England. They were, most of them, except in their subject matter, English books.

The list is large, and, in making some cursory comments, we do not wish to be understood as designating *all* who are worthy of notice, but only those who present themselves to our minds with some special claims. In history there has been nothing done to which the world at large has not been eager to award the full meed of its deserts. Mr. Prescott, for instance, has been greeted with as much warmth abroad as here. We are not disposed to undervalue his industry and power of clear and elegant arrangement. The richness and freshness of his materials is such that a sense of enchantment must be felt in their contemplation. We must regret, however, that they should have been first presented to the public by one who possesses nothing of the higher powers of the historian, great leading views, or discernment as to the motives of action and the spirit of an era. Considering the splendour of the materials the books are wonderfully tame, and every one must feel that having once passed through them and got the sketch in the mind, there is nothing else to which it will recur. The absence of thought, as to that great picture of Mexican life, with its heroisms, its terrible but deeply significant superstitions, its admirable civic refinement, seems to be quite unbroken.

Mr. Bancroft is a far more vivid writer; he has great resources and great command of them, and leading thoughts by whose aid he groups his facts. But we cannot speak fully of his historical works, which we have only read and referred to here and there.

In the department of ethics and philosophy, we may inscribe two names as likely to live and be blessed and honoured in the later time. These are the names of Channing and of Emerson.

Dr. Channing had several leading thoughts which corresponded with the wants of his time, and have made him in it a father of thought. His leading idea of "the dignity of human nature" is one of vast results, and the peculiar form in which he advocated it had a great work to do in this new world. The spiritual beauty of his writings is very great; they are all distinguished for sweetness, elevation, candour, and a severe devotion to truth. On great questions, he took middle ground, and sought a panoramic view; he wished also to stand high, yet never forgot what was above more than what was around and beneath him. He was not well acquainted with man on the impulsive and passionate side of his nature, so that his view of character was sometimes narrow, but it was always noble. He exercised an expansive and purifying power on the atmosphere, and stands a godfather at the baptism of this country.

The Sage of Concord has a very different mind, in every thing except that he has the same disinterestedness and dignity of purpose, the same purity of spirit. He is a profound thinker. He is a man of ideas, and deals with causes rather than effects. His ideas are illustrated from a wide range of literary culture and refined observation, and embodied in a style whose melody and subtle fragrance enchant those who stand stupified before the thoughts themselves, because their utmost depths do not enable them to sound his shallows. His influence does not yet extend over a wide space; he is too far beyond his place and his time, to be felt at once or in full, but it searches deep, and yearly widens its circles. He is a harbinger of the better day. His beautiful elocution has been a great aid to him in opening the way for the reception of his written word.

In that large department of literature which includes descriptive sketches, whether of character or scenery, we are already rich. Irving, a genial and fair nature, just what he ought to be, and would have been, at any time of the world, has drawn the scenes amid which his youth was spent in their primitive lineaments, with all the charms of his graceful jocund humour. He has his niche and need never be deposed ; it is not one that another could occupy.

The first enthusiasm about Cooper having subsided, we remember more his faults than his merits. His ready resentment and way of showing it in cases which it is the wont of gentlemen to pass by in silence, or meet with a good humoured smile, have caused unpleasant associations with his name, and his fellow citizens, in danger of being tormented by suits for libel, if they spoke freely of him, have ceased to speak of him at all. But neither these causes, nor the baldness of his plots, shallowness of thought, and poverty in the presentation of character, should make us forget the grandeur and originality of his sea-sketches, nor the redemption from oblivion of our forest-scenery, and the noble romance of the hunter-pioneer's life. Already, but for him, this fine page of life's romance would be almost forgotten. He has done much to redeem these irrevocable beauties from the corrosive acid of a semi-civilized invasion.*

* Since writing the above we have read some excellent remarks by Mr. W. G. Simms on the writings of Cooper. We think the reasons are given for the powerful interest excited by Hawk Eye and the Pilot, with great discrimination and force.

"They both think and feel, with a highly individual nature, that has been taught, by constant contemplation, in scenes of solitude. The vast unbroken ranges of forest to its one lonely occupant press upon the mind with the same sort of solemnity which one feels condemned to a life of partial isolation upon the ocean. Both are permitted that degree of commerce with their fellow beings, which suffices to maintain in strength the sweet and sacred sources of their humanity. * * * The very isolation to which, in the most successful of his stories, Mr. Cooper subjects his favourite personages, is, alone, a proof of his strength and genius. While the ordinary writer, the man of mere talent, is compelled to look around him among masses for his material, he contents himself with one man, and flings him upon the wilderness. The picture, then, which follows, must be one of intense individuality. Out of this one man's nature, his moods and fortunes, he spins his story. The agencies and dependencies are few. With the self-reliance which is only found in true genius, he

Miss Sedgwick and others have portrayed, with skill and feeling, scenes and personages from the revolutionary time. Such have a permanent value in proportion as their subject is fleeting. The same charm attends the spirited delineations of Mrs. Kirkland, and that amusing book, " A New Purchase." The features of Hoosier, Sucker, and Wolverine life are worth fixing; they are peculiar to the soil, and indicate its hidden treasures ; they have, also, that charm which simple life, lived for its own sake, always has, even in rude and all but brutal forms.

What shall we say of the poets ? The list is scanty ; amazingly so, for there is nothing in the causes that paralyze other kinds of literature that could affect lyrical and narrative poetry. Men's hearts beat, hope, and suffer always, and they must crave such means to vent them ; yet of the myriad leaves garnished with smooth stereotyped rhymes that issue yearly from our press, you will not find, one time in a million, a little piece written from any such impulse, or with the least sincerity or sweetness of tone. They are written for the press, in the spirit of imitation or vanity, the paltriest offspring of the human brain, for the heart disclaims, as the ear is shut against them. This is the kind of verse which is cherished by the magazines as a correspondent to the tawdry pictures of smiling milliners' dolls in the frontispiece. Like these they are only a fashion, a fashion based on no reality of love or beauty. The inducement to write them consists in a little money, or more frequently the charm of seeing an anonymous name printed at the top in capitals.

We must here, in passing, advert also to the style of story

goes forward into the wilderness, whether of land or ocean ; and the vicissitudes of either region, acting upon the natural resources of one man's mind, furnish the whole material of his work-shop. This mode of performance is highly dramatic, and thus it is that his scout, his trapper, his hunter, his pilot, all live to our eyes and thoughts, the perfect ideals of moral individuality."

No IX. Wiley and Putnam's Library of American books.—Views and Reviews by W. G. Simms.

current in the magazines, flimsy beyond any texture that was ever spun or even dreamed of by the mind of man, in any other age and country. They are said to be "written for the seamstresses," but we believe that every way injured class could relish and digest better fare even at the end of long days of exhausting labour. There are exceptions to this censure; stories by Mrs. Child have been published in the magazines, and now and then good ones by Mrs. Stephens and others; but, take them generally, they are calculated to do a positive injury to the public mind, acting as an opiate, and of an adulterated kind, too.

But to return to the poets. At their head Mr. Bryant stands alone. His range is not great, nor his genius fertile. But his poetry is purely the language of his inmost nature, and the simple lovely garb in which his thoughts are arranged, a direct gift from the Muse. He has written nothing that is not excellent, and the atmosphere of his verse refreshes and composes the mind, like leaving the highway to enter some green, lovely, fragrant wood.

Halleck and Willis are poets of society. Though the former has written so little, yet that little is full of fire,—elegant, witty, delicate in sentiment. It is an honour to the country that these occasional sparks, struck off from the flint of commercial life, should have kindled so much flame as they have. It is always a consolation to see one of them sparkle amid the rubbish of daily life. One of his poems has been published within the last year, written, in fact, long ago, but new to most of us, and it enlivened the literary thoroughfare, as a green wreath might some dusty, musty hall of legislation.

Willis has not the same terseness or condensed electricity. But he has grace, spirit, at times a winning pensiveness, and a lively, though almost wholly sensuous, delight in the beautiful.

Dana has written so little that he would hardly be seen in a more thickly garnished galaxy. But the masculine strength of feeling, the solemn tenderness and refined thought displayed in such pieces as the "Dying Raven," and the "Husband and Wife's Grave," have left a deep impression on the popular mind.

Longfellow is artificial and imitative. He borrows incessantly, and mixes what he borrows, so that it does not appear to the best advantage. He is very faulty in using broken or mixed metaphors. The ethical part of his writing has a hollow, second-hand sound. He has, however, elegance, a love of the beautiful, and a fancy for what is large and manly, if not a full sympathy with it. His verse breathes at times much sweetness; and, if not allowed to supersede what is better may promote a taste for good poetry. Though imitative, he is not mechanical.

We cannot say as much for Lowell, who, we must declare it, though to the grief of some friends, and the disgust of more, is absolutely wanting in the true spirit and tone of poesy. His interest in the moral questions of the day has supplied the want of vitality in himself; his great facility at versification has enabled him to fill the ear with a copious stream of pleasant sound. But his verse is stereotyped; his thought sounds no depth, and posterity will not remember him.

R. W. Emerson, in melody, in subtle beauty of thought and expression, takes the highest rank upon this list. But his poems are mostly philosophical, which is not the truest kind of poetry. They want the simple force of nature and passion, and, while they charm the ear and interest the mind, fail to wake far-off echoes in the heart. The imagery wears a symbolical air, and serves rather as illustration, than to delight us by fresh and glowing forms of life.

We must here mention one whom the country has not yet learned to honour, perhaps never may, for he wants artistic skill to give complete form to his inspiration. This is William Ellery Channing, nephew and namesake of Dr. C., a volume of whose poems, published three or four years ago in Boston, remains unknown, except to a few friends, nor, if known, would they probably, excite sympathy, as those which have been published in the periodicals have failed to do so. Yet some of the purest tones of the lyre are his, the finest inspirations as to the feelings and passions of men, deep spiritual insight, and an entire originality in the use of his means. The frequently unfinished and obscure state of his poems, a passion for forcing words out of their usual meaning into one which they may appropriately bear, but which comes upon the reader with an unpleasing and puzzling surprise, may repel, at first glance, from many of these poems, but do not mar the following sublime description of the beings we want, to rule, to redeem, to re-create this nation, and under whose reign alone can there be an American literature, for then only could we have life worth recording. The simple grandeur of this poem as a whole, must be felt by every one, while each line and thought will be found worthy of earnest contemplation and satisfaction after the most earnest life and thought.

Hearts of Eternity! hearts of the deep!
Proclaim from land to sea your mighty fate;
How that for you no living comes too late;
How ye cannot in Theban labyrinth creep;
How ye great harvests from small surface reap;
Shout, excellent band, in grand primeval strain,
Like midnight winds that foam along the main,
And do all things rather than pause to weep.
A human heart knows naught of littleness,
Suspects no man, compares with no man's ways,
Hath in one hour most glorious length of days,
A recompense, a joy, a loveliness;
Like eaglet keen, shoots into azure far,
And always dwelling nigh is the remotest star.

A series of poems, called "Man in the Republic," by Cornelius Mathews, deserves a higher meed of sympathy than it has received. The thoughts and views are strong and noble, the exhibition of them imposing. In plastic power this writer is deficient. His prose works sin in exuberance, and need consolidating and chastening. We find fine things, but not so arranged as to be seen in the right places and by the best light. In his poems Mr. Mathews is unpardonably rough and rugged; the poetic substance finds no musical medium in which to flow. Yet there *is* poetic substance which makes full chords, if not a harmony. He holds a worthy sense of the vocation of the poet, and worthily expresses it thus:—

To strike or bear, to conquer or to yield
Teach thou! O topmost crown of duty, teach,
What fancy whispers to the listening ear,
At hours when tongue nor taint of care impeach
The fruitful calm of greatly silent hearts;
When all the stars for happy thought are set,
And, in the secret chambers of the soul,
All blessed powers of joyful truth are met;
Though calm and garlandless thou mayst appear,
The world shall know thee for its crowned seer.

A considerable portion of the hope and energy of this country still turns towards the drama, that greatest achievement when wrought to perfection of human power. For ourselves, we believe the day of the regular drama to be past; and, though we recognize the need of some kind of spectacle and dramatic representation to be absolutely coincident with an animated state of the public mind, we have thought that the opera, ballet, pantomine and briefer, more elastic forms, like the *vaudeville* of the French theatre, or the *proverb* of the social party, would take the place of elaborate tragedy and comedy.

But those who find the theatres of this city well filled all the year round by an audience willing to sit out the heroisms of Rolla, and the sentimentalism and stale morality of such a piece as we were doomed to listen to while the Keans were here, ("Town and Country" was its name,) still think there is room for the regular drama, if genius should engage in its creation. Accordingly there have been in this country, as well as in England, many attempts to produce dramas suitable for action no less than for the closet. The actor, Murdoch, about to devote himself with enthusiasm and hope to prop up a falling profession, is to bring out a series of plays written, not merely *for* him, but because his devotion is likely to furnish fit occasion for their appearance. The first of these, "Witchcraft, a tragedy," brought out successfully upon the boards at Philadelphia, we have read, and it is a work of strong and majestic lineaments; a fine originality is shown in the conception, by which the love of a son for a mother is made a sufficient *motiv* (as the Germans call the ruling impulse of a work) in the production of tragic interest; no less original is the attempt, and delightful the success, in making an aged woman a satisfactory heroine to the piece through the greatness of her soul, and the magnetic influence it exerts on all around her, till the ignorant and superstitious fancy that the sky darkens and the winds wait upon her as she walks on the lonely hill-side near her hut to commune with the Past, and seek instruction from Heaven. The working of her character on the other agents of the piece is depicted with force and nobleness. The deep love of her son for her, the little tender, simple ways in which he shows it, having preserved the purity and poetic spirit of childhood by never having been weaned from his first love, a mother's love, the anguish of his soul when he too becomes infected with distrust, and cannot discriminate the natural magnetism of a strong nature from the spells and lures of sorcery, the final triumph of his faith, all offered the highest scope to genius and the power of moral perception in the actor. There are highly poetic intimations of those lowering days with their veiled skies, brassy light, and sadly whispering winds, very common in Massachusetts, so ominous and brooding seen from any point, but from the idea of witchcraft, invested with an awful significance. We do not know, however, that this could bring it beyond what it has appeared to our own sane mind, as if the air was thick with spirits, in an equivocal and surely sad condition, whether of purgatory or downfall; and the air was vocal with all manner of dark intimations. We are glad to see this mood of nature so fitly characterized.

The sweetness and *naiveté* with which the young girl is made to describe the effects of love upon her, as supposing them to proceed from a spell, are also original, and there is no other way in which this revelation could have been induced that would not have injured the beauty of the character and position. Her visionary sense of her lover, as an ideal figure, is of a high order of poetry, and these facts have very seldom been brought out from the cloisters of the mind into the light of open day.

The play is very deficient as regards rhythm; indeed, we might say there is no apparent reason why the lines should begin with capital letters. The minor personages are mere caricatures, very coarsely drawn; all the power is concentrated on the main characters and their emotions. So did not Shakspeare, does not ever the genuine dramatist, whose mind teems with "the fulness of forms." As Raphael in his most crowded groups can put in no misplaced or imperfect foot or hand, neither neglect to invest the least important figure of his backgrounds with every characteristic trait, nor could spare the invention of the most beautiful *coiffure* and accessories for the humblest handmaid of his Madonnas, so doth the great artist always clothe the whole picture with full and breathing life, for it appears so before his mental eye. But minds not perfectly artistical, yet of strong conceptions, subordinate the rest to one or two leading figures, and the imperfectly represented life of the others incloses them, as in a frame.

In originality of conception and resting the main interest upon force of character in a woman, this drama naturally leads us to revert to a work in the department of narrative fiction, which, on similar grounds, comes to us as a harbinger of the new era. This book is "Margaret, or the Real and Ideal," a work which has appeared within the past year; and, considering its originality and genuineness, has excited admiration and sympathy amazingly soon. Even some leading reviews, of what Byron used to speak of as the "garrison" class, (a class the most opposite imaginable to that of Garrison abolitionists,) have discussed its pretensions and done homage to its merits. It is a work of great power and richness, a genuine disclosure of the life of mind and the history of character. Its descriptions of scenery and the common people, in the place and time it takes up, impart to it the highest value as a representative of transient existence, which had a great deal of meaning. The beautiful simplicity of action upon and within the mind of Margaret, Heaven lying so clearly about her in the infancy of the hut of drunkards, the woods, the village, and their ignorant, simply human denizens, her unconscious growth to the stature of womanhood, the flow of life impelled by her, the spiritual intimations of her dreams, the prophecies of music in the character of Chilion, the *naive* discussion of the leading reform movements of the day in their rudimental forms, the archness, the humour, the profound religious faith, make of this book an aviary from which doves shall go forth to discover and report of all the green spots of promise in the land. Of books like this, as good, and still better, our new literature shall be full; and, though one swallow does not make a summer, yet we greet, in this one "Yankee novel," the sufficient earnest of riches that only need the skill of competent miners to be made current for the benefit of man.

Meanwhile, the most important part of our literature, while the work of diffusion is still going on, lies in the journals, which monthly, weekly, daily, send their messages to every corner of this great land, and form, at present, the only efficient instrument for the general education of the people.

Among these, the Magazines take the lowest rank. Their object is principally to cater for the amusement of vacant hours, and, as there is not a great deal of wit and light talent in this country, they do not even this to much advantage. More wit, grace, and elegant trifling, embellish the annals of literature in one day of France than in a year of America.

The Reviews are more able. If they cannot compare, on equal terms, with those of France, England, and Germany, where, if genius be rare, at least a vast amount of talent and culture are brought to bear upon all the departments of knowledge, they are yet very creditable to a new country, where so large a portion of manly ability must be bent on making laws, making speeches, making rail-roads and canals. They are, however, much injured by a partisan spirit, and the fear of censure from their own public. This last is always slow death to a journal; its natural and only safe position is *to lead;* if, instead, it bows to the will of the multitude, it will find the ostracism of democracy far more dangerous than the worst censure of a tyranny could be. It is not half so dangerous to a man to be immured in a dungeon alone with God and his own clear conscience, as to walk the streets fearing the scrutiny of a thousand eyes, ready to veil, with anxious care, whatever may not suit the many-headed monster in its momentary mood. Gentleness is dignified, but caution is debasing; only a noble fearlessness can give wings to the mind, with which to soar beyond the common ken, and learn what may be of use to the crowd below. Writers have nothing to do but to love truth fervently, seek justice according to their ability, and then express what is in the mind; they have nothing to do with consequences, God will take care of those. The want of such noble courage, such faith in the power of truth and good desire, paralyze mind greatly in this country. Publishers are afraid; authors are afraid; and if a worthy resistance is not made by religious souls, there is danger that all the light will soon be put under bushels, lest some wind should waft from it a spark that may kindle dangerous fire.

For want of such faith, and the catholic spirit that flows from it, we have no great leading Review. The North American was once the best. While under the care of Edward Everett, himself a host in extensive knowledge, grace and adroitness in applying it, and the power of enforcing grave meanings by a light and flexible satire that tickled while it wounded, it boasted more force, more life, a finer scope of power. But now, though still exhibiting ability and information upon special points, it is entirely deficient in great leadings, and the *vivida vis,* but ambles and jogs at an old gentlemanly pace along a beaten path that leads to no important goal.

Several other journals have more life, energy and directness than this, but there is none which occupies a truly great and commanding position, a beacon light to all who sail that way. In order to this, a journal must know how to cast aside all local and temporary considerations when new convictions command, and allow free range in its columns, to all kinds of ability, and all ways of viewing subjects. That would give it a life, rich, bold various.

The life of intellect is becoming more and more determined to the weekly and daily papers, whose light leaves fly so rapidly and profusely over the land. Speculations are afloat, as to the influence of the electric telegraph upon their destiny, and it seems obvious that it should raise their character by taking from them in some measure, the office of gathering and dispersing the news, and requiring of them rather to arrange and interpret it.

This mode of communication is susceptible of great excellence in the way of condensed essay, narrative, criticism, and is the natural receptacle for the lyrics of the day. That so few good ones deck the poet's corner, is because the indifference or unfitness of editors, as to choosing and refusing, makes this place, at present, undesirable to the poet. It might be otherwise.

The means which this organ affords of diffusing knowledge and sowing the seeds of thought where they may hardly fail of an infinite harvest, cannot be too highly prized by the discerning and benevolent. Minds of the first class are generally indisposed to this kind of writing; what must be done on the spur of the occasion and cast into the world so incomplete, as the hurried offspring of a day or hour's labour must generally be, cannot satisfy their judgment, or do justice to their powers. But he who looks to the benefit of others, and sees with what rapidity and ease instruction and thought are assimilated by men, when they come thus, as it were, on the wings of the wind, may be content, as an unhonoured servant to the grand purposes of Destiny, to work in such a way at the Pantheon which the Ages shall complete, on which his name may not be inscribed, but which will breathe the life of his soul.

The confidence in uprightness of intent, and the safety of truth, is still more needed here than in the more elaborate kinds of writing, as meanings cannot be fully explained nor expressions revised. Newspaper writing is next door to conversation, and should be conducted on the same principles. It has this advantage: we address, not our neighbour, who forces us to remember his limitations and prejudices, but the ideal presence of human nature as we feel it ought to be and trust it will be. We address America rather than Americans.

A worthy account of the vocation and duties of the journalist, is given by Cornelius Mathews. Editors, generally, could not do better than every New Year's day to read and insert the following verses.

As shakes the canvass of a thousand ships,
Struck by a heavy land-breeze, far at sea,

Ruffle the thousand broad sheets of the land,
  Filled with the people's breath of potency.

A thousand images the hour will take,
  From him who strikes, who rules, who speaks, who sings,
Many within the hour their grave to make,
  Many to live, far in the heart of things.

A dark-dyed spirit he, who coins the time,
  To virtue's wrong, in base disloyal lies,
Who makes the morning's breath, the evening's tide,
  The utterer of his blighting forgeries.

How beautiful who scatters, wide and free,
  The gold-bright seeds of loved and loving truth!
By whose perpetual hand, each day supplied,
  Leaps to new life the empire's heart of youth.

To know the instant and to speak it true,
  Its passing lights of joy, its dark, sad cloud,
To fix upon the unnumbered gazers' view,
  Is to thy ready hand's broad strength allowed.

There is an inwrought life in every hour,
  Fit to be chronicled at large and told.
'Tis thine to pluck to light its secret power,
  And on the air its many-colored heart unfold.

The angel that in sand-dropped minutes lives,
  Demands a message cautious as the ages,
Who stuns, with dusk-red words of hate his ear,
  That mighty power to boundless wrath enrages.

This feeling of the dignity of his office, honour and power in fulfilling it, are not common in the journalist, but, where they exist, a mark has been left fully correspondent to the weight of the instrument. The few editors of this country who, with mental ability and resource, have combined strength of purpose and fairness of conduct, who have never merged the man and the gentleman in the partisan, who have been willing to have all sides fully heard, while their convictions were clear on one, who have disdained groundless assaults or angry replies, and have valued what was sincere, characteristic and free, too much to bend to popular errors they felt able to correct, have been so highly prized that it is wonderful that more do not learn the use of this great opportunity. It will be learned yet; the resources of this organ of thought and instruction begin to be understood, and shall yet be brought out and used worthily.

We see we have omitted honoured names in this essay. We have not spoken of Brown, as a novelist by far our first in point of genius and instruction as to the soul of things. Yet his works have fallen almost out of print. It is their dark, deep gloom that prevents their being popular, for their very beauties are grave and sad. But we see that Ormond is being republished at this moment. The picture of Roman character, of the life and resources of a single noble creature, of Constantia alone, should make that book an object of reverence. All these novels should be republished; if not favorites, they should at least not be lost sight of, for there will always be some who find in such powers of mental analysis the only response to their desires.

We have not spoken of Hawthorne, the best writer of the day, in a similar range with Irving, only touching many more points and discerning far more deeply. But we have omitted many things in this slight sketch, for the subject, even in this stage, lies as a volume in our mind, and cannot be unrolled in completeness unless time and space were more abundant. Our object was to show that although by a thousand signs, the existence is foreshown of those forces which are to animate an American literature, that faith, those hopes are not yet alive which shall usher it into a homogeneous or fully organized state of being. The future is glorious with certainties for those who do their duty in the present, and, lark-like, seeking the sun, challenge its eagles to an earthward flight, where their nests may be built in our mountains, and their young raise their cry of triumph, unchecked by dullness in the echoes.

Since finishing the foregoing essay, the publication of some volumes by Hawthorne and Brown have led to notices in "The Tribune," which, with a review of Longfellow's poems, are subjoined to eke out the statement as to the merits of those authors.

MOSSES FROM AN OLD MANSE: By NATHANIEL HAWTHORNE.—In Two Parts. New-York: Wiley and Putnam. 1846.

WE have been seated here the last ten minutes, pen in hand, thinking what we can possibly say about this book that will not be either superfluous or impertinent.

Superfluous, because the attractions of Hawthorne's writings cannot fail of one and the same effect on all persons who possess the common sympathies of men. To all who are still happy in some groundwork of unperverted Nature, the delicate, simple, human tenderness, unsought, unbought and therefore precious morality, the tranquil elegance and playfulness, the humour which never breaks the impression of sweetness and dignity, do an inevitable message which requires no comment of the critic to make its meaning clear. Impertinent, because the influence of this mind, like that of some loveliest aspects of Nature, is to induce silence from a feeling of repose. We do not think of any thing particularly worth saying about this that has been so fitly and pleasantly said.

Yet it seems *un*fit that we, in our office of chronicler of intellectual advents and apparitions, should omit to render open and audible honour to one whom we have long delighted to honour. It may be, too, that this slight notice of ours may awaken the attention of those distant or busy who might not otherwise search for the volume, which comes betimes in the leafy month of June.

So we will give a slight account of it, even if we cannot say much of value. Though Hawthorne has now a standard reputation, both for the qualities we have mentioned and the beauty of the style in which they are embodied, yet we believe he has not been very widely read. This is only because his works have not been published in the way to ensure extensive circulation in this new, hurrying world of ours. The immense extent of country over which the reading (still very small in proportion to the mere working) community is scattered, the rushing and pushing of our life at this electrical stage of development, leave no work a chance to be speedily and largely known that is not trumpeted and placarded. And, odious as are the features of a forced and artificial circulation, it must be considered that it does no harm in the end. Bad books will not be read if they are bought instead of good, while the good have an abiding life in the log-cabin settlements and Red River steamboat landings, to which they would in no other way penetrate. Under the auspices of Wiley and Putnam, Hawthorne will have a chance to collect all his own public about him, and that be felt as a presence which before was only a rumor.

The volume before us shares the charms of Hawthorne's earlier tales; the only difference being that his range of subjects is a little wider. There is the same gentle and sincere companionship with Nature, the same delicate but fearless scrutiny of the secrets of the heart, the same serene independence of petty and artificial restrictions, whether on opinions or conduct, the same familiar, yet pensive sense of the spiritual or demoniacal influences that haunt the palpable life and common walks of men, not by many apprehended except in results. We have here to regret that Hawthorne, at this stage of his mind's life, lays no more decisive hand upon the apparition—brings it no nearer than in former days. We had hoped that we should see, no more as in a glass darkly, but face to face. Still, still brood over his page the genius of revery and the nonchalance of Nature, rather than the ardent earnestness of the human soul which feels itself born not only to see and disclose, but to understand and interpret such things. Hawthorne intimates and suggests, but he does not lay bare the mysteries of our being.

The introduction to the "Mosses," in which the old manse, its inhabitants and visitants are portrayed, is written with even more than his usual charm of placid grace and many strokes of his admirable good sense. Those who are not, like ourselves, familiar with the scene and its denizens, will still perceive how true that picture must be; those of us who are thus familiar will best know how to prize the record of objects and influences unique in our country and time.

"The Birth Mark" and "Rapaccini's Daughter," embody truths of profound importance in shapes of aerial elegance. In these, as here and there in all these pieces, shines the loveliest ideal of love, and the beauty of feminine purity (by which we mean no mere acts or abstinences, but perfect single truth felt and done in gentleness) which is its root.

"The Celestial Railroad," for its wit, wisdom, and the graceful adroitness with which the natural and material objects are interwoven with the allegories, has already won its meed of admiration. "Fire-worship" is a most charming essay for its domestic sweetness and thoughtful life. "Goodman Brown" is one of those disclosures we have spoken of, of the secrets of the breast. Who has not known such a trial that is capable indeed of sincere aspiration toward that only good, that infinite essence, which men call God. Who has not known the hour when even that best beloved image cherished as the one precious symbol left, in the range of human nature, believed to be still pure gold when all the rest have turned to clay, shows, in severe ordeal, the symptoms of alloy. Oh, hour of anguish, when the old familiar faces grow dark and dim in the lurid light—when the gods of the hearth, honoured in childhood, adored in youth, crumble, and nothing,

nothing is left which the daily earthly feelings can embrace—can cherish with unbroken faith! Yet some survive that trial more happily than young Goodman Brown. They are those who have not sought it—have never of their own accord walked forth with the Tempter into the dim shades of Doubt. Mrs Bull-Frog is an excellent humourous picture of what is called to be "content at last with substantial realities!!" The "Artist of the Beautiful" presents in a form that is, indeed, beautiful, the opposite view as to what *are* the substantial realities of life. Let each man choose between them according to his kind. Had Hawthorne written "Roger Malvin's Burial" alone, we should be pervaded with the sense of the poetry and religion of his soul.

As a critic, the style of Hawthorne, faithful to his mind, shows repose, a great reserve of strength, a slow secure movement. Though a very refined, he is also a very clear writer, showing, as we said before, a placid grace, and an indolent command of language.

And now, beside the full, calm yet romantic stream of his mind, we will rest. It has refreshment for the weary, islets of fascination no less than dark recesses and shadows for the imaginative, pure reflections for the pure of heart and eye, and like the Concord he so well describes, many exquisite lilies for him who knows how to get at them.

ORMOND; or, The Secret Witness.
WIELAND; or, The Transformation. By Charles Brockden Brown. Library of Standard Romance. W. Taylor & Co., 2 Astor House.

We rejoice to see these reprints of Brown's novels, as we have long been ashamed that one who ought to be the pride of the country, and who is, in the higher qualities of the mind, so far in advance of our other novelists, should have become almost inaccessible to the public.

It has been the custom to liken Brown to Godwin. But there was no imitation, no second-hand in the matter. They were congenial natures, and whichever had come first might have lent an impulse to the other. Either mind might have been conscious of the possession of that peculiar vein of ore without thinking of working it for the mint of the world, till the other, led by accident, or overflow of feeling, showed him how easy it was to put the reveries of his solitary hours into words and upon paper for the benefit of his fellow men.

"My mind to me a kingdom is."

Such a man as Brown or Godwin has a right to say that. It is no scanty, turbid rill, requiring to be daily fed from a thousand others or from the clouds! Its plenteous source rushes from a high mountain between bulwarks of stone. Its course, even and full, keeps ever green its banks, and affords the means of life and joy to a million gliding shapes, that fill its deep waters, and twinkle above its golden sands.

Life and Joy! Yes, Joy! These two have been called the dark masters, because they disclose the twilight recesses of the human heart. Yet their gravest page is joy compared with the mixed, shallow, uncertain pleasures of vulgar minds. Joy! because they were all alive and fulfilled the purposes of being. No sham, no imitation, no convention deformed or veiled their native lineaments, checked the use of their natural force. All alive themselves, they understood that there is no joy without truth, no perception of joy without real life. Unlike most men, existence was to them not a tissue of words and seemings, but a substantial possession.

Born Hegelians, without the pretensions of science, they sought God in their own consciousness, and found him. The heart, because it saw itself so fearfully and wonderfully made, did not disown its Maker. With the highest idea of the dignity, power and beauty of which human nature is capable, they had courage to see by what an oblique course it proceeds, yet never lose faith that it would reach its destined aim. Thus their darkest disclosures are not hobgoblin shows, but precious revelations.

Brown is great as ever human writer was in showing the self-sustaining force of which a lonely mind is capable. He takes one person, makes him brood like the bee, and extract from the common life before him all its sweetness, its bitterness, and its nourishment.

We say makes *him*, but it increases our own interest in Brown that, a prophet in this respect of a better era, he has usually placed this thinking royal mind in the body of a woman. This personage too is always feminine, both in her character and circumstances, but a conclusive proof that the term *feminine* is not a synonym for *weak*. Constantia, Clara Wieland, have loving hearts, graceful and plastic natures, but they have also noble thinking minds, full of resource, constancy, courage. The Marguerite of Godwin, no less, is all refinement, and the purest tenderness, but she is also the soul of honour, capable of deep discernment and of acting in conformity with the inferences she draws. The man of Brown and Godwin has not eaten of the fruit of the tree of knowledge and been driven to sustain himself by sweat of his brow for nothing, but has learned the structure and laws of things, and become a being, rational, benignant, various, and desirous of supplying the loss of innocence by the attainment of virtue. So his woman need not be quite so weak as Eve, the slave of feeling or of flattery: she also has learned to guide her helm amid the storm across the troubled waters.

The horrors which mysteriously beset these persons, and against which, so far as outward facts go, they often strive in vain, are but a representation of those powers permitted to work in the same way throughout the affairs of this world. Their demoniacal attributes only represent a morbid state of the intellect, gone to excess from want of balance with the other powers. There is an intellectual as well as a physical drunkenness, and which no less impels to crime. Carwin, urged on to use his ventriloquism, till the presence of such a strange agent wakened the seeds of fanaticism in the breast of Wieland, is in a state no more foreign to nature than that of the wretch executed last week, who felt himself drawn as by a spell to murder his victim because he had thought of her money and the pleasures it might bring him, till the feeling possessed his brain that hurls the gamester to ruin. The victims of such agency are like the soldier of the Rio Grande, who, both legs shot off and his life-blood rushing out with every pulse, replied serenely to his pitying comrades that "he had now that for which the soldier enlisted." The end of the drama is not in this world, and the fiction which rounds off the whole to harmony and felicity before the curtain falls, sins against truth, and deludes the reader. The Nelsons of the human race are all the more exposed to the assaults of fate that they are decorated with the badges of well-earned glory. Who, but feels as they fall in death, or rise again to a mutilated existence, that the end is not yet? Who, that thinks, but must feel that the recompense is, where Brown places it, in the accumulation of mental treasure, in the severe assay by fire that leaves the gold pure to be used sometime—somewhere.

Brown, man of the brooding eye, the teeming brain, the deep and fervent heart; if thy country prize thee not and has almost lost thee out of sight, it is that her heart is made shallow and cold, her eye dim, by the pomp of circumstance, the love of gross outward gain. She cannot long continue thus, for it takes a great deal of soul to keep a huge body from disease and dissolution. As there is more soul thou wilt be more sought, and many will yet sit down with thy Constantia to the meal and water on which she sustained her full and thoughtful existence, who could not endure the ennui of aldermanic dinners, or find any relish in the imitation of French cookery. To-day many will read the words, and some have a cup large enough to receive the spirit, before it is lost in the sand on which their feet are planted.

Brown's high standard of the delights of intellectual communion and of friendship correspond with the fondest hopes of early days. But in the relations of real life, at present, there is rarely more than one of the parties ready for such intercourse as he describes. On the one side there will be dryness, want of perception or variety, a stupidity unable to appreciate life's richest boon when offered to its grasp, and the finer nature is doomed to retrace its steps, unhappy as those who having force to raise a spirit cannot retain or make it substantial, and stretch out their arms only to bring them back empty to the breast.

POEMS. By HENRY WADSWORTH LONGFELLOW; with Illustrations by D. HUNTINGTON. Philadelphia; Carey & Hart, Chesnut-st. 1845.

POETRY is not a superhuman or supernatural gift. It is, on the contrary, the fullest and therefore most completely natural expression of what is human. It is that of which the rudiments lie in every human breast, but developed to a more complete existence than the obstructions of daily life permit, clothed in an adequate form, domesticated in nature by the use of apt images, the perception of grand analogies, and set to the music of the spheres for the delight of all who have ears to hear. We have uttered these remarks, which may, to many of our readers, seem truisms, for the sake of showing that our definition of poetry is large enough to include all kinds of excellence. It includes not only the great bards, but the humblest minstrels. The great bards bring to light the more concealed treasures, gems which centuries have been employed in forming and which it is their office to reveal, polish, and set for the royal purposes of man; the wandering minstrel with his lighter but beautiful office calls the attention of men to the meaning of the flowers, which also is hidden from the careless eye, though they have grown and bloomed in full sight of all who chose to look. All the poets are the priests of Nature, though the greatest are also the prophets of the manhood of man. For, when fully grown, the life of man must be all poetry; each of his thoughts will be a key to the treasures of the universe; each of his acts a revelation of beauty, his language will be music, and his habitual presence will overflow with more energy and inspire with a nobler rapture than do the fullest strains of lyric poetry now.

Meanwhile we need poets; men more awakened to the wonders of life, and gifted more or less with a power to express what they see, and to all who possess, in any degree, those requisites we offer and we owe welcome and tribute, whether the place of their song be in the Pantheon, from which issue the grand decrees of immortal thought, or by the fireside, where hearts need kindling and eyes need clarifying by occasional drops of nectar in their tea.

But this—this alone we claim, and can welcome none who cannot present this title to our hearing; that the vision be genuine, the expression spontaneous. No imposition upon our young fellow citizens of pinchbeck for gold! they must have the true article, and pay the due intellectual price, or they will wake from a life-long dream of folly to find themselves beggars.

And never was a time when satirists were more needed to scourge from Parnassus the magpies who are devouring the food scattered there for the singing birds. There will always be a good deal of mock poetry in the market with the genuine; it grows up naturally as tares among the wheat, and, while there is a fair proportion preserved, we abstain from severe weeding lest the two come up together; but when the tares have almost usurped the field, it is time to begin and see if the field cannot be freed from them and made ready for a new seed-time.

The rules of versification are now understood and used by those who have never entered into that soul from which metres grow as acorns from the oak, shapes as characteristic of the parent tree, containing in like manner germs of limitless life for the future. And as to the substance of these jingling rhymes, and dragging, stumbling rhythms, we might tell of bombast, or still worse, an affected simplicity, sickly sentiment, or borrowed dignity; but it is sufficient to comprise all in this one censure. The writers did not write because they felt obliged to relieve themselves of the swelling thought within, but as an elegant exercise which may win them rank and reputation above the crowd. Their lamp is not lit by the sacred and inevitable lightning from above, but carefully fed by their own will to be seen of men.

There are very few now rhyming in England, not obnoxious to this censure, still fewer in our America. For such no laurel blooms. May the friendly poppy soon crown them and grant us stillness to hear the silver tones of genuine music, for, if such there be, they are at present almost stifled by these fifes and gongs.

Yet there is a middle class, composed of men of little original poetic power, but of much poetic taste and sensibility, whom we would not wish to have silenced. They do no harm, but much good, (if only their minds are not confounded with those of a higher class,) by educating in others the faculties dominant in themselves. In this class we place the writer at present before us.

We must confess to a coolness towards Mr. Longfellow, in consequence of the exaggerated praises that have been bestowed upon him. When we see a person of moderate powers receive honours which should be reserved for the highest, we feel somewhat like assailing him and taking from him the crown which should be reserved for grander brows. And yet this is, perhaps ungenerous. It may be that the management of publishers, the hyperbole of paid or undiscerning reviewers, or some accidental cause which gives a temporary interest to productions beyond what they would permanently command, have raised such an one to a place as much above his wishes as his claims, and which he would rejoice, with honourable modesty, to vacate at the approach of one worthier. We the more readily believe this of Mr. Longfellow, as one so sensible to the beauties of other writers and so largely indebted to them, *must* know his own comparative rank better than his readers have known it for him.

And yet so much adulation is dangerous. Mr. Longfellow, so lauded on all hands—now able to collect his poems which have circulated so widely in previous editions, and been paid for so handsomely by the handsomest annuals, in this beautiful volume, illustrated by one of the most distinguished of our younger artists—has found a flatterer in that very artist. The portrait which adorns this volume is not merely flattered or idealized, but there is an attempt at adorning it by expression thrown into the eyes with just that which the original does not possess, whether in face or mind. We have often seen faces whose usually coarse and heavy lineaments were harmonized at times into beauty by the light that rises from the soul into the eyes. The intention Nature had with regard to the face and its wearer, usually eclipsed beneath bad habits or a bad education, is then disclosed, and we see what hopes Death has in store for that soul. But here the enthusiasm thrown into the eyes only makes the rest of the face look more weak, and the idea suggested is the anomalous one of a dandy Pindar.

Such is not the case with Mr. Longfellow himself. He is never a Pindar, though he is sometimes a dandy even in the clean and elegantly ornamented streets and trim gardens of his verse. But he is still more a man of cultivated taste, delicate though not deep feeling, and some, though not much, poetic force.

Mr. Longfellow has been accused of plagiarism. We have been surprised that any one should have been anxious to fasten special charges of this kind upon him, when we had supposed it so obvious that the greater part of his mental stores were derived from the works of others. He has no style of his own growing out of his own experiences and observations of nature. Nature with him, whether human or external, is always seen through the windows of literature. There are in his poems sweet and tender passages descriptive of his personal feelings, but very few showing him as an observer, at first hand, of the passions within, or the landscape without.

This want of the free breath of nature, this perpetual borrowing of imagery, this excessive, because superficial, culture which he has derived from an acquaintance with the elegant literature of many nations and men out of proportion to the experience of life within himself, prevent Mr. Longfellow's verses from ever being a true refreshment to ourselves. He says in one of his most graceful verses:

> From the cool cisterns of the midnight air
> My spirit drank repose;
> The fountain of perpetual peace flows there,
> From those deep cisterns flows.

Now this is just what we cannot get from Mr. Longfellow. No solitude of the mind reveals to us the deep cisterns.

Let us take, for example of what we do not like, one of his worst pieces, the Prelude to the Voices of the Night—

> Beneath some patriarchal tree
> I lay upon the ground;

His hoary arms uplifted be,
And all the broad leaves over me
Clapped their little hands in glee
With one continuous sound.

What an unpleasant mixture of images! Such never rose in a man's mind, as he lay on the ground and looked up to the tree above him. The true poetry for this stanza would be to give us an image of what was in the writer's mind as he lay there and looked up. But this idea of the leaves clapping their little hands with glee is taken out of some book; or, at any rate, is a book thought, and not one that came in the place, and jars entirely with what is said of the tree uplifting its hoary arms. Then take this other stanza from a man whose mind *should* have grown up in familiarity with the American *genius loci.*

Therefore at Pentecost, which brings
The Spring clothed like a bride,
When nestling buds unfold their wings,
And bishop's caps have golden rings,
Musing upon many things,
I sought the woodlands wide.

Musing upon many things—ay! and upon many books too, or we should have nothing of Pentecost or bishop's caps with their golden rings. For ourselves, we have not the least idea what bishop's caps are;—are they flowers?—or what? Truly, the schoolmaster was abroad in the woodlands that day! As to the conceit of the wings of the buds, it is a false image, because one that cannot be carried out. Such will not be found in the poems of poets; with such the imagination is all compact, and their works are not dead mosaics, with substance inserted merely because pretty, but living growths, homogeneous and satisfactory throughout.

Such instances could be adduced every where throughout the poems, depriving us of any clear pleasure from any one piece, and placing his poems beside such as those of Bryant in the same light as that of the prettiest *made* shell, beside those whose every line and hue tells a history of the action of winds and waves and the secrets of one class of organizations.

But, do we, therefore esteem Mr. Longfellow a wilful or conscious plagiarist? By no means. It is his misfortune that other men's thoughts are so continually in his head as to overshadow his own. The order of fine development is for the mind the same as the body, to take in just so much food as will sustain it in its exercise and assimilate with its growth. If it is so assimilated—if it becomes a part of the skin, hair and eyes of the man, it is his own, no matter whether he pick it up in the woods, or borrow from the dish of a fellow man, or receive it in the form of manna direct from Heaven. "Do you ask the genius," said Goethe, "to give an account of what he has taken from others. As well demand of the hero an account of the beeves and loaves which have nourished him to such martial stature."

But Mr. Longfellow presents us, not with a new product in which all the old varieties are melted into a fresh form, but rather with a tastefully arranged Museum, between whose glass cases are interspersed neatly potted rose trees, geraniums and hyacinths, grown by himself with aid of in-door heat. Still we must acquit him of being a willing or conscious plagiarist. Some objects in the collection are his own; as to the rest, he has the merit of appreciation, and a re-arrangement, not always judicious, but the result of feeling on his part.

Such works as Mr. Longfellow's we consider injurious only if allowed to usurp the place of better things. The reason of his being overrated here, is because through his works breathes the air of other lands, with whose products the public at large is but little acquainted. He will do his office, and a desirable one, of promoting a taste for the literature of these lands before his readers are aware of it. As a translator he shows the same qualities as in his own writings; what is forcible and compact he does not render adequately; grace and sentiment he appreciates and reproduces. Twenty years hence, when he stands upon his own merits, he will rank as a writer of elegant, if not always accurate taste, of great imitative power, and occasional felicity in an original way, where his feelings are really stirred. He has touched no subject where he has not done somewhat that is pleasing, though also his poems are much marred by ambitious failings. As instances of his best manner we would mention "The Reaper and the Flowers," "Lines to the Planet Mars," "A Gleam of Sunshine," and "The Village Blacksmith." His two ballads are excellent imitations, yet in them is no spark of fire. In "Nuremberg" are charming passages. Indeed, the whole poem is one of the happiest specimens of Mr. L.'s poetic feeling, taste and tact in making up a rosary of topics and images. Thinking it may be less known than most of the poems we will quote it. The engraving which accompanies it of the rich old architecture is a fine gloss on its contents.

NUREMBERG.

In the valley of the Pegnitz, where across broad meadow lands
Rise the blue Franconian mountains, Nuremberg, the ancient, stands.
Quaint old town of toil and traffic—quaint old town of art and song—
Memories haunt thy pointed gables, like the rooks that round them throng;
Memories of the Middle Ages, when the Emperors, rough and bold,
Had their dwelling in thy castle, time defying, centuries old;
And thy brave and thrifty burghers boasted in their uncouth rhyme,
That their great imperial city stretched its hand through every clime.
In the court-yard of the castle, bound with many an iron band,
Stands the mighty linden, planted by Queen Cunigunda's hand.
On the square the oriel window, where in old heroic days,
Sat the poet Melchior, singing Kaiser Maximilian's praise.
Every where I see around me rise the wondrous world of Art—
Fountains wrought with richest sculpture, standing in the common mart;
And above cathedral doorways, saints and bishops carved in stone,
By a former age commissioned as apostles to our own.
In the church of sainted Sebald sleeps enshrined his holy dust,
And in bronze the Twelve Apostles guard from age to age their trust;

In the church of sainted Lawrence stands a Pix of sculpture rare,
Like the foamy sheaf of fountains, rising through the painted air.
Here, when Art was still Religion, with a simple reverent heart,
Lived and laboured Albert Durer, the Evangelist of Art;
Hence in silence and in sorrow, toiling still with busy hand,
Like an emigrant he wandered, seeking for the Better Land.
Emigravit is the inscription on the tomb-stone where he lies;
Dead he is not, but departed, for the Artist never dies.
Fairer seems the ancient city, and the sunshine seems more fair,
That he once has trod its pavement—that he once has breathed its air!
Through those streets so broad and stately, these obscure and dismal lanes,
Walked of yore the Master-singers, chanting rude poetic strains.
From remote and sunless suburbs came they to the friendly guild,
Building nests in Fame's great temple, as in spouts the swallows build.
As the weaver plied the shuttle, wove he to the mystic rhyme,
And the smith his iron measures hammered to the anvil's chime;
Thanking God, whose boundless wisdom makes the flowers of poesy bloom
In the forge's dust and cinders—in the tissues of the loom.
Here Hans Sachs, the cobbler-poet, laureate of the gentle craft,
Wisest of the Twelve Wise Masters, in huge folios sang and laughed.
But his house is now an ale-house, with a nicely sanded floor,
And a garland in the window, and his face above the door;
Painted by some humble artist, as in Adam Paschman's song,
As the old man grey and dove-like, with his great beard white and long.
And at night the swarth mechanic comes to drown his cank and care,
Quaffing ale from pewter tankards in the master's antique chair.
Vanished is the ancient splendour, and before my dreamy eye
Wave these mingling shapes and figures, like a faded tapestry.
Not thy Councils, not thy Kaisers, win for thee the world's regard;
But thy painter, Albert Durer, and Hans Sachs, thy cobbler bard.
Thus, oh, Nuremberg! a wanderer from a region far away,
As he paced thy streets and court-yards, sang in thought his careless lay;
Gathering from the pavement's crevice, as a flow'ret of the soil,
The nobility of labour, the long pedigree of toil.

This image of the thought gathered like a flower from the crevice of the pavement, is truly natural and poetical.

Here is another image which came into the mind of the writer as he looked at the subject of his verse, and which pleases accordingly. It is from one of the new poems, addressed to Driving Cloud, "chief of the mighty Omahaws."

Wrapt in thy scarlet blanket I see thee stalk through the city's
Narrow and populous streets, as once by the margin of rivers
Stalked those birds unknown, that have left us only their foot-prints.
What, in a few short years, will remain of thy race but the foot-prints?

Here is another very graceful and natural simile:

A feeling of sadness and longing,
That is not akin to pain,
And resembles sorrow only
As the mist resembles rain.

Another—

I will forget her! All dear recollections,
Pressed in my heart like flowers within a book,
Shall be torn out and scattered to the winds.

The drama from which this is taken is an elegant exercise of the pen, after the fashion of the best models. Plans, figures, all are academical. It is a faint reflex of the actions and passions of men, tame in the conduct and lifeless in the characters, but not heavy, and containing good meditative passages.

And now farewell to the handsome book, with its Preciosos and Preciosas, its Vikings and knights, and cavaliers, its flowers of all climes, and wild flowers of none. We have not wished to depreciate these writings below their current value more than truth absolutely demands. We have not forgotten that, if a man cannot himself sit at the feet of the muse, it is much if he prizes those who may; it makes him a teacher to the people. Neither have we forgotten that Mr. Longfellow has a genuine respect for his pen, never writes carelessly, nor when he does not wish to, nor for money alone. Nor are we intolerant to those who prize hot-house bouquets beyond all the free beauty of nature; that helps the gardener and has its uses. But still let us not forget—Excelsior!!

SWEDENBORGIANISM.

NOBLE'S APPEAL IN BEHALF OF THE VIEWS HELD BY THE NEW (or Swedenborgian) CHURCH. Second edition, 1845. Boston: T. H. Carter & Co.—Otis Clapp.

ESSAYS BY THEOPHILUS PARSONS. Boston: Otis Clapp, School-st. 1845.

THE CORNER STONE OF THE NEW JERUSALEM, by B. F. BARRETT. New York: Bartlett and Wellford, Astor House; John Allen, 139 Nassau-street, 1845.

THE claim to be the New Church, or peculiarly the founders of a New Jerusalem, is like exclusive claims to the title of Orthodox. We have no sympathy with it. We believe that all kinds of inspiration and forms of faith have been made by the power that rules the world to coöperate in the development of mental life with a view to the eventual elucidation of truth. That ruling power overrules the vanity of men, or just the contrary would ensue. For men love the letter that killeth better than the spirit that continually refreshes its immortal life. They wish to compress truth into a nut-shell that it may be grasped in the hand. They wish to feel sure that they and theirs hold it all. In vain! More incompressible than light, it flows forth anew, and, while the preacher was finishing the sermon in which he proclaimed that now the last and greatest dispensation had arrived, and that all the truth could henceforward be encased within the walls of a church—it has already sped its way to unnumbered zones, planted in myriad new-born souls the seeds of life, and wakened in myriads more a pulse that cannot be tamed down by dogma or doctrine, but must always throb at each new revelation of the glories of the infinite.

Were there, indeed, a catholic church which should be based on a recognition of universal truths, simple as that proposed by Jesus, Love God with all thy soul and strength, thy neighbour as thyself; *such* a church would include all sincere motions of the spirit, and sects and opinions would no more war with one another than roses in the garden, but, like them, all contentedly grace a common soil and render their tribute to one heaven.

Then we should hear no more of *the* church, creed, or teacher, but of *a* church, creed or teacher. Each man would adopt contentedly what best answered his spiritual wants, lovingly granting the same liberality to others. Then the variety of opinions would produce its natural benefit of testing and animating each mind in its natural tendency, without those bitter accompaniments that make theological systems so repulsive to religious minds.

Religious tolerance will, probably, come last in the progress of civilization, for, in those interests which search deepest, the weeds of prejudice have struck root deepest, too. But it will come; for we see its practicability sometimes proved in the intercourse between friends; and so shall it be between parties and groups of men, when intercourse shall have been placed on the same basis of mutual good-will and respect for one another's rights. Then those ugliest taints of spiritual arrogance and vanity shall begin to be washed out of this world.

As with all other cases, so with this! We believe in no new church *par excellence*. Swedenborgians are to us those taught of Swedenborg, a great, a learned, a wise, a good man—also one instructed by direct influx from a higher sphere, but one of a constellation, and needing the aid of congenial influences to confirm and illustrate his.

That the body of his followers do not constitute a catholic church would be sufficiently proved to us by the fact, asserted by all who come in contact with them, that they attach an exaggerated importance to the teachings of their master, which shuts them in a great measure from the benefit of other teachings, and threatens to make them bigots, though of such mild strain as shows them to be the followers of one singularly mild and magnanimous.

For Swedenborg was one who, though entirely open and steadfast in the maintenance of his pretensions, knew how to live with kings, nobles, clergy, and people, without being the object of persecution to any. They viewed with respect, if not with confidence, his conviction that he was "in fellowship with angels.' They knew the deep discipline and wide attainments of his mind. They saw that he forced his convictions on no one, but relied for their diffusion upon spiritual laws. They saw that he made none but an incidental use of his miraculous powers, and that it was not to him a matter of any consequence whether others recognized them or not; for he knew that those whom truth does not reach by its spiritual efficacy cannot be made to believe by dint of signs and wonders.

Thus his life was, for its steady growth, its soft majesty, and exhibition of a faith never fierce and sparkling, never dim, a happy omen for the age. Thus gently and gradually may new organizations of great principles be effected now! May it prove that, at least in the more advanced part of the world, revolutions may be effected without painful throes! Such a life was in correspondence with his system, which is one of gradation and harmony.

I have used the word system, and yet it is not the right one. The works of Swedenborg contain intimations of a system, but it is one whose full development must be coincident with the perfection of all things. Some great rules he proffers, some ways of thinking opens; we have centre and radii, but the circumference is not closed in.

This is to us the greatness of Swedenborg and the ground of our pleasure in his works, that in them we can expatiate freely; there is room enough. We can take what does us good, and decline the rest: we may delight in his theory of forms or of correspondences, may be aided in tracing the hidden meanings of symbols, or animated by the poetic energy of his vision, without being bound down to things that seem to us unimportant. We can converse with *him* without acquiescing in the declaration that all angels have, at some time, been men, or the like, which seem to us groundless and arbitrary. It is not so with his followers; they are like the majority of disciples; if you do not know the master before knowing them, his true face will be hidden from you forever. Their minds being smaller, they lay the chief stress on what is least important in his instructions, and do not know how to express the best even of what they have received; being too mighty for them to embrace they cannot reproduce it, though it acts upon their lives.

So it is with all the books at the head of this notice. Noble's Appeal has been, we understand, a famous book among the followers of Swedenborg. We did not find it sufficiently interesting to give it a thorough reading. It is addressed to those who object to Swedenborg from a low platform. It arrays arguments and evidences with skill, and in a good spirit, and contains particulars, as to matters of fact, that will interest those who have not previously met with them. It quotes Swedenborg's letter to Mr. Hartley, written with such a beautiful dignity, and giving so distinct an idea of the personal presence of the writer, also the letter of Kant with regard to one of Swedenborg's revelations as to a matter of fact, (the fire at Stockholm.) The letter has been quoted a hundred times before, but it always remains interesting to see the genuine candour with which a great mind can treat one so opposite to its own, and pleasant to see how far such an one is above the necessity felt by lesser minds of denying what they cannot explain.

We have often been asked what we thought of these pretensions in Swedenborg. We think, in the first place, none can doubt his sincerity, and in few cases could we have so little reason to doubt the correctness of perception in the seer. Swedenborg must be seen by any one acquainted with his mind to be in an extraordinary degree above the chance of self-delusion. As to the facts, the evidence which satisfied Kant might satisfy most people, one would suppose. As to the power of holding intercourse with spirits enfranchised from our present sphere, we see no reason why it should not exist, and do see much reason why it should rarely be developed, but none why it should not *sometimes*. Those spirits are, we all believe, existent somewhere, somehow, and there seems to be no good reason why a person in spiritual nearness to them, whom such intercourse cannot agitate, or engross so that he cannot walk steadily in his present path, should not enjoy it, when of use to him. But it seems to us that the stress laid upon such a fact, for or against, argues a want of faith in the immortality of souls. Why should those who believe in this care so very much whether one can rise from the dead to converse with his friend! We see that Swedenborg esteemed it merely as a condition of a certain state of mind, a great privilege as enlarging his means of attaining knowledge and holiness. For ourselves, it is not as a seer of ghosts, but as a seer of truths that Swedenborg interests us.

But to return to the books. They show the gradual extension of the influence of Swedenborg, and the nature of its effects. In Mr. Parsons's case they are good. His mind seems to have been expanded and strengthened by it. Parts of his book we have read with pleasure, and think it should be a popular one among the more thoughtful portion of the great reading public. As to Mr. Barrett's discourse, the basis of Swedenborgianism had seemed to us broader than such a corner stone would lead us to suppose. Generally, we would say, read Swedenborg himself before you touch his interpreters. In him you will find a great life, far sight, and a celestial spirit. You will be led to think, and great and tender sympathies be gratified in you. Then, if you wish to prop yourself by doctrines taken from his works, and hasten to practical conclusions, you can do so for yourself, and from Swedenborg *himself* learn how to be a Swedenborgian; but we hope he may teach you rather to become an earnest student of truth as he was, for it is so, and not by crying; "Lord, Lord," that you can know him or any other great and excelling mind. But, whatever the result be, read him first, and then you may profit by comparison of your own observations with those of other scholars; but, if you begin with them, it is, even more than usual, in such cases, the blind leading the blind. Confucius had among the host one perfect disciple; others have been, in some degree, thus favoured, but Swedenborg had none such, and he is not far enough off yet for the common sense of mankind to have marked out what is of leading importance in his thoughts. Therefore, search for yourselves; it is a mighty maze, but not without a plan, and the report of all guide-books, thus far, is partial.

METHODISM AT THE FOUNTAIN.

THE LIFE OF CHARLES WESLEY. Comprising a Review of his Poetry, and Sketches of the Rise and Progress of Methodism, with Notices of Contemporary Events and Characters. By THOMAS JACKSON. New-York, 1844.

THIS is a reprint of a London work, although it does not so appear on the title-page. We have lately read it in connection with another very interesting book, Clarke's "Memoirs of the Wesley Family," and have been led to far deeper interest in this great stream of religious thought and feeling by a nearer approach to its fountain-head.

The world at large takes its impression of the Wesleys from Southey. A humbler historian has scarce a chance to be heard beside one so rich in learning and talent. Yet the Methodists themselves are not satisfied with this account of their revered shepherds, which, though fair in the intention, and tolerably fair in the arrangement of facts, fails to convey the true spiritual sense, and does not, to the flock, present a picture of the fields where they were first satisfied with the food of immortals.

A better likeness, if not so ably painted, may indeed be found in chronicles written by the disciples of these great and excellent men, who, as characters full of affection no less than intellect, need also to be affectionately, no less than intellectually, discerned, in order to a true representation of their deeds and their influence.

The books we have named, and others which relate to the Wesleys, are extremely interesting, apart from a consideration of the men and what their lives were leading to, from the various and important documents they furnish, illustrative of the symptoms and obscurer meanings of their times.

In the account of the family life of the rectory of Epworth, where John and Charles Wesley passed their boyish years, we find a great deal that is valuable condensed. And we look upon the picture of home and its government with tenfold interest, because the founders of the Methodist church inherited, in a straight line, the gifts of the Spirit through their parentage, rather than were taught by angels that visited them now and then unawares, or received the mantle from some prophet who was passing by, as we more commonly find to have been the case in the histories of distinguished men. This is delightful; for we long to see parent and child linked to one another by natural piety—kindred in mind no less than by blood.

The father of the Wesleys was worthy so to be in this, that he was a fervent lover of the right, though often narrow and hasty in his conceptions of it. He was scarce less, however, by nature a lover of having his own will. The same strong will was tempered in the larger and deeper character of his son John, to that energy and steadfastness of purpose which enabled him to carry out a plan of operations so extensive and exhausting through so long a series of years and into extreme old age.

This wilfulness, and the disposition to tyranny which attends it, the senior Mr. Wesley showed on the famous occasion when he abandoned his wife because her conscience forbade her to assent to his prayers for the then reigning monarch, and was only saved from the consequences of his rash resolve by the accident of King William happening to die shortly after. Still more cruel, and this time fatal, was the conduct it induced in marrying one of his daughters, against her will and judgment, to a man whom she did not love, and who proved to be entirely unworthy of her. The sacrifice of this daughter, the fairest and brightest of his family, seems most strangely and wickedly wilful; and it is impossible to read the letter she addressed to him on the subject without great indignation against him, and sadness to see how, not long ago, the habit of authority and obedience could enable a man to dispense with the need and claim of genuine reverence.

Yet he was, in the main, good, and his influence upon his children good, as he sincerely sought, and encouraged them to seek, the one thing needful. He was a father who would never fail to give noble advice in cases of conscience; and his veneration for intellect and its culture was only inferior to that he cherished for piety.

As has been generally the case, however, with superior men, the better part, both of inheritance and guidance, came from the mother. Mrs. Susannah Wesley was, as things go in our puny society, an extraordinary woman, though, we must believe, precisely what would be, in a healthy and natural order, the ordinary type of woman. She was endowed with a large understanding, the power of reasoning and the love of truth, animated by warm and generous affections. Her mental development began very early, so that, at the age of thirteen, she had made, and on well-considered grounds, a change in her form of theological faith. The progress so early begun, did not, on that account, stop early, but was continued, and with increasing energy, throughout her whole life. The manifold duties of a toilsome and difficult outward existence, (of which it is enough to say that she was the mother of nineteen children, many of whom lived to grow up, the wife of a poor man, and one whose temper drew round him many difficulties) only varied and furthered her improvement by the manifold occasions thus afforded for thought and action. In her prime she was the teacher and cheerful companion of her children, in declining years at once their revered monitor and willing pupil. Indeed, she was one that never ceased to grow while she stayed upon this earth, nor to foster and sustain the growth of all around her. Even the little pedantries of her educational discipline did more good than harm, as they were full of her own individuality. And it would seem to be from the bias thus given that her sons acquired the tendency which, even in early years, drew to them the name of Methodists. How much too may not be inferred from the revival effected by her in her husband's parish during his absence, in so beautiful and simple a manner! How must impressions of that period have been stamped on the minds of her children, sure to recur and aid them whenever on similar occasions the universal voice should summon them to deviate from the usual and prescribed course, and the pure sympathies awakened by their efforts be the sole confirmation of their wisdom! How wisely and temperately she defends herself to her husband, winning the assent even of that somewhat narrow and arbitrary mind! With wisdom, even so tempered by a heart of charity and forbearance, did John and Charles Wesley maintain against the world of customs the bold and original methods which the deep emotions of their souls dictated to them, and won its assent; at least we think there is no sect on which the others collectively look with as little intolerance as on Methodism.

(It may be remarked *par parenthese* that the biographer, Mr. Jackson, who shows himself, in many ways, to be a weak man, is rather shocked at Mrs. Wesley on those occasions where she shows so much character. His opinions however, are of no consequence, as he fairly lays before the reader the letters and other original documents which enable him to judge of this remarkable woman, and of her children, several of them no less remarkable—As we shall not again advert to Mr. Jackson, but only consider him as a cup in which we have received the juice of the Wesleyan grape, we will mention here his strange use of the work *superior* in ways such as these: "This book will be read with superior interest"; Lady —— met him with superior sympathy," &c.)

The children of the Epworth Rectory were, almost without exception, of more than usual dignity and richness of mind and character. They all were aspiring, and looked upon a human life chiefly as affording materials to fashion a temple for the service of God. But, though alike in the main purpose and tendency, their individualities were kept distinct in the most charming freshness. A noble sincerity and mutual respect marked all their intercourse, nor were the weaker characters unduly influenced by the stronger. In proportion to their mutual affection and reverence was their sincerity and decision in opposing one another, whenever necessary; so that they were friendly indeed. The same real love which made Charles Wesley write on a letter assailing John, "Left unanswered by John Wesley's brother," made himself the most earnest and direct of critics when he saw or thought he saw any need of criticism or monition.

The children of this family shared, many of them, the lyric vein, though only in Charles did it exhibit itself with much beauty. It is very interesting to see the same gift taking another form in the genius for Music of his two sons. The record kept by him of the early stages of development in them is full of valuable suggestions, and we hope some time to make use of them in another connection. It is pleasant to see how the sympathies of the father melted away the crust of habitual opinions. It was far otherwise with the uncle, where the glow of sympathy was less warm.

The life of the two brothers was full of poetic beauty in its incidents and conduct. The snatching of the child, destined to purposes so important, "as a brand from the burning;" their college life; Charles's unwillingness to be "made a saint of all at once;" and his subsequent yielding to the fervour of his brother's spirit,—John Wesley's refusal to bind himself to what seemed at the time a good work, even for his mother's sake, because the Spirit within, if it did not positively forbid, yet did not say "I am ready," thus sacrificing the outward to the inward duty with a clear decision rare even in great minds,—their voyage to America, intercourse with the Moravians and Indians,—the trials to which their young simplicity and credulity there subjected them, but from which they were brought out safe by obeying the voice of Conscience, —their relations with Law, Böhler and Count Zinzendorf,—the manner of their marriages, their relations with one another and with Whitfield,—all are narrated with candour and fullness, and all afford subjects for much and valuable thought. As the mind of John Wesley was of stronger mould and in advance of his brother's, difference of opinion sometimes arose between them, and Charles, full of feeling, protested in a way calculated to grieve even a noble friend.—His conduct with regard to his brother's marriage seems to have been perfectly unjustifiable, and his heart to have remained strangely untaught by what he had felt and borne at the time of his own. Even after death his prejudices acted to prevent his mortal remains from resting beside those of his brother. In all those cases where John Wesley found his judgment interfered with, his affections disappointed or even deeply wounded, as was certainly the case in the breaking off his first engagement, while he felt the superior largeness and clearness of his own views, as he did in exercising the power of ordination, and when he wrote on the disappointment of his wish that the body of his brother should be interred in his own cemetery, because it was not regularly "consecrated earth;" "That ground is as holy as any in England," still the heart of John Wesley was always right and noble; still he looked at the motives of the friend, and could really say and wholly feel in the spirit of Christian love, "Be they forgiven for they know not what they do."

This same heart of Christian love was shown in the division that arose between the brothers and Whitfield; and owing to this it was that division of opinion did not destroy unity of spirit, design and influence in the efforts of these good men to make their fellows good also. "The threefold cord," as they loved to call it, remained firm through life, and the world saw in them one of the best fruits of the religious spirit, mutual reverence in conscientious difference. This rarest sight alone would have given them a claim to instruct the souls of men.

We wish indeed that this spirit had been still better understood by them, and that, in ceasing to be the pupils of William Law, they had not felt obliged to denounce his mode of viewing religious truth as "poisonous mysticism." It is human frailty that requires to reäct, thus violently, against that we have left behind. The divine spirit teaches better, shows that the child was father of the man, and that which we were before has prepared us to be what we now are.

One of the deepest thinkers of our time believes that the exaggerated importance which each man and each party attaches to the aims and ways which engage him or it, and the far more odious depreciation of all others, are needed to give sufficient impetus and steadiness to their action. He finds grand correspondence in the laws of matter with this view of the laws of mind to illustrate and sustain his belief. Yet the soul craves and feels herself fit for something better, a wisdom that shall look upon the myriad ways in which men seek their common end—the development and elevation of their natures,—with calmness, as the Eternal does. For ourselves, in an age where it is still the current fallacy that he who does not attach this exaggerated importance to some doctrinal way of viewing spiritual infinities, and the peculiar methods of some sect of enforcing them in practice, has no religion, we see dawning here and there a light that predicts a better day—a day when sects and parties shall be regarded only as schools of thought and life, and while a man perfers one for his own instruction, he may yet believe it is more profitable for his brethren differently constituted to be in others. It will then be seen that God takes too good care of his children to suffer all truth to be confined to any one church establishment, age, or constellation of minds, and it will be not only assented to in words, but believed in soul, that the Laws and Prophets may be condensed, as Jesus said, into this simple law, "Love God with all thy soul, thy fellow-man as thyself;" and that he who is filled with this spirit and strives to express it in life, however narrow cut be his clerical coat, or distorting to outward objects, no less than disfiguring to himself, his theological spectacles, has not failed both to learn and to do some good in this earthly section of existence. When this much has once been granted; when it is seen that the only true, the only Catholic Church, the Church whose communion, invisible to the outward eye, is shared by all spirits that seek earnestly to love God and serve Man, has its members in every land, in every Church, in every sect; and that they who have not this, in whatever tone and form they cry out, "Lord, Lord," have in truth never known Him; then may we hope for less narrowness and ignorance in the several sects, also, for all and each will learn of one another, and dwelling together in unity still preserve and unfold their life in individual distinctness. Such a platform we hope to see ascended by the men of this earth, of this or the coming age. At any rate, disengagement from present bonds, must lead to it, and thus we trust, the Wesleys have embraced William Law and found that his "poisonous mysticism" had its truth and its meaning also, while he rejoices that their minds, severing from his, took a different bias and reached a different class for which his teachings were not adapted. And thus, passing from section to section of the truth, the circle shall be filled at last, and it shall be seen that each had need of the other and of all.

Charles and John Wesley seemed to fulfil toward their great family of disciples the offices commonly assigned to Woman and Man. Charles had a narrower, tamer, less reasoning mind, but great sweetness, tenderness, facility and lyric flow, "When successful in effecting the spiritual good of the most abject, his feelings rose to rapture." Soft pity filled his heart, and none seemed so near to him as the felon and the malefactor, because for none else was so much to be done.

His habitual flow of sacred verse was like the course of a full fed stream. In extreme old age, his habits of composition are thus pleasingly described:

"He rode every day (clothed for Winter, even in Summer,) a little horse, grey with age. When he mounted, if a subject struck him, he proceeded to expand and put it in order. He would write a hymn thus *given* him on a card (kept for that purpose) with his pencil in short hand. Not unfrequently he has come to the house on the City road, and having left the pony in the garden in front, he would enter, crying out 'Pen and ink! pen and ink!' These being supplied, he wrote the hymn he had been composing. When this was done, he would look round on those present, and salute them with much kindness, ask after their health, give out a short hymn, and thus put all in mind of eternity. He was fond of that stanza upon these occasions,

"There all the ship's company meet," &c.

His benign spirit is, we believe, gratified now by finding that company larger than he had dared to hope.

The mind of John Wesley was more masculine; he was more of a thinker and leader. He is spoken of as credulous, as hoping good of men naturally, and able to hope it again from those that had deceived him. This last is weakness unless allied with wise decision and force, generosity when it is thus tempered. To the character of John Wesley it imparted a persuasive nobleness, and hallowed his earnestness with mercy. He had in a striking degree another of those balances between opposite forces which mark the great man He kept himself open to new inspirations, was bold in apprehending and quick in carrying them out. Yet with a resolve once taken he showed a steadiness of purpose beyond what the timid scholars of tradition can conceive.

In looking at the character of the two men, and the nature of their doctrine we well understand why their spirit has exercised so vast a sway, especially with the poor, the unlearned and those who had none else to help them. They had truth enough and force enough to uplift the burdens of an army of poor pilgrims and send them on their way rejoicing. We should delight to string together, in our own fashion, a rosary of thoughts and anecdotes illustrative of their career and its consequences, but, since time and our limits in newspaper space forbid, cannot end better than by quoting their own verse, for they are of that select corps, "the forlorn hope of humanity," to whom shortcoming in deeds has given no occasion to blush for the lofty scope of their words.

"Who but the Holy Ghost can make
 A genuine gospel minister,
A bishop bold to undertake
 Of precious souls the awful care?
The Holy Ghost alone can move
 A sinner sinners to convert,
Infuse the apostolic love
 And bless him with a pastor's heart."

APPENDIX

THE TRAGEDY OF WITCHCRAFT.

As the tragedy of Witchcraft has not been published, nor is likely to be, while the dramatic interests of the country are unprotected by any copyright law, it may not be amiss to afford the reader a further opportunity of passing his judgment on this production by a few extracts, and the publication of a contemporary comment on the play, with a letter in the Evening Post, giving an account of its first performance.

"The curtain rises in the new play upon a scene in a wood, and we are immediately introduced to the witch-haunted atmosphere of the era, for the spirit of that great persecution was abroad, as it were, in the air, and surrounded everything as a mysterious Presence. The first words between two of the yeomanry are tinctured with the popular superstition. We feel from the very moment that there is a general blight, a tendency to evil that cannot be resisted. This is the perfection of the Tragic interest, and it never leaves us through the piece. It was a time of Superstition, when the Prince of the Powers of the Air set up his throne in Salem, clung to the skirts of the dark wood, hung threatening in the blackness of the cloud, interpreted his mysteries in the flight of birds, hung out his inscriptions in the withered folds of old women's faces, to be read by conceited interpreters of Heaven's law, and hypocritical men of cruelty. A fearful time that. In the play all this is felt, as the talk of the characters keeps continually approaching, by a species of fascination, as it were, the fatal subject. Day by day it gathers strength. From distant regions, it is heard of in the neighbouring villages, and gradually approaches, like some fell disease, closing in upon the life—the devoted town of Salem, and within that town of Salem, at its very heart, the lives and persons of a man and woman of no ordinary mould among those townspeople, the hero and heroine of the play—the Mother and Son of the story. There are several passions at work in the Drama—there is Bigotry seeking its victim, Christianity borrowing weapons from Hell to circumvent the Devil—the jealousy of the lover serving God and *his* passion, too, at the same time, and calling Revenge—Religion—there are petty cowardice and curiosity, but far above them all, striking a root in nature deeper even than the miscalled devotion of those times, the relation between a mother and her son—the untaught emotion of boyhood rising up bolder and stronger than the inveterate hardihood and selfish hypocrisy of manhood. By this simple element of strength one human being at least is saved, and the expedients of that miserable age shattered and almost driven back from their strongholds.

How all this and more is done those who have seen or will soon witness this tragedy, will be at no loss to understand. Mr. Murdoch is labouring to a purpose and with the author. The play is a beautiful example of development. All is elaborately wrought out, the details are numerous, and the result simplicity.

The plot is simply this. A proud woman of great independence and superior education, retires, when age and trouble have begun to set their marks upon her, to the comparative solitude of Salem. She bore trouble in her heart, was among the townspeople, but not of them, loved lonely walks on the hill side, gathered old Indian relics, which she kept out of reverence for the past. "The fee grief due to her single breast" was remorse for an act of pride, by which her husband had fallen in a duel. A word from her might have prevented the calamity, and she had not spoken it.

With such elements, and the material the meddlesome town naturally afforded, and the vile poison of witchcraft already introduced into the land, how easily was this woman implicated. She walked alone and talked much with herself—it was a trick of witchcraft. She possessed little Indian figures, which she called after the names of the local characters of the town—the magistrates and constables, whose religion was to be set at work either through fear or the insult—these were the instruments of incantation, like the waxen images of ancient necromancy. She laughed at the folly of her persecutors—it was of course hardened wickedness. The *atmosphere* is so choking, that the son yields and for a moment believes his mother's guilt, but when he listens to her explanation of the silent grief, the lonely walks, he spurns the whole brood in language and acts of unmeasured indignation. This is the triumph of the actor, as well as of the moral element in the fifth act. But evil men have had their counsel and completed their deed. The Witch is condemned to die!

"*Gideon.* The deed is done! Ruin upon a sacred head
Is piled, and ye are evermore accursed—
What have ye done—thou sepulchre of all belief
(*To Deacon Gidney.*)
And truth, stares not this lie you have enacted
Stark and o'erwhelming as a dead man's face
Against your path! What have ye proven
To drive this penalty against a venerable breast?
Some solitary walks, sacred as night,
Familiar love for hills and woods and fields,
A way through life out of your beaten path
But ever in the road to the pure Truth
And goodness of a heart troubled too much
In conscience for a deed that would have been
A feather's weight upon your brutish souls.
(*To the People.*)
Ye are the most accursed deceivers,
Most pitiful deluded men, this clime
Or century hath hatched. Ye have enfogged,
Darkened, and led astray my childish love,
Made this aged mother seem a horror and a hag
To one, who, drop by drop, would once have died—and will—
To save or serve her! Blasted this blest place
And made its men and women beasts of prey,
Hunting each other to chains and flames and deaths.

This passage tells much of the story. There are other incidents and personages. The Deacon is strongly marked, so is that feeble little shadow of him and the justice, petty officer Pudeater. The Deacon is described

A sturdy gentleman of solemn port,
Whose eyes are lobster-like in gaze, whose paunch
Is full and hungry ever, his step
Demure and confident as though he trod
On holy pavements always.

The little official is the type of timid, obsequious sextons, who hang upon the eyelids of the vestry and the clergyman, or any in authority. He always appears in character, and is sure of being laughed at. He bears about him with the best grace in the world the utmost extent of the ridiculous.

As a specimen of the dialogue, we give the first scene between the Deacon and Ambla, in which he seeks to entrap her.

"*Deacon.* I should be sorry to know your age was racked
With pains, and vexed with old unquietness:
Sleep you well o' nights?
Ambla. I'm thankful for the rest
I find, and if the other villagers take
What I lose I'm thankful still.
Deacon. You seek your bed
Early, I hope, as doth become your age.
Ambla. A little walk on Maple Hill, a meditation
At the down-falling of the sun, and I
Am lapped in sleep.
Deacon. Dream you much now,
My aged friend—we at our age, that is, at yours,
Sometimes forego our dreams.
Ambla. I have not dreamed
A dream, for three and twenty years,
Except awake.
Deacon. Was there no vision in your sleep last night?
You heard of Margaret Purdy's death at Groton?
Her spectre, 'tis given out, passed over this house
Of yours—in a white flame at midnight.
Ambla. An angel, she, to honor so this low
Unworthy roof!
Deacon. You think well, then, of her, do you?
She was no praying woman, I am told.
Ambla. There is a silent service, sir, I've heard
It said, keeps up its worship at the heart
Although the lips be closed.
Deacon. What! prayer irregular and chance begot!
Sad orthodoxy! I, Deacon Perfect Gidney,—
A humble pattern to this lowly parish,
Am used to have a different way—
I snuff my candle with a prayer,
And with a prayer wind up my watch,
And go to prayer at striking of the clock,
The great one, my learned grandfather's gift,
In the Hall; and kindle with a prayer
My morning fire.

This is compact and straightforward, nothing wanting, nothing superfluous. The American writer who can sustain five acts of a play at this standard is an acquisition!

The scattered poetic beauties of single lines and figures, exercises of an original fancy, are numerous and always aid the dramatic element.

Passages like the following are sufficient proofs of a new poet and dramatist somewhere among us.

(*A Lover.*)

I would not give its balmy pains,
For calmest health: its pangs delicious,
Troubles full of joy, wakenings electrical
At dead of night, its dreams by day,
These are its bounties—

(*Gideon, of his Mother.*)

With what a smile she used, when shouting to her,
I came back from my first childish strayings
To the woods—to open wide her garden gate,
Young Salem's first of gardens tending,
And bring me in.
Chief was she in her majestical mild port
Of all women; guide to the lost and sad,
Helper to all poor neighbourhood—
Kindling her welcome fire, earliest
In this lone place, for wayfarers,
Of all creeds, all colours, and all climes.

(*A son's watchful guardianship*).

Yes, yes—we know his weapon
Plays about that low-roofed house, free
And familiar as the breaking day.

(*Gideon's affection for his mother.*)

Ambla. Be calm, my son, nor love me too much!
Gid. Too much! the universe can hold it not!—
When from your hand I go, I die a death
At every step; you seem to hold the roof-tree
With your arm, to hang above the fields and whiten them:
Nor could I through the noon-day harvest toil,
Knew I your lap would not receive
My weary head when night draws on.
*   *   *   *   *   *
Gid. Then there's calamity at hand that colors everything.

(*No evil spirits in the New World*).

Believe it not!
Believe it not!—Clear, crystal and unstained,
The gracious Power upholds this round of Earth
New found and beautiful: no foul nor ugly thing,
Hath power, I'm sure, in this new land—
Goblin nor witch!

He sweeps apast me
With his glittering scythe and victor-arm.

If she be not, and these are hunters
For the sport's sake, if they pursue her,
Panther-like for the wild beauty
Of her ways.
* * * * * *
Though I could see an hundred witches
'Gainst the white moon flying.

(*The Spirit of Witchcraft*).

There have been doings dark as night,
And close as death: murders and deadliest crimes
Which the clear eye of day has seen not!
Acts to outface the bloody wolf, *and scare*
The ravenous lion with his unappeasable mane!
Night's ear hath many counsels of the dark,
She hears the whispers of the self-reproached,
And blacker grows!
* * * * * *
When boy and girl pluck flowers together,
Together wade, white-ankled in the shining stream.

Gid. (*of his mother.*)
Some silent place will miss her;
Out of these woods and from these stillnesses
A power with her may pass, bearing a light away!

Who reverences not the Past, Hereafter
Shall not reverence, nor hold to have had
A present time.

Must is a lion that turns back
To tear its driver, you know, no less than hunt
What goes before.

What say you to a great-antlered elk
Tangling his horns amid the branches
Of the hemlock wood? to speckled swimmers
In still-water stream?

The Earth hath foothold
For the unsubstantial dark alone.

She passes and with th' invisible spirit talks,
And dallies with the hands of unfamiliar things.

Gid. What wonder now is this
Ambla. Sometimes it wanders the wood, sometimes
The free-flowered air: come softly on!—&c. &c.

From the Evening Post, New York, May 6th.

THE NEW DRAMA OF WITCHCRAFT.—We have received a letter from a correspondent in Philadelphia, touching the new play produced in that city on Monday evening last:

PHILADELPHIA, Tuesday, May 5, 1846.

Mr. Murdoch's new play of Witchcraft was performed last evening at the Walnut street theatre, to one of the most crowded houses of the season. The play had been prominently announced and spoken of in several of the morning papers, and had evidently created great expectation in advance. Tier above tier, from the orchestra to the gallery, rose the vast surface of heads. Here we thought was the material to try fully the new play. If it could hold the attention of this crowded body, it would be a success far beyond the approval of the few packed critical friends who generally attend on such occasions. The critics were not wanting either; the intellect of Philadelphia was well represented on the occasion. The curtain rose on a woodland scene in old Salem, and presently Mr. Murdoch appeared in his character of Gideon Bodish. He was never dressed or looked to greater advantage than in his closely fitting russet coat; his attitudes were after his manner exceedingly graceful, his voice music itself. In scene after scene, in every act, he drew down repeated applause, as he delivered one passage after another of singular poetic beauty, or fierce indignant eloquence.

It was evident from the first moment that the play was wholly unlike the ordinary efforts under the name of the "American Drama." It was bold, confident, original in illustration, and in the incidents and developments of the plot. The stage situations were new. The confirmation of Gideon's doubts of his mother's guilt of witchcraft at the crisis of the play by a species of sacred divination, an augury from a chance opened passage of the Bible, and the solemn introduction of a child to confront the accused in the grand trial scene, as they were managed, were proofs of undoubted genius on the part of the author.—The play was sown all over with the happiest poetical expressions, not merely in the leading parts, but with an unaccustomed prodigality on the part of a modern dramatist were thrown away, for stage purposes, on the lips even of the supernumeraries. Take such lines as these in the mouth of the mother, as she solves one of the perplexities of the piece her apparent guilt; not that of witchcraft, but the life-long remorse for the murder of her husband in a duel, whom she might have saved by declaring her innocence, which she was too proud to prove:

He thought that I had sinned
Against his love with that gay paramour,
Who was no more than birds are to the tree
They hover o'er, to me who lived in mine
Own thoughts above suspicion's climbing,

or this illustration, finely delivered by Murdoch, of the dark silent approach of the superstition upon the soul—

The night sits on this gloomy heart—
I see an Indian on a hill top standing,
Part of the silent fixedness of things;
He breaks the mighty calm, wherein he stood
Slow striding down the mountain's side.
Swifter and darker as he nears us we regard him,
Flashing and red, woe's living thunder cloud,
And now, and now, he bends above us—
Dusk murder in the very person of itself—
So creeps this hideous witchcraft on me.

Or such bits of descriotion as the following, a perfect picture in the limits of a sentence;

You recollect old Tituba, the shrivelled squaw,
Who wigwamed gloomily by the wood's edge
Some summers past—

or so perfect an illustration as this of the gathering suspicions of his mother's life in Gideon's conversation—

Ever in his speech
There lived and moved as in the river stream
The fish, darkly and yet swift gliding
Old Ambla's form,

Yet these were not the chief merits, but accessories only to the dramatic action; they never came to interrupt, but to aid the character and story. The longer single passages, or any just exhibition of the dialogue, would lead me beyond the limits of a letter.

In the general style of the acting—leading parts were taken by Mrs. Wallack, our old favourite Richings, and a very successful comical tipstaff by Chapman—and especially in the grouping and stage appointments no American play that we have seen has appeared to equal advantage. The scenery had been drawn on the spot at Salem, and Mr. Murdoch had been accompanied in his researches for the dress and costume of the period by Rev. Mr. Upham, the author of a book on the Salem Witchcraft. The bill states the costumes to have been "taken from portraits, paintings, &c. in possession of the Salem Historical Library association." The Deacon, a Justice, an old goodwife were admirable.

We have rarely witnessed a performance where the interest excited was better sustained. The uproarious elements in the pit and galleries, of which we were fearful, were subdued to perfect silence; the laugh at the comic characters, the Deacon's bloated presumption and Chapman's comicalities, was quickly changed to the earnest or pathetic as Gideon or the Mother entered the scene. It was a long and satisfactory study. At the close, Mr. Murdoch was loudly called for, made a short speech to the effect that he rejoiced in the warm reception he had received that evening; that he attributed this solely to the merits of the unknown American author, who did not wish to be known as a dramatic writer, and for whom he had pledged to maintain, and would strictly, the anonymous.

www.ingramcontent.com/pod-product-compliance
Lightning Source LLC
LaVergne TN
LVHW010147110826
845151LV00002B/449

* 9 7 8 1 4 2 5 5 3 7 7 4 6 *